DANGEROUS
DIFFERENCES

Mac Laird

To Don and Joy Hansen
of Williamsburg. You
will find some
familiar places here.
Best Wishes,
Mac Laird
May 2010

A
story of the
search for understanding
in the New World
of 1700.

To my son, Jeff, for his
love of the outdoors
and
his deep appreciation
of things natural.

This novel is a work of fiction. References to real names of actual people are explained in Author's Note. All other names, characters, places, dialogue, and incidents portrayed in this book are the product of the author's imagination.

Cartography © 2010 by Jeffrey M. Laird

Library of Congress Control Number: 2009910181

Cover design and photo by Quail High Books

Published by Quail High Books

ISBN **978-0-9825443-0-3**

http://www.quailhigh.com

AUTHOR'S NOTE

DANGEROUS DIFFERENCES is set in the piedmont country of the eastern wilderness and in Williamsburg in the year 1700. By this time, the capital of the Virginia colony had been relocated six miles west from the site of the original capital, Jamestown, to the more favorable terrain and climate of Middle Plantation. There the town was established and named Williamsburg.

During the time of this novel, September, October and November of 1700, Francis Nicholson was Governor of Virginia, James Blair was President of the College of William and Mary, and Thomas Cowles was Sheriff of James City County. The events, dialogue, and behavior appearing with these names, however, is entirely a product of my imagination as are all other names, characters, and events.

Although sachem, werowance, emperor, king, and other words denoting leadership actually appeared in the speech and writing of the times, the title "Chief" is simpler, widely understood, and I use it throughout to denote "leader." The word "Indian" encompasses the people of two continents and dozens, if not hundreds of cultures, but I use it in this book to denote only the collective indigenous people of Southeastern America.

M.L.
Williamsburg, 2010

v

FOREWARD

No history is more explosive and tragic, more enlightening and rewarding, and more complicated than the culture clash of the Europeans and Native Americans in the 169 years before the colonies won their independence in 1776. In the years before that, Great Britain, France, Spain, and even the Netherlands and Sweden, sent troops, traders, trappers, explorers, and settlers to the New World with the promise of unlimited land, trees, fur, and the freedom to worship as they pleased.

In that pre-revolutionary period, natives of the New World, mistakenly named Indians by Columbus because he thought he had found India, ran a gauntlet of encounters with an endless wave of strangers. Encounters of wonder, welcome, and curiosity quickly turned into warfare, disease, and defeat for the natives. Both they and the arriving Europeans suffered great losses, but in less than 100 years the ratio of Native American to European had completely reversed, and still more settlers poured into the New World. By 1700, the Anglo population in the New World had grown to over 250,000, over 50,000 in the tidewater area of Virginia alone. Out of the struggle between these two cultures came a way of life rooted in the concept of private property, a robust commerce, Christianity, an unwavering pioneer spirit, freedom, and the *pursuit of happiness*. America.

Unlike the five-nation confederation of the Iroquois to the north and the large well-organized Cherokee nation to the south, Indian tribes of Virginia and parts of North

Carolina and Maryland cherished their independence. They generally lived in small groups in towns or villages, and sometimes they moved when the firewood and game near them played out. They also moved because European settlers were fast consuming Indian-cleared lands, sometimes by trade, sometimes by government grant, but frequently by simply "squatting" on what appeared to them as unused land.

Dangerous Differences is about daily living in the Virginia colony and one generation of Saponi Indians located in the piedmont country of western North Carolina on the Yadkin River in the year 1700. These strong people lived without police, parliaments, jails, poverty, nobles, prefects, lawsuits, and debts or debtors. They felt a deep responsibility to their children, aged, needy, sick, and disabled. Instead of the commerce systems, law libraries, and government organizations so well understood in Europe, they were guided by the songs of their elders, by stories handed down from generation to generation, and by the awesome power and manifestations of nature. They had no written language, no books, and few pictorial records. Neither did they understand the concept of personal property. They relied on the abundant riches of the Eastern forests, streams, and fields of maize, beans, and squash for sustenance. And although they were strong, capable, and resourceful hunter-gatherers, and even grew certain crops, they did not embrace labor-for-hire, accumulate property, or compete for wealth as known by the white strangers.

The settlers marveled at how resistant Indians were to winter weather, having no need for the warmth, space, and shelter of log and stone buildings. The Indians were just as amazed that the farmers worked from dawn to dark in vast fields of tobacco, growing far more than they could consume. They did not see the sense of the settlers' immovable houses with so many rooms for so few people. Differences such as these fed the flames of misunderstanding and eventually snuffed out hope for peaceful coexistence.

Within 100 years of the 1607 arrival of the English at Jamestown, the white man had claimed most of the coastline of North America from Canada to Florida. Vast Indian populations, yielding to the weapons, tools, and diseases of the white man almost disappeared—that quick, within those few years.

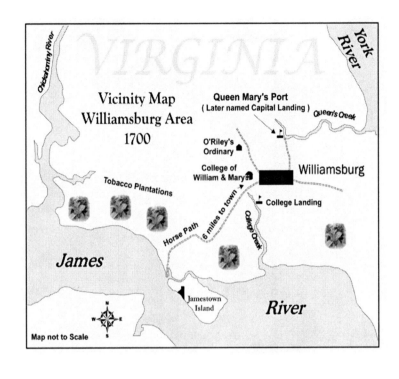

Virginia Indian
Locations
1700

SHAWNEE

MOUNTAINS

APPALACHIAN

South Fork

Appalachian Trail

Manahoac

MONACAN

Nahyssan/Tuscarora
Battleground

NAHYSSAN

Williamsburg

Atlantic

Ocean

Saponi Trail

Nottoway

Virginia

North Carolina

OCCANEECHI

Delaware
Maryland

Chesapeake Bay

TUTELO

Tayamiti Held Captive

Shamoti

Sissipahaw

Saponi Town

SAPONI

Catawba

TUSCARORA

Machapunga

Pamlico

Outer Banks

Pamlico Sound

Map Scale:

0   25   50   100 Miles

X

1

Sensing danger, the young Saponi Indian froze and focused on the sudden silence of the dry, autumn forest. He had learned patience through rigorous training and could remain motionless as long as it took. The unusual silence warned him that he was not alone. There on the edge of an open meadow of wild flowers and long grass, the sumac and young hardwood saplings blended with his chestnut brown coloring. He squinted into the wilderness before him, moving his black eyes slowly to check his position and escape route.

He eased the rabbit hanging from the game strap to his right side to free his legs for the speed he might need. The hickory bow in his left hand was nocked with his longest flint-tipped arrow. Eleven more feathered arrows of various tips and lengths lay inside the otter-skin quiver strapped across his bare back. Around the rim of the quiver, arrow shafts rested in tiny bone slots designed to separate the delicate turkey feathers for quick, silent, damage-free withdrawal. A deerskin loincloth hung loosely from his hips leaving his strong legs, slightly flexed, free, and ready.

It was high privilege for a youth to be allowed to go alone into the hunting grounds, even higher privilege to be permitted to hunt there. This hunt a well-earned preliminary to the huskanaw, a rigorous program of training and trials to prepare him for warrior status. Many times, he had come here with his father, Custoga, and his grandfather, Choola, to learn the way of the wilderness.

He made no sound or movement. Only the occasional rustle of colored leaves giving way to light air movements disturbed the silence. Then came the call of the black-billed cuckoo, rapid, repetitive *coocoocoo*, followed by a single chirp. Kadomico relaxed and smiled. It was the signal of his friend, Tree Son.

He answered the call, moved back to the trail, and waited.

"Your father sent me." Tree Son's muffled voice projected so that Kadomico could not be certain of its location. It seemed to come from yonder thicket, but he knew Tree Son's ability to play tricks with his voice, and the game was on. He listened carefully, scanning the scene for a likely concealment. Still uncertain, Kadomico's eyes kept returning to the old white oak tree not twenty paces from him. If he was wrong, he was the loser. He decided to risk it. In the strongest, most commanding voice he could manage, he said, "Tree Son, you stand behind the great oak, and my arrow is aimed where your belly will be if you leave that position."

"Kadomico, it is true. The great white oak protects me, but your arrow is aimed five Tree Sons too low to reach my belly." The reply came from the upper branches of the tree, barely concealing the pleasure of success; his tactic had worked.

"The trees favor you, Tree Son. Come down, and tell me why you have spoiled my hunt," Kadomico said.

Tree Son, using the climbing skills that had earned him his name, descended. By the time his moccasins touched the autumn leaves on the forest floor, he began to deliver the news he carried from Kadomico's father, Custoga, Chief of the Saponi tribe.

"Your father has called the council and will speak to them and to you today when the shadow is smallest and the sun is highest. I am sent to bring you, and I know only that the fires in the longhouse burned late last night."

While Tree Son spoke, Kadomico unstrung his bow, tied it to the quiver straps with soft buckskin thongs and turned into the trail. He trotted lightly, gathering his thoughts. In his mind, he flashed through possible explanations of being called back from the hunt. It was not a punishment. Custoga would have dealt with that as a family matter unless it had tribal consequences. He was still too young to be given warrior status. He knew of no ceremonies in which he was to be included. What then? He was glad to be running. It kept his mind focused.

Kadomico had not bothered with food before beginning his hunt, and he thought that probably Tree Son had also not eaten. As they approached a wide section of the trail, he took a handful of parched maize from his pouch and dropped back to pass it to Tree Son. Neither spoke.

Moving forward again, Kadomico ran easily over flat ground in the deep forest preparing for the climb of the first of three hills in his homeward path. Although they ran well apart now, they moved as one, aware of the hawk riding the morning thermals, alert to places where moccasins or rattlers might be, taking notice of movements and sounds around them. The cool of mid-morning, the wind in their faces, and the clear sky eased their task but did not distract their attention to the trail.

Kadomico increased the pace. They jumped the occasional blow-down and splashed through shallow creek beds before starting up the last hill. There they slowed and ran unobserved over the bare-earth trail until they reached the top where, in a small clearing, the trail forked. The westward view revealed the Yadkin River twisting down from its source of cold, clear springs high in the Blue Mountains. Beyond the river, smoke of the cooking fires marked the location of the Saponi town.

In Custoga's roundhouse with its reed-thatched roof and bark-covered walls, Kadomico's mother, Tanaka, cleared away the last of the mid-morning meal of venison and squash, removed the empty pottery dish and gave Custoga a pouch of tobacco. He looked up from his sitting position on the clean, smooth, hard-packed, earth floor, and gave his wife a troubled look.

"Woman, you are silent," he said.

"All has been said, Custoga. The English and the ways of the English are ever more upon us. Twice we have moved in my lifetime, and they continue to advance. More and more we need them, and we need to understand them and to learn how to live in their presence. Yesterday we spoke of their offer to accept our son in their place of learning they call school. There they will teach him about talking papers, English ways and their God." Tanaka paused to gather the right words.

"You are right to send my only son to them. In his first summer, I named him Kadomico "Of the People" because everyone came to him like birds to their feeding fields, even before he walked. Soon he will lead us. What he learns there will prepare him, but my heart will remain heavy until I see him safely back by your side. Today, make Kadomico proud of his task and of you. You can do no more."

Custoga, as always, found reassurance in Tanaka's words. He said, "Kadomico and Tree Son will be here soon. I will speak with him before council. He will leave tomorrow with two braves who will see him safely there. They will need food for three days."

During this talk, White Water, the eight-year-old sister of Kadomico, had finished folding away her bed of fur and the blanket Custoga had brought her from a trade he had made two years ago at an English fort on the James River. She was now sweeping the doorway with a small brush broom made from the branches of a dogwood tree, her mind filled with the vision of Kadomico and Tree Son certain to be returning on the east trail. Carefully clearing away the last bit of debris, she hung the broom neatly in its place near the doorway, and without speaking, without even thinking, she yielded to the impulse, *meet them.* She slipped past the hide covering over the doorway and quickened her pace as she turned onto the brown earth path. Her buckskin skirt shifted comfortably with each stride as she ran toward the trail where she expected to meet Kadomico.

Reminded of the turbulence and beauty of cascading water, Tanaka had named her White Water soon after she was born. By the time she was four winters, her arms and legs were long and beautiful, the muscles flowing smoothly under deeply tanned skin. Her first steps were a run rather than a walk, and she loved it. Her first word was "Don't" and her little hands were often clenched into fists of determination. After those first steps, she ran when she could, even short trips across the hut. Now, at the age of eight, she could outrun most anyone her age, including boys, and did so at every opportunity. White Water, a joyful free spirit of inexhaustible energy, oblivious of her gender, and unable to suppress her extraordinary physical powers, loved the feel of speed. She excelled in jumping and swimming as well. Now she sped to the East trail to meet Kadomico and Tree Son.

She ran across the field of maize, struck the trail, and entered the forest, running up a gentle incline toward the summit where she intended to wait for them, but less than half way, she saw Kadomico descending the hill, fast closing the distance between them. Waving a greeting, she slowed, made a graceful turnabout, and skipped along until he caught up. She fell in behind him laughing at his annoyance and surprise at seeing her there alone on the trail, but she knew he was, as always, glad to see her.

Even though she knew she could not outrun her brother, when they reached the fields separating them from the town and the river, she could hardly wait to challenge him. It was enough to know that the gap between their speeds was closing, ever so slowly, but closing.

When the way opened for a race across the field, she moved up with her right hand raised. As she reached his side, not even glancing towards him, she straightened her arm before her, pointed, and let her legs have their way. Kadomico gave her five paces before he increased his pace just enough to trail slightly behind her. Nearing the river, he moved up by her, reached out, and swept her up in his arms, her legs still churning. He slowed to a walk and put the laughing White Water down just as Tree Son came up shaking his head.

"Has this little one no respect for us warriors?" he said. "Does she not know that her place is with the women? Kadomico, I think we must punish her."

"You can't even catch me, Tree Son," she said standing just out of reach, eager for another race.

"Go, little sister. Tell our mother I am near, and see if you can escape what she has in mind for you for running alone in the forest." Handing the rabbit to White Water, he added, "Take this. The skin will be yours. Remove it carefully."

She was so delighted to have the gift and to be the one to bring the news of Kadomico's return that it took her a moment to realize that it also meant that she would face her mother alone. Not even the rabbit would soften Tanaka's disapproval of White Water's thoughtless, impulsive exuberance, a matter of concern since her birth. White Water wanted to walk through the town with Kadomico, even if at a respectful distance behind. She would proudly carry the game and be seen returning from a successful hunt with her brother, already admired for his developing wilderness and shooting skills.

Kadomico and Tree Son walked the narrow, well-worn path toward the town, now visible on high ground beyond the maize field. Several women worked the field in the hot September sun, gathering maize.

White Water dropped back, playing for time, and spoke faster than necessary,. "I will remove the skin so cleanly that it will be unblemished except the place made by my brother's arrow, and I will remove the feet and dry them for a necklace. I will prepare the meat for our mother so that she has only to add it to the cooking bowl. My Brother, I . . . ."

Kadomico stopped, arm outstretched, forefinger pointed straight at the town. White Water knew there was no choice. Side-stepping Kadomico's reach, she fell into an easy trot toward home, eager to be seen, if not with her brother, at least with the kill.

Custoga had just returned from a talk with his father Choola and was preparing for the council meeting when White Water eased into the room. She respectfully acknowledged her father, and moved quietly to Tanaka who was tending the ashes of the morning fire.

"Kadomico and Tree Son have returned," she said. Tanaka was silent.

"Kadomico said I can have the skin," she said, holding the rabbit up for Tanaka to see. Still silence.

White Water turned to leave. "I will prepare the rabbit for you, my mother."

"White Water, leave your brother's kill there," Tanaka said, and without looking at her daughter she pointed to a large white stone near the ashes. "Leave now. Go to the place of bathing. Wait there. I will be a long while. Think. We will talk when I come. Go."

White Water was shocked. She wanted so much to be present when Kadomico arrived. She did not understand all that was said between her parents that morning, but she knew it involved Kadomico and that it was of solemn concern to her parents. Now she would not even be the one to prepare the rabbit, but when she tried to speak, Tanaka turned her back in rejection, her severest punishment. White Water fell silent.

With trembling chin, she fought back tears as she walked downhill to the clearing where the cascading water of a small creek met the Yadkin River. There she found a place from which she could watch the path and hope Tanaka would relent. Two women, seated on a flat limestone outcropping, their feet resting in the cool, clear water of the little stream, were scrubbing pots with hard, young pine cones gathered in the early summer.

2

Over the last half of the seventeenth century, the Saponi, a tribe of about three hundred souls including fifty warriors, had been forced steadily south from their northern homeland by fierce and powerful Iroquois raiders and by the endless westward advancement of the European settlers. Moving ever south and hugging the hills of the Appalachian Mountains, three times in fifty years they had relied on the great Eastern wilderness for new places to live in peace and plenty, unaware that its endless resources were not endless at all.

Now they were settled in the North Carolina hill country of the great Blue Mountains near the river called Yadkin. Here both Kadomico and Tree Son were born thirteen winters ago. Here also rose the small Saponi town of bark-and skin-covered houses, protected by the wilderness to the south, the mountains to the west, and the river to the north. Eastward lay the territory of the fierce Tuscarora tribe with whom an uneasy friendliness kept the Saponi constantly alert. The women planted and tended fields of squash, beans, and maize, and maintained the households. The forest and river provided the meat and fish to be smoked and dried against the winter. The men fashioned weapons and tools, trained to become protectors of the tribe and to hunt and fish for food in the wilderness forest and streams. They had little to do with crop raising, house building, or child rearing except when their strength and endurance were needed for clearing new ground for crops, gathering materials for houses, and training boys in warfare, hunting, and fishing.

Now the braves hunted and trapped for fur, especially beaver and muskrat, to trade with the white man. Trading had always been a highly prized and respected activity among the Indians, and so it was with the Saponi. By the year 1700, copper kettles, iron tools, and cloth, mere curiosities not so long ago, were considered necessities. Moreover, thanks to this new commerce with the Europeans, the products were easily available in exchange for the coveted animal furs. With these changes in their lives came warmer and cleaner housing, better and faster food preparation, and vastly improved equipment for hunting and fishing and weapons of war. Along with these improvements came unavoidable dependence on the very people who threatened their cherished lands.

Characteristic of traders throughout the world, the Indians tried to control trade in their areas. East of the Saponi near the North Carolina-Virginia line, the Occaneechi made it dangerous for strangers to travel through their territories without permission. Further southeast the powerful Tuscarora, with their 1200 warriors, maintained a cautious but vigorous fur trade with the English. They were excellent trappers, and they often collected fur from other tribes. Nor were they above raiding for it if it suited them.

The Saponi had understandings with the Occaneechi and an uncertain peace with the fierce Tuscarora. Sometimes they traded with them. In recent years, the English had come to the Saponi to trade.

Custoga had watched this growth of trading with some satisfaction as he saw his people benefit from the English products. A few of his warriors had developed shooting skills. The thunderous firesticks of the English could kill a deer at a long distance, and the longknives hanging from their sides could sever a man's head. With their steel hammers they could break stone, even crush a beaver-tooth knife; their sharp axes could bring down a tree and chop it into firewood. Guns, iron, cloth, and fire-resistant copper kettles were welcome wonders to almost all of the Saponi—but not to Choola.

Choola, father of Custoga, spent these dim days of his twilight years working hickory, locust, and ash into bows with graceful recurve ends. He also made arrows of many kinds, armed with heads shaped specifically to deal with the target: rounded flint to glance off bone for bear, deer, and warriors; blunted ends for stunning small game and birds; and a variety of arrows feathered and tipped just for target practice. Choola enjoyed wide acclaim among Eastern Indians for his craftsmanship, and he loathed the strange products of the English. He believed they were demonic and cursed. To use them was to defy the natural gods of heaven and earth. And although an Indian could eventually fell a big tree with his stone axe or burn it at the base until it fell, there was rarely a need to do so. Wind and flood left trees of every size and kind on the forest floor for canoes, firewood, paddles, bows, and other wooden necessities.

The settlers felled and burned trees and cleared the land, turning forests into fields. To Choola, this was senseless destruction of the life-giving forest, ignored by the ignorant to their eventual peril. He remembered the time when his people enjoyed the abundance of the wilderness: wood, bone, and stone for tools and weapons; and for food, roots, leaves, berries, honey, juices, and nuts; animals for more food, clothing, and shelter and for their bark and reed covered roundhouses. All these and more were offered by the land. There were streams of pure, sweet water; plants with healing qualities; and there were caves for shelter and for storage through the menacing cold of winter and heat of summer.

Choola remembered when his people had set controlled fires to the valley meadows to burn off intrusive saplings and weeds and renew the grazing land for great herds of antelope and deer. Often the Indians built grass fires to drive the big game into a wedge where groups of hunters clubbed, speared, or killed them with arrows. This had been their way down through the ages. The elders and priests told the stories many times, and Choola had memorized them and had become one of the favorite storytellers. They believed the forest to be as freely available as air and water. They respected tribal hunting grounds, especially those near towns, and they guarded their own hunting ground, but territories not clearly in use or near towns were available to all. In those lands, they often joined communal gatherings in fall or winter for seasonal kills and preparation of smoked and dried meat for the coming hard days of ice and snow.

To Choola it was simple—take the animals, fish, and fowl of the forest and find refuge in it against storm and attack, then leave it to replenish itself. Like the mountains, rivers, and heavenly bodies, the forest was a gift of the great deity of all things good.

Choola had watched the gradual decline of self-sufficiency among his people as they grew steadily dependent on copper kettles, warm blankets, and iron axes. The firesticks were even more worrisome. Warriors were becoming skilled with the English firesticks, but they were of no value without the lead and powder made only by the white man. And fewer and fewer braves now knew how to make and use the bow, arrow, and spear, those inexhaustible weapons offered by the wilderness and sufficient to their needs until the English came with their deadly firesticks, steel axes, and saws. They could quickly clear a section of wilderness for a farm on what was once the land of the tribes of the Powhatan nation. They made farms even in the hill country of the Blue Mountains. They came in great numbers, clearing, planting, bargaining—often fighting—for more land of which there was never enough to satisfy them. The bargains were the worst of it. Choola spit at the notion of exchanging land for talking paper.

"Father, I come." Kadomico spoke as he entered the house and found Custoga alone.

"You are here," Custoga said. It was a customary greeting. "We will go soon to council in the longhouse. There I will speak of the way of the English and the way of the Saponi. I will speak about the English wish to teach us about the use of talking papers and to know their great God. You, my son, will leave tomorrow to a place of the English near the great water. There you will attend the teachings of the English and see how they live, council, and worship. When you are done you will return, and together we will lead our people."

"As my father wishes." That was all Kadomico dared say, so great was the swelling in his throat. Questions competed with the fears and uncertainties flooding his brain for attention. He followed Custoga to the door. There, facing them, stood Tanaka. She nodded approval and understanding to Kadomico as they passed, then turned away toward the place of bathing.

From the nearby field of maize, Tree Son watched. As powerfully as his curiosity urged, he knew he must wait until Kadomico was finished at the tribal council.

As Custoga and Kadomico approached the longhouse, Custoga motioned to Choola standing nearby to follow. The three of them entered. There in the center, a stone-rimmed circle filled with hardwood coals smoldered. Warm air rose toward an opening in the thatched roof. Horns, carved masks, and the dried heads of various beasts hung on the sidewalls, carefully separated by artfully woven reed mats of red and yellow checkerboard patterns. On the floor beneath each section of wall were stone-lined rectangles filled with fresh pine straw and large enough to admit one or two worshippers.

Deep pallets made from the thick skins of bear, cougar, and buffalo lay near the fire for seating. Two groups of three senior Saponi warriors, separated by the circle of fire, formed two lines facing each other across the fire. Custoga and Choola entered and took the places reserved for them at the head of the assembly. Kadomico remained standing behind Custoga.

The priest produced a long pipe, lighted the bowl of tobacco, and passed it to the warrior next to him. The Indians smoked and chatted until each had drawn from the pipe. Then, as if by some invisible signal, silence fell over the assembly and Custoga began to speak. In a low, powerfully projected voice, he began his message to the council of Saponi warriors.

"Tomorrow we join the Occaneechi, Tutelo, Keyaunwee, and Shakori for the winter hunt. This time the place is five nights away. Each winter the distance is more, the deer and bear are fewer, and we fight off attacks by other hunters and watch the smoke of the cooking fires of the English houses draw nearer. We are steadily losing our people to war and sickness. Now we Saponi are half the number we were when my son, Kadomico, was born. Even the great Powhatan are fallen. Only two of many Powhatan towns and settlements remain, and those are confined to a small place they call a reservation. Still the English farmers, traders, and trappers come west. The Blue Mountains are now at our backs, and we must find new ways to protect our people, hunting grounds, and fields. Tomorrow Kadomico will go to a place of the English where he will join their sons and learn about the talking papers and about their God. They call it school."

There was a low murmur of surprise from the warriors seated around the fire. Custoga hesitated, and then continued.

"The English are now governed by Nicholson and his council in a place near the Chickahominy. Nicholson himself sent the trader to me and certain other tribal chiefs to send him their first sons for this training. He said they would have very good food and shelter, all free. He promised to be ready this summer with good clothes of the English, books, and learning. He said they will have care in health and sickness, visits by their families will be welcome, and the school will be open for inspections at all times. And each can have a servant or member of his tribe remain with him to speak their language and be sure they remember the Indian way. He spoke of what the best Englishmen's sons learn as though the same is good for all tribes."

Custoga paused, but nobody stirred.

13

"Kadomico will go tomorrow with Red Wolf and Tree Son. One will remain as long as Kadomico wishes. On the north trail they will meet Shanda, son of a Tutelo chief, and also be joined by Hawk, son of an Occaneechi chief. When they reach the Appomattox they will turn east toward the confluence of the Appomattox and the James Rivers. There they will be met by Sam Layton, the English guide, a trader well known and respected among the tribes. From there Layton will escort the group to Williamsburg to meet the master of the school named for the King and Queen, William and Mary."

Custoga fell silent and waited for the responses he knew would vary widely in these troubled times.

In the soft light of the windowless longhouse, oak coals of the dying fire glowed red under coats of white ash as the youngest of the six senior warriors, Red Wolf, raised his tomahawk and spoke. "This is the only thing the English understand. Words, papers, and councils are their way of fighting for the land and destroying our people. Before I go to them, live with them, and learn to be like them, I will join the French or the Spanish and fight them. It is better to die like men than to dwindle away by little bits."

Watauga, sitting opposite Red Wolf, reached out with a long willow wand and stirred the coals thoughtfully as though their slow disintegration was a sad omen. "The time for uniting and fighting is past. The white man is here to stay and in such numbers and with such strength they cannot be overcome. Now the French and English fight each other, and we Saponi must join one or the other or perish. Custoga speaks wisely. Kadomico will see the way of the English, and we will be better able to protect our people."

Custoga was searching the faces before him for a sign of where this council would stand on the issue when Choola rose, stretching to his full height. His eyes showed plainly the deep sadness within him as he began to speak in a low voice, pronouncing the words evenly. "There was no white man when I was young. The Saponi were many, and our warriors were strong and feared by the Mohawk, Seneca, and Cherokee. They left us in peace because of our strength. Our hunting grounds were plentiful, and although there was often war among the tribes and many raids of towns, there was seldom a cause for the Saponi to take to the warpath. Our town once stood in the protective hills of the great mountains of the north. Our people grew food in fertile fields and took meat from the forest and streams, and it was plentiful. As it was with our ancestors, so it was with us—when I was young." Choola paused in remembrance, letting the deep sadness give way to rising anger, typical of his manner when this subject came up.

He continued, his voice rising. "Gradually, our way has changed. Now our women seek the clothes of the white woman, cook in copper and iron and make beds of blankets. Our braves use firesticks, iron beaver traps, and tomahawks and knives and weaken us further because they are losing the way of making and using their own hunting bows and war clubs and seek only the firesticks, powder, and ball of the Longknives. When I was young, the Saponi were strong and able to protect the tribe. Now the great nations of Iroquois, Cherokee, and Shawnee face the French, English, and Spanish even as they face each other to make their boundaries. Watauga is right, it is too late to turn back, we are too few to fight alone, and there is no place left to retreat except higher into mountains where the land is steep and the winters kill. Kadomico must go. He will learn the way of the English and show the way of the Saponi. It is a first step."

Choola paused, and then looking directly at his grandson, he began again. "But let Kadomico understand, we have seen what happened to Chief Opechancanough and the Powhatan people after the English came. After many summers of war, they finally captured Opechancanough and proceeded to destroy more than two hundred of the Powhatan towns. Now the Powhatan are few and live in small places the English call reservations. So, beware and let Kadomico understand, the English will never accept the Saponi as an equal, and no Saponi will accept the English as his master."

15

Kadomico stood transfixed, leaning forward, as if to embrace his grandfather as well as his words.

"Kadomico will learn the way of the English and help us find the best way for the Saponi to protect their people and hunting grounds. In doing this, he will not depart from the way of the Saponi, forget his people or bow to the English. It must be done, else we face the fate of others before us—death by war, disease, or starvation. We will wait for Kadomico to return."

The frozen stillness of Choola's face did not mask the sadness in his eyes as he eased back to his seat, crossed his legs, and folded his arms. His words of concession to the strength of the English fell heavy on the assembly, men unaccustomed to conceding without a fight. To them it smacked of allying with the very force threatening them, or worse yet, submission, heretofore unthinkable. Anger, sadness, and confusion stirred among them as they listened to their most outspoken and respected old warrior.

In spite of the confusion and uncertainty they were feeling, they did understand what Choola had said. They could wait and see what would become of Kadomico's visit to Williamsburg.

Custoga sensed the reluctant acceptance of the council and spoke. "Kadomico will go tomorrow. Red Wolf and Tree Son will go with him. Red Wolf will see the firesticks, English warriors and their strength. And our priests will call on the gods of evil to stop the white man."

3

Tanaka felt the warm earth under her bare feet as she walked the short well-worn path through the open meadow of long grass and wildflowers to the bathing place. Just ahead shrubs of pokeberry, elderberry, honeysuckle, and crimson sumac rose above the long grass to form a dense barrier to the stands of sycamore, dogwood, and willow bordering the clear, cold water of the bathing stream. The deeply shaded stream continuously divided itself into twisting paths over gravel and sand, splashed around limestone outcrops, and formed tiny musical cascades of white droplets before resting in a wide stretch of quiet, shallow water convenient to the bathers and women washing clothes. Saponi women kept a very large section of that bank clear of brush and long grass. From there they could hear and see the town, a matter of safety and convenience. Two women, just leaving the creek, met Tanaka, nodded a greeting and moved on.

Nearing the stream, Tanaka's thoughts shifted from deep concern about Kadomico's future to White Water. She noticed the elderberry bushes, reminding her that the lush black fruit must be gathered soon. Her brow wrinkled with concern at White Water's recent impetuosity. In a land so dense with trees that a squirrel might travel for days without touching ground, help was usually out of reach. As a rule, only armed braves traveled alone in the wilderness, and then, only with good reason:

training, hunting or on a special mission. Tanaka, to balance the freedom of natural expression with appropriate restraint, preferred to let the eight-year-old White Water learn from her mistakes. But she was quick to react in the case of safety or serious tribal transgressions such as interrupting elders and disrespecting others.

White Water sat on the smooth first limb of a giant sycamore felled by a storm from long ago. When she saw her mother she stood, head slightly bowed. When they were an arm's length apart, Tanaka spoke without emotion.

"Did you not know Saponi women are forbidden to be alone outside the town, not even in the maize fields and especially not the forest?"

Lifting her head to look directly into Tanaka's eyes, hoping to find understanding and forgiveness there, White Water said, "Yes, my Mother, I know this, but I think I forgot. I thought Kadomico would be near the maize field where the women worked today, and when he was not, I just went a little way on the trail."

Tanaka ignored the excuse and said, "When two or more are together they can help each other if one is hurt. More important, raiding or unfriendly hunting parties can easily take an unarmed woman. You went alone into the woodlands. You disobeyed the rule of our people and me. You were careless. And you put yourself and your people at risk. I am deeply disappointed. To help you remember never to do it again, you will go with the women each day and gather maize until the season is past. They go to the fields at sun-up. I will wake you before first light so you will have time to do your morning chores."

White Water was not unhappy to hear this. To go into the fields with the women would be fun. She did not yet know that rising so early would be difficult, and after the first hour in the field she would grow tired, and the working women would scold her for gathering so little maize. But at this moment, she was deeply distressed because she had failed her mother. She fought back the tears welling behind her closed eyes; she was determined to show no emotion.

High above the town, Kadomico stood on a massive gray stone outcropping embedded high above the gentle rapids of the river called Yadkin. As he faced the first light of dawn, tears streamed from eyes stained red after a sleepless night. Again this morning, his father was plain-spoken as he said goodbye, and Kadomico understood that this assignment was a matter of great service to the Saponi, somehow profoundly important to their future. He was eager to obey and to make his father and people proud, but he was unable to choke back his sadness when he thought of leaving the forest, the river, and the other young braves in training to become warriors and hunters. Was he not to become a warrior? If not, what? He had no vision of what it would be like to live among the English or to attend their school. He understood he was to study the marks they called writing, and that this was somehow crucial to his people, but how long would such a thing take? How many and what other Indians, friend or enemy, would be there? Would he also learn to shoot the thunderous firestick and handle the longknives of the English?

Finally, he accepted within himself the instructions of his father, and he resolved to do his best. Turning his face upward to the heavens, he raised outstretched hands to the sky, and prayed for understanding of the task before him. The sun rose fire-red, sending its first rays blazing through the misty dawn to dry the last tear Kadomico would permit.

He breathed in deeply. Gentle air currents, scented by the fallen leaves and moist riverbank, filled his lungs and gave him a feeling of renewed strength. He took a last look at the green valley beneath him. Between patches of morning fog he saw the river twisting through the valley, a black thread in a sea of green.

Beside him, the whispering water mingled with the rustle of leaves and Kadomico smiled. A warm surging confidence swept over him in a moment of divine transformation charged with the presence of the Great Spirit. The questions, uncertainties, and sadness had vanished, and in their place he felt a strong sense of purpose, an eagerness to face the task before him. He turned and entered the dense forest, running almost soundlessly over the small animal track.

Tree Son and Red Wolf were waiting for him at the trail head. When he came into view, they turned southeast, toward Occaneechi country, trotting into the forest single file, well apart.

4

In the summer of 1676, Sam Layton was two years old when Seneca raiders burned his family's frontier farm to the ground, killed the animals, set fire to the crop bins, and killed and scalped everyone except little Sam. The Seneca took him west near the Ohio Valley and traded him to the Shawnee. There he was adopted by a Shawnee family and raised just as though he had been born into the family. Sam had no memory of the massacre of his English family, but he would never forget the day when at age eight, six mounted colonial militia rode into the Shawnee town, pow-wowed with the Shawnee council, and took him away.

That morning his Shawnee mother had hung a medallion of polished white crystal around his neck. Within the crystal, was a flame-shaped flair of red and green. Holding both his shoulders, she had looked deeply into his eyes and whispered, "Do not forget." The words meant nothing special to him at that moment, but they would remain with him the rest of his life. After that things happened quickly and no one explained to him that his life with the Shawnee was over.

Among the Indians, captives were frequently adopted to replace family members lost to battle, accident, or disease. Child captives were greatly favored for adoption because they were most easily absorbed into a family. By 1667, settler defense and strength had grown so that when they learned of a captive, often from a traveler but sometimes from an Indian expecting favor or reward, they dispatched parties of militia to the rescue. Sometimes the militia bargained, paid a ransom, or traded for a captive, but when necessary they took the captive by force. Understandably, child captives were greatly distressed to be torn from the only family they knew, but in many cases, adults also refused to go with the militia.

The scene that morning in the Shawee town was noisy. Strangely clothed men saddled horses, primed rifles, and checked their longknives, scabbards and saddle packs. Sam, clad only in a soft deerskin loincloth and barefoot, had stood hesitant and uncertain with his Shawnee family at the front of the small gathering. When the riders mounted, the horses stamped and pranced in the dusty lane and cast a sort of spell over the crowd. Like Sam, most of them had never seen a horse. As he watched, a huge militiaman, his eyes barely visible behind a turned-down hat shading a thick black beard, had handed the reins of his horse to a companion rider and stepped away. Nodding politely, he touched the brim of his hat, moved closer to Sam and his mother, and spoke softly in their language.

He said, "It is time. The boy will be with his people." It was the best he could do with Shawnee words. Sam had understood enough to be frightened and turned away just as he felt the gentle grip on his upper arm. The bearded giant turned him around and swung him high into the air behind a mounted English rifleman.

The instant the horse turned away from the small group of family and friends, Sam heaved himself upward behind the saddle and twisted away from the horse. He hit the ground running toward the woods, instinctively choosing the densest part to eliminate pursuit. He ran with all his might, but he failed to see Chokan, and ran straight into the outstretched arms of the big warrior. Chokan tried but failed to reassure Sam as he carried the kicking and struggling youngster back to the waiting militia. The bearded man sat him firmly behind the mounted rifleman, pulled his arms around the rider's waist and tied his hands loosely.

After five days on the wilderness trail east, they reached a frontier fort. There the militia handed Sam over to another militia group that was about to return to the settlements in coastal Virginia. Once there, the authorities declared him an orphan and placed him with the Layton farm family from which he repeatedly tried to run away. After the first attempt, they watched him closely, and each time he tried to leave, they stopped him. The punishment was usually a beating by his adopted father. The humiliation was worse than the beatings. The Shawnee punished their enemies that way but never their own people, and the beatings merely strengthened Sam's resolve to reject the way of the white man.

Months passed before he spoke, and then only when necessary, always without emotion. No Shawnee warrior would give his captor the satisfaction of seeing his distress. His stoicism only fueled the Laytons' determination to raise him right, which only fueled his own determination to reject the way of proper table manners, strange clothing, and frequent prayers and church services.

In time, Sam stopped running away and became more cooperative and respectful, but he steadfastly refused to accept his adopted parents as parents or address them as mother or father as they suggested. He did well in school, did his share of chores, attended church as directed, and dressed as they asked, but every night, in the privacy of his bed, he prayed to his own Creator with the stone his Indian mother had given him clasped firmly, secretly in his hand. Even after six years, Sam felt no ties to his adopted parents. Yet, six years of life in the family of a white man, the undeniable white skin beneath his clothing, the freckles on his cheeks, and the chestnut colored hair were undeniable manifestations of his true heritage.

He made only one friend among the English, a schoolmate named Jock Adams. Jock had also been raised in captivity, rescued, and returned to a life on the small tobacco farm of the Adams family who adopted him. The militia rescued him the same year they rescued Sam. Captured at the age of three, he had spent five years with the northern Iroquois Indians. Algonquian being his native language at the time of rescue, he and Sam learned English together, and Sam even learned Jock's Algonquian tongue. When they could, they hunted and fished together and met often in church and school and secretly shared stories of their Indian lives. And while Sam rejected the Laytons, the childless Adams so cherished their adopted son that Jock grew to trust them, then to depend on them, and finally, to return their love and affection. Jock became a proper English son. The boys understood the differences in their family life and rarely spoke of it.

Sam grew strong on the farm, and although he was shorter than Jock, who had a long, lanky frame, he was muscular, solid through the chest and shoulders with powerful arms and legs. In typical Shawnee fashion, Sam continued to train for strength and endurance.

He had quickly learned how the settler family guaranteed their winter food by keeping chickens, cows, and hogs. He noticed the great variety of plants grown in the kitchen gardens, some of them similar to the maize, bean, and squash in the fields of the Shawnee but lacking the in-season plants, roots, nuts, and berries of the forest which were vital, abundant, and prized by every Shawnee woman.

Watching his adopted father, Sam learned to use a team of oxen to till the soil, move great logs, and haul by wagon or slide. Of all the animals living on the farm, the lively spirit and beauty of the horse captured his understanding, admiration, and respect. Soon, boy and horse worked together with very little exchange of voice or gesture. To the astonishment of his adopted father, the horse came to Sam on sight, followed him to or from the feeding stall, and even helped him to work the bridle, harness, or saddle by shifting his weight and backing or stepping conveniently.

Sam embraced school enthusiastically, and after the second year became a voracious reader; he led his class in grades, and was often advanced early to the next level. But, as compelling as his white skin and life in a white family was, even more compelling to him were the values he had developed during the six formative years with his Indian family: his faith in nature and the gods of nature; his love and respect for his Indian family; and his loyalty to his tribe.

He was revolted by the white man's hatred, fear, and treatment of Indians. He saw it every day, and it continually reinforced his resolve to refuse the so-called civilized way. But he also knew that marauding Indians murdered hundreds of Virginians, scalped the white settlers, captured their women and children, destroyed their livestock and crops, and burned their buildings. And he had heard the settler men speak often of the sneak attacks by the Powhatans in 1622 and again in 1644 after twenty-two years of peace and friendship.

Sam had finally come to terms with the inevitable truth: he was a Shawnee Indian born of white parents. But, after six years of living with the settlers, he also understood that he would forever be different from his Shawnee people. It troubled him to know all this, and he struggled with the contradicting realities of hate and love he found among the Shawnees and the settlers. He knew comfort and peace only when he was alone in the wilderness. There among the trees and mountain streams he clearly belonged. There he felt an abiding strength and understanding.

In the passage of time and despite the longing in his heart, Sam slowly realized that the Shawnee life he had once known was over, and as much as he missed that life, he had come to like working with horses, wagons, and plows. Also, he had come to understand that the white man's strength lay in his overwhelming numbers and his command of an inexhaustible supply of guns and ammunition. Beyond that, these Virginians could grow vast quantities of food and tobacco, make glass, fashion tools from iron, and build strong structures of wood, stone, and brick. He saw that the ships of many sails provided a continuous supply of goods from distant lands called Europe, Africa, and Asia. Sam learned fast about the expanding commerce among the Virginia settlers and with those other countries.

But Sam also became convinced that he would never be accepted by the white man. Nor did he wish to be. He refused to adopt the Anglican religion of the Laytons. Instead, he believed deeply in the heavenly Creator of his Shawnee people, the Creator of all the land, sky, and waters. He believed in the Creator of Mother Earth. He had learned at the knee of his Shawnee mother and countless ceremonial tributes that the Creator provides all the needs of man and then leaves him to himself to make the best of it. His Shawnee mother taught him that the storms, droughts, floods, and fires were the work of the devil who demanded sacrifice and acknowledgment. She had reminded him never to forget, and he would not.

Eventually, Sam accepted that he was destined to be different in both the Indian's and white man's worlds. In his fourteenth year, he began to plan his own future.

One September day in 1688, Sam at age 14, faced his adopted father in the barnyard as he sorted out freshly shucked maize for various livestock.

"Sir, could I have a word?"

Knowing full well Sam would not stop until the stock had been penned and fed, the gates latched, and the various troughs filled with fresh water, Angus Layton nevertheless re-emphasized the importance of all that by replying, "We can talk when the chores are done."

"They are done, sir."

"Well, then. What is it?"

"The crops are in now. I will leave tomorrow and go farther west than we have ever been to trap and trade beaver this winter."

Sam waited for the response. After a short silence, he continued, "It will be a good thing if I have the musket I have been using and some powder and shot, and I think my share of the fur we have stashed would be a fair trade."

Layton would lose his most valuable farm hand at a time when he intended to expand his holdings. But after six years of watching Sam grow, this personal declaration of independence did not surprise him. Nor did he think he could stop him or change his mind, but it was worth a try.

"Well lad, I figured you for more sense than that. You wouldn't get one day into the woods until some Iroquois would have my rifle and your scalp. And you know well as me puttin' guns in the hands of Indians is the same as murdering our own. That's why it's against the law to sell, trade, or give Indians guns and powder, and here you are asking me to break the law, and worse yet, make it so some unsuspecting settler gets murdered.

"If it's more beaver you want, we can set aside some time to trap together this winter like always, and still open new ground for tobacco next year." Layton hesitated, cleared his throat, and continued, "Besides, time's coming when you can have your own share of this farm."

Sam did not miss the hesitation in his adopted father's voice. He just looked away not wanting to see the conflict in Layton's eyes. As usual, his share, if any, would be the smallest, poorest of the lot, after his father's two natural children.

He ignored the half-hearted offer and replied, "The gun and ammunition will be safe with me, and because I will travel alone, I will be invisible to enemies. The sheriff will not hold you responsible for arming a family member against the dangers of wilderness travel, but either way, I will leave before first light to be clear of settlements. You can say I have gone to trap in a new land beyond the frontier. It is the truth."

"I forbid you to go," Layton said, then turned his back and walked away.

When Sam rose an hour before first light, the musket, powder, and ball lay alongside his pallet with a wrapper of bread, beef jerky, and dried apples.

Sam walked away from his settler home and family knowing that he would not return and knowing that except for the work he did, he would not be missed. They had fed, clothed, and schooled him equally with the other children. But his refusal to deny his Shawnee upbringing and to join the family in prayers, singing, and celebrations of birthdays and holidays set him apart. He had responded to gestures of love and affection stoically, neither accepting nor denying them until they finally stopped altogether. Eventually, he took his place in the family as a valuable worker on the farm, in school as a good student and a voracious reader, and in the community of Virginia frontier settlers as "the boy who was raised by Indians."

Each night before he fell asleep, he remembered the Shawnee town, his Indian family, and the strong determined face of his Indian mother that morning when she pressed the brilliant stone into his hand, looked into his eyes, and whispered, "Do not forget."

As he walked toward the western mountains that warm autumn morning, with each footfall raising tiny splashes of white trail dust around the calloused pads of his bare feet, his eyes were fixed on the mountain pass two days dead ahead. Beyond lay a fifteen mile-wide valley of grassland. On the western side, the Shenandoah River, a serpentine ribbon of clear water, tumbled over limestone and gravel moving north to join the Potomac River, then east to the Chesapeake Bay. The Shenandoah River and its tributaries attracted beaver with fur of the best quality, and Sam expected to find huge colonies of them.

His route west led past two frontier farms, then into Monacan and Manahoac hunting grounds, and over the Blue Mountains. After that, it was just a day's walk across the rich valley grasslands to the river where he planned to begin trapping beaver and muskrat. The mountain posed the most danger to

Sam. The ferocious Iroquois regularly traveled the crest of these mountains raiding for fur, weapons, and ammunition, but especially for slaves and captives to replenish their dwindling number. Sam and his weapon would be a prize worth taking.

The quickest way would lead him through the mountain pass before him, but it was also likely that others would travel that way. He left the trail, and, careful to avoid the occasional open spaces, prepared to scale the less steep terrain well south of the pass. After about an hour, he came to a vast slide of shale directly in his path and decided to detour rather than expose himself on the open shale. The climb was nearly straight up in places but so well forested with wild azalea and laurel beneath the hardwood he had only to pull himself upward one arm length at a time. He slowed his pace and moved steadily upward, careful not to dislodge rock or debris.

He was still a short climb before the top when he sensed danger—no sign, no sound—just hair rising on the back of his neck sent him into a frozen position, listening, not even moving his head to help his eyes search. Nothing. He waited a long while before he began to ease down and flatten out in the laurel-strewn ground. Once he thought he heard a limb rustle as though pushed out of the way and released, but he couldn't be sure.

When he felt the danger was past, he resumed his climb and topped out on the well-worn Appalachian Trail. Hastily checking for sign of travelers, he found nothing until he checked off-trail. There along the edge of a flat stone half-buried lay a single blade of freshly broken grass. He carefully freed it from the clump, and eased backward down into the hardwood cover, where he stopped long enough to examine the blade. Grass disturbances from weather and animals were not uncommon along the trail, but this blade had been crushed—much like a careless footfall. It was enough to reassure him that his instincts were correct.

He moved on down the steep mountainside until he reached the beginning of the valley. There he knew he was visible from the mountain behind him and from the valley stretching before him, but in that vast valley grassland, he felt reasonably free from ambush. He started through the knee-high switch grass and chest-high golden rod at a fast trot. Because he could see as well as be seen, it was safe traveling until he reached the woodlands near the river. Just before entering the woodlands, he changed directions, and running along the edge of the undergrowth, he doubled his pace. At the first opening, he turned toward the river. He was unprepared for the breathtaking scene of clear green and blue waters splashing white around giant limestone outcrops, rippling over gravel beds, running and falling northward into a vista of green hardwoods under a clear blue sky.

Sam was home. Here he would camp and take as many beaver pelts as he could before the first snowfall. He planned to build a raft or a canoe and float his cargo to one of the trading posts.

Almost immediately after he arrived at the river, a party of Shawnee hunters confronted him, and upon hearing his story in their native language, they led him to their town west of the river where he was joyfully accepted. He was welcomed with a celebration complete with dancing, singing, feasting, prayers, and sacrifices of tobacco and choice foods: venison, fish, fowl, maize, beans, honey, berries, and nuts. Afterwards, Sam and his Indian friends trapped beaver together and gathered a large cache of fur. That November, they paddled down the Potomac River to a trading post at Trummel Town, near the fall line on the northern boundary of Virginia.

Sam set up his base in the Shawnee town, took an Indian wife in his eighteenth year, and continued to prosper. Because of his unusual command of the Algonquian and English languages and his understanding of both cultures, he soon became a respected go-between for the English and the Indian leaders of various tribes in the Eastern territory. That led to his eventual mastery of the Siouan language in the southern piedmont country and the Algonquian dialects of the Iroquois and Virginia Powhatan Indians. By his twentieth year, Sam Layton was known and trusted by several colony Governors and by many Iroquois, Shawnee, and other Eastern Indian leaders. Because he could read English print and explain it to the Indians, Sam developed a well-informed and accurate view of the complexities of coexistence between the hunter/gatherers and the land-hungry farmers.

In the rivers and the mountains just beyond the frontier, he knew peace, family, friendship, and there he felt the presence of the Great Spirit, the creator of that mystical wilderness of boundless beauty and endless sustenance. There he belonged.

Now, in the fall of 1700, far from the Shenandoah Valley and his Shawnee home, he stood by his birch bark canoe and gazed out over the James River. This river was once known as the Powhatan River, which to Sam's mind was a much more musical and worthy name than "James."

Just a week ago, a frontier scout had found him on the south fork trapping fur just south of the confluence of the north and south forks of the Shenandoah River. The scout brought a message from Virginia's Governor Nicholson. Would Sam come to Williamsburg for a special job as interpreter and escort to visiting Indians? Could he come right away? Sam turned his furs and trap line over to his Shawnee partner. He pondered the trip and decided he would go by water rather than overland. The scout readily agreed when he saw the birch bark canoe.

"I've heard of canoes like that. Made of bark right off a tree," he said, pausing to admire the craftsmanship. "Never saw one, though. Even the lashings are perfect and she sets the water like she's a part of it."

The scout paused again, drinking in the lines of the canoe and the intricate designs carved and painted in the gold-colored bark siding, then said, "Sure is a beauty. How'd you come by it?"

Sam told him the whole story. He had first seen it on a trading trip into the region of the St. Lawrence River three years ago. Immediately, he knew he must have it. Although there were canoes all about him, the grace and beauty of this one caught the eye of every paddler. It was light enough that one man could easily carry it. The end stems were mirror images of each other, curving up gracefully from the water, then turning back over the protected dry-well beneath. Its fourteen feet of ribs and gunwales were lashed precisely with finely twisted spruce root, then covered for protection by single pieces of thin cedar top rail which had been split from the heart of straight-grained white cedar and set firmly in place by carved maple thwarts. A single sheet of white birch bark covered the shell, the smooth inner bark on the outside of the canoe. The price was all the fur he had with him—an entire winter's trapping. Even so he had bargained and negotiated two days before the owner, a French trader, agreed.

"I was glad to pay the price," Sam added. "It's the best canoe I ever expect to see. The Ojibwa made it, and they're the best makers you'll find. They live on the north shore of Lake Superior where such bark as this is plentiful. The owner was a French trader willing to trade only because he needed a craft capable of more cargo."

Sam and the Governor's messenger loaded the canoe with their provisions and weapons and left the following morning for Williamsburg. In three days, they shot through the rapids of both the Shenandoah and Potomac rivers, portaged around the Potomac fall line, and rode the currents into the Chesapeake Bay. There they struck a course of easy paddling for the York River, then upstream to Queen's Creek and followed the creek on to Capitol Landing near Williamsburg.

Still dressed in buckskins, moccasins, and with shoulder-length hair, Sam met with Governor Nicholson in his small rented house near the college. From similar work in the past, these two men knew, trusted, and were comfortable with each other.

"Welcome, Sam. Welcome. Welcome. I am pleased you came," Nicholson said, moving briskly into the room with outstretched hand from his half-removed waist coat, the other hand busy freeing his throat from the confinement of shirt and collar. The beginning of a generous belly fought the trousers he wore above white knee-length stockings and buckled shoes.

"Governor," Sam said it with sincere respect. He stood holding his wide brim sun hat by his side and shook hands with Nicholson. He looked the governor straight in his eyes in a way that reassured Nicholson he could be counted on. Sam greatly respected the Governor's efforts to contain settler animosity and the smoldering belief among some that "the only good Indian was a dead Indian." The past uprisings and massacres in Virginia were not easily forgotten.

"Sit down, Sam. Let's get something wet in here. Then I'll tell you why I sent for you."

He began to explain that when the moon was full, maybe in two more days, he wanted Sam to meet some young western frontier Indian boys escorted by braves of their tribes. They would expect him where the Appomattox and the James Rivers meet and escort the group to Williamsburg. The boys, at the invitation of Governor Nicholson, were to attend the English school and learn the language and Christianity. Sam was to introduce them to the schoolmaster and remain as interpreter until they were settled. The Governor worried about the safety of the frontier Indians as they came near the colony of settlers. Sam, with his knowledge of both languages and understanding of the Indian/settler problem, would see to the safe arrival of the Indians and get them off to a good start.

Sam pondered the Governor's enthusiasm to get Indian boys in an English classroom and shook his head. Governor Nicholson said, "The King himself wrote of this schooling the savages, 'It is so good and pious a work.'" As much as he believed the sincerity of the King of England and the efforts of the Governor to bridge the gap between the Indian and English, Sam was doubtful. Indian boys, conditioned to live as comfortably with darkness, rain, snow, ice, and wind as with fair weather and sunlight, would find it difficult to accept the confinement of a schoolroom. Add to that the typical humiliating corporal punishment, the prevailing hostile attitude of most English toward Indians, and the hours of sitting still in class and you've got yourself a problem, thought Sam. He remembered how he hated the first suit of clothes forced on him and the agonizing instructions in the Anglican Church.

But Sam accepted his assignment. He carried his canoe from Capitol Landing to College Landing and made his way to the James River, then upstream to the mouth of the Chickahominy River. There he set his bow at an angle to the current and paddled a straight line across to the other side. Aware that he was completely exposed while crossing, his eyes kept sweeping the southern bank for movement. He listened intently for telltale signals between those who might be watching him. Neither hearing nor seeing them only heightened his alertness, and he let the current move him further downstream until he found the mouth of a familiar stream, wide and deep enough to make a protective moat for landing. Still there was no sound, no movement on the bank. He slipped the canoe silently between rocks and through the shallow water on the downstream side of the creek. Grasping the gunnels on either side of the canoe, he stepped forward, out onto the rocky shore and dragged the canoe almost clear of the water.

"LAY…Ton, you will live a long time," came the voice of Kajika, a dangerous Tuscarora warrior with whom Sam had once traded.

Sam stopped and looked in the direction of the voice. On the other side of the creek lay a large clearing between the river on one side and the wide mouth of the creek on the other. Beyond the clearing, a thick wall of saplings covered with honeysuckle vine and briars blocked the way to a stand of sycamore and walnut trees. He was not an easy target, he thought—arrow or musket ball—but he could pay a high price for a lucky shot. His nearest cover was too far. Nor did he know the strength of the Tuscarora—more likely several warriors than just one. He stayed put, turned his back to the clearing, slung his backpack into place over his shoulder and squatted down to stow the bowline in the canoe, presenting the smallest possible target to the clearing. While his right hand rested near the flintlock pistol in his belt, his left hand worked the bowline near the musket laying in the bow of the canoe.

He said, "Kajika, it is you. Come. You can tell me how it is with the Tuscarora. It has been a long time. I am here to meet Occaneechi, Tutelo, and Saponi braves and go with them to the place of the English chief."

No response. Sam waited until the natural sounds of the forest resumed before he rose and scouted the area thoroughly for sign. Finding none on either side of the creek, he felt satisfied he was alone, but to find Tuscarora braves this far north meant trouble. Kajika may have backed off when he learned Occaneechi and Saponi parties could be in the area even now. However, it also meant he might try to locate them and determine their strength before he made his next move. And it may be they could best do that by letting Sam lead them to the parties. Was Kajika waiting?

Sam thought through it. The party he was to meet would be well into their trip down the Appomattox. He figured his position was half a day's walk to the meeting place and about the same if he paddled back upstream. The river was very wide at this point. He could be out of range in a few paddle strokes. Certainly Sam's weapons would tempt Kajika, but Sam had seen the envy in many an eye that admired his canoe. For that Kajika would risk most anything.

Sam stayed busy with the articles in the canoe, gradually positioning it where he wanted it. He walked to the bow, lifted it as though to bring it farther ashore, and with both feet firmly gripping the wet sand, gave the canoe a sudden shove. He ran with it back into the river and with two more steps threw himself over the gunwale into the bottom of the canoe, now caught in the current and rapidly moving away from the shore.

It happened so quickly that Kajika, watching intently from the other side of the creek, jerked forward in surprise, neither firing his musket nor drawing his bow. Instead, he glared at the canoe caught moving away with the current. He watched it recover and set a course upstream Kajika returned to the nine warriors waiting in the cover of the woodland and they began to follow the canoe upstream.

With knees planted firmly on either side of the centerline of the keel and leaning back against the center thwart, Sam paddled to the middle of the wide flat water of the James, never changing sides with his paddle. By twisting his wrist at the end of the paddle in a J-pattern with each stroke, the bow of the canoe maintained an arrow-straight course upstream. The light canoe drew only inches of draft and answered handsomely to each stroke. He paddled steadily on, well aware that Kajika would not give up easily.

5

Moving steadily northeast toward a point just below the headwaters of the Appomattox River, Red Wolf guided his party safely west of the towns of the enemy Tuscarora and other tribes of questionable friendliness.

Early on the morning of the second day, Hawk, son of the Occhaneechi chief, and his escort, a warrior named Wiwohka, appeared on the trail ahead of them. Without breaking stride, Red Wolf signaled them to align themselves single file, and the group of five now ran steadily on over the trail toward the Appomattox. As singles, they left less trail sign and made less sound.

Red Wolf finally signaled a halt and waited for Wiwohka to approach. They grasped forearms in greeting.

Red Wolf said "We will reach the river by nightfall. It is good to have you with us, Wiwohka. I do not expect the Iroquois or Tuscarora raiders on this trail, but it is possible. A Shawnee trader from the north came to our town and told us of raids near the mountains during the last moon."

"It is good to travel with the Saponi, Red Wolf. We must return in time to join the hunt this winter," Wiwohka said. "The Occaneechi and Saponi are good hunters. Together we will again bring back a winter supply of deer and bear."

While Red Wolf and Wiwohka talked quietly, Hawk, with the faintest of smiles on his face, approached Kadomico. "I am Hawk, son of the chief of the Occaneechi."

Kadomico liked Hawk instantly. He saw a young brave near his own age, already with a full chest of muscle and arms of great strength for one so young. But it was the smiling eyes that captivated him. Deep set under rich full brows and lashes, his eyes spoke loudly his sincerity and friendliness. Unknown to Kadomico at the time, those same eyes, driven by his trigger-quick temper, could radiate a murderous hatred.

"I am to go to Williamsburg to see the way of the English," continued Hawk softly. He looked away as though envisioning himself marching past the staring white strangers. "And *they* will see that the Occaneechi are mighty hunters and warriors."

"I am Kadomico, son of Custoga, Chief of the Saponi."

The two had fallen into an unspoken pact, one that would serve them well in the strangeness of the forthcoming days among the English, but there was much left to learn about each other. Kadomico would grasp all opportunities to learn. Hawk would look only for weapons and better ways to wage war against the white man. To Hawk, all white men were a menace, and he had no use for them or their strange ways. He had learned to hate white men at the knee of his mother and from many warriors in his town. It had become a strong, uncompromising hate, but so well disguised that his father had chosen him to go to the English to learn, a matter perfectly acceptable to Hawk, but for a vastly different reason. Hawk simply wanted the English out of his country. Nothing else mattered.

By nightfall of the second day, a young Indian of the Tutelos named Shanda joined them. He was younger than Kadomico and slender of build, even for a boy. He took a trail position directly behind Kadomico but did not speak. Shanda was not at all certain he would see his people again. He only knew that he was to go with this group and that their mission was of great importance to his people. When they stopped for a brief time, he approached

Kadomico. "I am Shanda, son of the Chief of the Tutelo. Have you traveled far?"

"We have traveled two suns. Red Wolf will lead us until near darkness. I am Kadomico, son of Custoga, Chief of the Saponi. There, high in that tree, is Tree Son, my friend. He will return with Red Wolf after we arrive in the town of the white people. I will stay and…." Kadomico stopped abruptly. His eyes had found the warrior accompanying Shanda, a warrior of such great stature Kadomico could not help but stare at his broad shoulders, great height, and gleaming weapons. When the warrior moved, the muscles of his back traveled like wavelets across his shoulders nudging the quiver of arrows and flowing into arms the size of some men's legs.

"His name is Wapiti," Shanda said. "He is the greatest warrior of all the Tutelos. Among our people his tomahawk throw is the best. He can cut straws at many paces and his arrows go farther than any other. Many cannot even draw the bow he carries, and no man has ever defeated him in battle or game."

Kadomico admired the bow carried by Wapiti. Slightly longer than his arm, it was made of Osage Orange wood, backed with rattlesnake skin, and was shorter than usual to ease movement in the dense underbrush of wilderness travel. It fit snugly to his shoulders; the quiver strapped under the bow next to his right shoulder carried a dozen man-killing iron-tipped arrows and four more with bone or blunt tips for small game and fowl. A razor-edged knife of tempered steel, nearly the length of his forearm, hugged his left hip in a buckskin sheath with the antler grip thrust forward for an easy cross-draw. On his right hip, he carried a polished steel tomahawk with a hand-worn, slightly curved, black locust handle. Two scalps hung from his belt. Although they spoke a mixture of Algonquian dialects, this diminished tribe of Tutelos was strongly allied with the Saponi. Kadomico was enthralled. He felt Wapiti's strength and power and believed that in time he would be like that. Seeing the three eagle feathers in Wapiti's warlock, he thought, soon I will wear a fine feather and carry the steel tomahawk.

Although they were all armed, ready, and moving in a defensive pattern, they did not wear war paint, a clear message they were not on the warpath, as were many raiding parties in that area, especially the Iroquois, the Monacan, and the Tuscarora.

They trotted northward toward the Appomattox River; from there, they would follow the river southeast to the place on the James River where Sam Layton would join them for the final leg of the trip. Red Wolf had hunted most of this country at one time or another. The underbrush, hills, and ravines smacked of ambush, and he sometimes moved ahead, listened to the ground, climbed hills or trees to check the terrain. Others watched the foliage and grasses for signs of recent passage. Once, when he spied a party of Indians in the distance, Red Wolf sent his people into a ravine to wait out their passing. They were probably hunters, possibly Iroquois, not likely to be friendly.

About mid-day, just before reaching the river, Red Wolf sat down with Wiwohka and Wapiti in a stand of giant pine trees to confer on their location and the run down the Appomattox to the James. A raft could take two days. Bark canoes would be much faster. Elm bark had the greater strength and pliability, but hickory bark would also serve their purpose. Failing to find good bark, they would settle for a raft. They thought that materials for one or the other would be available. With seven workers, either could be built in a day.

The terrain about them was hilly with thick underbrush, occasionally broken by swampy sections. They had only three days before the moon would be full, one day for building the raft or canoe and two for travel. A canoe or two small ones, drawing only inches of water and able to navigate tight passages in the rock-strewn river, could make the trip in much less time than a raft. They decided to split up and cover the last three or four hours of travel looking for the best material available for their craft. Separated into three groups, they remained in sight of each other and moved forward.

Well before dark, the moist air and gently sloping terrain told them they were near the river. At the first sound of falling water, they stopped until Red Wolf gave the signal to reassemble. Each had sighted elm and hickory trees with straight-grained bark suitable for canoes.

When they reassembled, Red Wolf pointed to Tree Son, Hawk, Shanda, and Kadomico. "Go to the river, two upstream, two downstream. Make no sound. Follow it. Look for sign. Come back here before the sun reaches the mountain. If you find others or sign of others, make no contact. Remain out of sight. Do not signal."

The boys paired up and left silently, aware that Red Wolf and the others watched their manner and moves. Near the river, they separated. Kadomico and Tree Son started upstream.

When the warriors gained the bank of the Appomattox River, Wiwohka spoke "The river is low. There will be places where we will walk and carry."

Although it was clear to Red Wolf from the near fullness of last night's moon they had little time to spare, he gave it no weight in his planning. It would take whatever time it would take. He planned the surest, not the fastest, way to complete the trip. There was plenty of hostile wilderness yet to be faced.

"The long canoe can be built faster than two small ones, but it will not travel well over the rocks, falls, and shallow stretches of this river," he said.

Wiwohka said, "On the trail, I cut into two elm trees with bark good for canoes, but the sap has slowed, and the bark cannot be removed in one piece until the new growing season when the sap will again run heavy and loosen the bark."

"The water is too low for rafts," Red Wolf said. "We must continue running." He pointed downstream. "The Nahyssan, brothers to Saponi and Tutelo, are there. Less than half a sun. We will stop there and try to trade for canoes."

As the sun dropped behind the hills to their back, Wiwohka and Wapiti started downstream to locate Shanda and Hawk on the packed-earth of the riverbank trail. It was kept open by animals and the occasional hunter—easy traveling except for the occasional swampy ground with dense undergrowth that slowed their pace or forced them to find a way around. Wapiti, well known for his speed and endurance on the trail, set out at twice the pace of Wiwohka to alert the Nahyssans of their visit.

Red Wolf started upstream to summon Kadomico and Tree Son for the night trip ahead of them. He found them investigating tracks and disturbed bank soil.

"Three men, two with strange footwear," Kadomico said as he pointed to heel marks of boots. "One with moccasins. The canoe is heavy, maybe dugout. There are the ashes of the campfire." He pointed in the direction of a thick undergrowth of small trees and shrubs.

"Maybe two suns," Tree Son said. "Ashes have been wet."

Red Wolf was pleased with the details of the report. He nodded approval but squatted for a closer look. There in the soft ground near the water, the print of a moccasin was so clear that considerable detail was exposed.

"What tribe is the moccasin?" he asked.

The boys knew immediately they had overlooked some detail. Often the pattern of lacing revealed the tribe. They had been taught the patterns of several tribes, especially those of the enemy Iroquois. Both boys looked carefully at the print, but they could not identify the pattern.

"It is not Iroquois," Tree Son said.

"It could be Cherokee," Kadomico replied as he noticed the similarity with the pattern of the southern tribes.

"Tree Son is right," Red Wolf said. "He speaks well. Kadomico, if you do not know, it is better to remain silent. It is the moccasin of the Susquehanna people, enemy of the Iroquois and friends of the Saponi. This was a white trader camp guided by a Susquehanna brave. The canoe was loaded with fur, and you can see here, it traveled downstream. And you are right, it has been two suns."

At full darkness they stopped, took a little food from their pouches, dozed, and rested. The moon, one day from being full, rose casting a warm coverlet of soft light over the virgin timber of the dense forest. Walking the river bank on the clean, bare earth of animal trails, they took one more short rest before dawn to give Wapiti plenty of time to alert the Nahyssans.

Their early morning reception at the Nahyssan town was traditionally cordial. They were escorted past the cooking fires of several women to Yahou-Lakee, aged chief of the Nahyssan, and his council of elders in the principal roundhouse of the town. There they received an elaborate feast of bread, venison, turkey, and fish served with bowls of stewed maize, beans, and squash. They sat on furs and woven fabrics from trades with the English and arranged in a circle described by stones fencing a small fire. They cast small sacrifices of food and tobacco into the fire and whispered short prayers. Little clouds of smoke drifted upward as they passed the pipe of peace in silence while delicacies of meat, dried fruit, and nuts were spread before them.

When the serving women left, the priest raised his arms up and outward and prayed in Siouan:

> *Great Father of the forest, the waters, and the skies above, you have given us the sun to warm these lands of beauty and plenty. Winter comes now with cold winds and snow. When the days are short and the nights are long make us warm. Let us walk the trails that lead us to deer and antelope that our people will have food. For these things we thank you and the Mother of Earth.*

When the prayer was over Yahou-Lakee began to speak. "Our people are honored to have the warriors of our brothers in the south and to have the son of my friend, Chief Custoga of the Saponi. What we have is yours."

The priest sprinkled a mixture into the fire that caused a light flash and white smoke. Yahou-Lakee began to eat, followed respectfully by the council members and guests.

When Red Wolf had eaten a little of the venison and stew, he signaled his readiness to speak by folding his arms and withdrawing from the food.

Yahou-Lakee responded. "Here we are fewer than ever, as you can see. We have lost many of our people to raids by the white man, Iroquois, and Tuscarora. Winter food is scarce; now the forest has little game. In the land of the Saponi, the hunting is much better, the whites are not there, and the land of the Saponi remains the land of the Saponi. Why does Red Wolf come here?"

Red Wolf said, "We accept these rich gifts of food in the name of your brothers to the south and your friend, Custoga, Chief of the Saponi. Nicholson of Williamsburg, Chief of the English, wishes to train the sons of the Chiefs of the Saponi, Tutelo, and Occhaneechi in the way of the English. He says it is a good thing for us. We think not, but we have seen most of the people of Powhatan vanish, they who were as many as the stars when the English came. Now, only a few remain, and they live in tiny places the English call reservations. We have been told they work for the English and are fed by the English. Now, we see ever-westward movements of these white strangers, hungry for the land they take and fence for their use only; they do not even permit their own brothers to use the land they take. I say fight, but Custoga and the elders seek better understanding of the English first."

Pointing to each in turn, he continued, "Kadomico, Shanda, and Hawk go there to receive this training Nicholson speaks of, to observe the English, and to return to help us find a way to continue our own way of life and to protect our hunting grounds, towns, and fields. When the moon is full, soon now, we are to go downstream where the rivers come together and meet Sam Layton, a Shawnee man sent by Nicholson. He will speak for us and stay with the sons of the chiefs until they are settled."

Yahou-Lakee's face flamed red as he spoke. "When I was but six winters at my mother's knee, there were three towns of Nahyssan. Our warriors were many. Until only a few winters ago, the Powhatan and settlers feared us. On one raid they lost half the men they threw at us, and ran terrified at our strength. But the settlers came back, so many that if one fell in battle two would replace him. When we retreated beyond our towns, they killed our wives and children. After that, we moved west and south, seeking new hunting grounds, then further south and east and warred with the Tuscarora for hunting grounds. Now we have returned north and west as far as we are able to go. Each time we moved we lost more people to the sickness and war, sometimes with other tribes, often with the English.

"We have now been here a few winters in an uneasy peace. Traders come for our furs, maize, and meat. They see our fields and speak of tobacco which brings them much wampum. They use their own fields for tobacco and cannot feed themselves so they come to us with beads, iron, cloth, and copper. If we refuse to trade they send soldiers to raid our stores. It is but a little more time before we must fight or leave. Tell Custoga, if he says come, the Nahyssans will join him."

Kadomico absorbed every word and began to realize the importance of the work before him. Looking at those about him, he saw great strength and endurance in these men. They were one with storms, ice, wind, rain, and blistering heat. They needed little to keep going. They shot deer at great distances, outran them, finished them off, and carried them back to the towns for food. They slept on the forest floor in mid-winter ice and snow, swam swollen rivers, and lived for days on the products of the wilderness. They could run all day and into the night without rest. Kadomico's training included these things, and thinking of them, he felt invincible. The English could be stopped. He felt immensely proud to be the son of Custoga, to be Saponi, to be an Indian, and to have been chosen for this important work.

Red Wolf answered Yahou-Lakee. "I will tell Custoga. Now we must go, but we need two canoes to carry us to the meeting place."

Yahou-Lakee stood and whispered to the warrior nearest him. The warrior nodded and vanished immediately. Yahou-Lakee faced Red Wolf. "You will have two canoes with two

Nahyssan warriors in each. They will carry you and bring you back if you wish. Or return for you whenever you say."

"We are grateful for your generosity." Red Wolf rose and offered his forearm to Yahou-Lakee in a gesture of peace and unity.

Tonawanda, Tenskwataw, Tadewi, and Chava, all heavily armed, stout Nahyssan braves, manned the two dugout canoes, bow and stern. The smoothly hewn poplar was brightly painted with the marks of the Nahyssan at each end. Highly polished and well oiled inside and out, they were built with a generous beam but short enough for good maneuverability in rapids.

Kadomico had noticed the muskets carried by two of the Nahyssans. He whispered to Hawk, "Is that the firestick I have heard our braves speak of?"

"It is," Hawk said. "There are two of them in our town. They make a loud noise, but only if you have powder for them. What they hit, they usually kill."

"What is powder?" Kadomico asked.

"I don't know. It is fine, like black dust, and only the English have it. I have heard that their chief forbids them to trade it with us, but some of them trade anyhow."

Kadomico resolved to learn more about this.

Anxious to be of service to the visitors, smiling Nahyssan women and children loaded baskets of leftovers into the canoes. Among them was a young buckskin-clad girl of extraordinary beauty who waded to the canoe where Kadomico knelt ready to paddle. She placed a tiny basket next to him, leaning forward in such a way her waist-length, shimmering black hair spilled over her shoulder and brushed his thigh. When she straightened, their eyes met, and Kadomico felt his blood rise in a bewildering way and with such overwhelming intensity that, for an instant, the vision before him seemed unreal.

Then, the canoe turned slowly into the current, and the magic of the moment faded. The girl stood transfixed in the knee-deep water, her buckskin skirt gathered in one hand well above her knees. Her mother finally broke the spell by taking her hand.

Within each canoe a paddle rested at the passenger positions. In addition, cedar poles with fire-hardened points lay along the length of each canoe. The cedar poles would replace paddles in the shallow stretches of the river. Expertly used by one standing in the stern, the canoe could be maneuvered through the rapids and rock-strewn sections of the river, upstream or downstream.

Red Wolf, well aware of their good fortune and his obligation to revisit Yahou-Lakee on the return trip with appropriate gifts, rested his paddle while the Nahyssan brave in the stern guided the sleek dugout past protruding rocks in the shallow water toward the safety and easier travel of mid-stream.

On reaching mid-stream, Kadomico still held the paddle poised as if spellbound. The warrior seated behind him, Tonawanda, tapped him on the shoulder.

"Her name is Sayen," he said, then sternly, "Paddle."

Kadomico responded immediately by matching the others stroke-for-stroke, but a warm, bright vision of Sayen remained with him long after she faded from view.

As they traveled downstream, the strange sights splashed through Kadomico's mind and around his vision of Sayen. Not even when he saw an occasional horse-drawn wagon or oxen snaking huge logs toward building sites, or slides made of hewn oak logs loaded with firewood, maize, or tobacco, did his vision fade. Nor was his vision of the beautiful Nahyssan girl disturbed when the breathtaking scene of wide water at the mouth of the river came into view—it was so vast a vista that he had no word for it. The vision of Sayen remained even while he wondered if this was the great water of the east and why it felt as though she was sharing the experience with him.

He had learned her name from the Nahyssan paddler behind him, but he had yet to learn that that fierce, copper-skinned, armed-for-battle warrior whose paddle strokes seemed as easy as breathing, was Sayen's father, Tonawanda, senior warrior of the Nahyssan.

6

S am Layton gained the mouth of the Appomattox River just before dark. On high ground beyond the south shore lay the burned-out remains of an Appomattuck town of long ago. Directly in the mouth of the river, a low-laying unoccupied island divided the Appomattox current into two wide streams. Occasional fields of tobacco broke the wilderness on both sides of the river, clearly marking the westward movement of the settlers and their passion for that cash crop.

Sam carefully chose a campsite, keeping in mind that Kajika and the Tuscarora warriors had probably followed him up-river. There remained enough forest here to conceal them. He chose the bank of the island offering the best westward observations toward the Appomattox. Sure enough, as he beached his canoe and busied himself with collecting firewood, he heard the faint bird call on the south shore that probably was not a bird calling. The Tuscaroras proved to be fast travelers. It was not likely they would swim to the island after dark for the canoe, weapons, and whatever other loot they might favor. Since a surprise attack was not possible, maybe Kajika wouldn't like the odds and leave— maybe.

Sam decided against a fire, left the canoe clearly visible, and strapped on his rucksack of food and ammunition. Carrying his arms, including a bow and arrows, he stepped only on stone or driftwood until he reached the cover of a thick patch of bayberry

48

shrubs and tall reeds. Now concealed, he settled down within easy shot of the canoe, made himself comfortable and watched the south shore satisfied he could hear and see any disturbance of the quiet, smoothly flowing water. He squinted at the sky, glad this night promised the good visibility of a full moon in a clear sky. He drank a little water from a skin he carried, ate some dried fruit, meat, and chinquapin nuts from last year, and squinted into the evening's misty silence for sign on the south shore. At first there was only the silence, then he saw a bird flush from the deep grass at the edge of the woods, nothing more, but enough to alert Sam that something or someone was there. He would stay alert.

Across the expanse of water and unseen in a thicket of young cedar and bayberry brush, Kajika had watched catlike and motionless as Sam beached his canoe on the island in the mouth of the Appomattox River and set up camp. With his nine warriors stationed well behind him, Kajika also searched for a way to attack. Like many others, Kajika believed if a warrior died in combat at night he would spend eternity in darkness. As much as he feared that unthinkable prospect, he thought seriously about a silent swim to the island after dark, but quickly yielded to his better judgment and abandoned the idea. If discovered they would be helpless targets in deep water, and Layton would be high, dry, and well armed.

Kajika's Tuscarora town was named Katearas, meaning a place of great Indian trade and commerce. It lay south where for many years the Tuscarora maintained an independent but tenuous control of a thriving Indian trade operation in southern Virginia and the Carolinas. Eventually, the Carolina militia and allied tribes would drive the Tuscarora north where they would finally join the five-nation Iroquois, but for now, they remained a fierce ruthless tribe. Their settler and Indian neighbors wisely gave them a wide berth.

When they left their town, their chief had made it plain to Kajika's war party that weapons and powder would be the most valuable prizes—the more iron weapons and thunderous firesticks in their arsenal, the more secure their people. In addition, strength in arms meant a stronger bargaining position in council with their ally, the five-nation Iroquois Confederacy. Still, Kajika knew the greatest prize would be Layton's canoe.

Kajika scanned the scene before him, still pondering a way to approach Layton. He finally concluded that while Sam's canoe was uncommonly magnificent and his rifle, pistol, and knives were probably of the best quality—well worth a fight—this was not the time. While he thought, the day grew gray and grayer still, a reminder to settle down for the night. It looked as though Sam had already settled.

Unseen by Sam, two canoes were moving straight toward his island. Just beyond the vast confluence of the two rivers, the paddlers set a fast pace in ever widening quiet water. By the time they became visible he could hear the dip of the paddles. They were so near to passing on that Sam had to hustle to be seen in the mist; he waved his hat for them to come in. With a little back-paddling the canoes slowed to a dead stop mid-stream within hailing distance.

He called out to them: "I am Sam Layton."

It was enough. Red Wolf's canoe beached first, and he lifted himself free of the dugout and stepped into the sandy shallows. He raised his open hand in peace and greeting. The others remained seated.

"I am Red Wolf of the Saponi."

"It is plain to see Red Wolf is well-chosen for this important mission. I have heard of your bravery in battle and your skill with the bow and arrow."

This unexpected compliment caught Red Wolf off-guard, and he nearly let it be known that he was pleased to hear these words. Catching himself, he remained straight-faced and replied, "And I have heard of you, Sam Layton. With me are three sons of chiefs, each with a tribe brother. They will go to Williamsburg. There their brothers will stay with them until it is right for them to leave."

"The leader of the English is Nicholson." Sam replied. "He is called Governor and lives in Williamsburg. The Governor sends his greetings. He will welcome you himself in Williamsburg. I am to take you there and remain as long as needed,".

He observed with despair the eleven strong, armed hunters, who could become fierce warriors instantly, and who were not only satisfied with themselves, but so proud they would fight to the death to revenge an insult or injury to themselves, a member of their family or their tribe. The English intended to convert them to Christianity, teach them to speak the King's English, clothe their nakedness, and make them subjects of the British King. King William had said, "It is a good and pious thing."

Sam could see neither the sense nor the likelihood of it, but now after almost a hundred years, the constant murders and massacres on both sides argued heavily for a change. And if not this, what? The good intentions of both sides counted for something. He understood the need to change even though he was not sure what changes were needed. He suddenly felt a touch of gratitude that it was not his problem. Enough that he still had some risky miles to go to get them to Williamsburg.

"It is but a half day's travel downriver to Jamestown and only two hours more on to Williamsburg. If your people wish, we can camp here until morning, leave fresh, and arrive before sunset," Sam said.

He hoped that after talking to them, they would be better prepared for the strange sights and sounds before them: horses, wagons, buggies, vendors, clothed citizens, houses, cattle, pigs, and chickens, shops with stacks of merchandise, longknives, pistols, and muskets. Sam knew that an Indian from beyond the frontier observing so many knives or ears of maize lying unused in a public place might openly take one for his own use and fight to keep it, if challenged. The Indians beyond the frontier knew little of the white man's laws, his concept of private property, or his notion of ownership and exclusive use of land. And they could be easily and unknowingly offended, in which case revenge was mandatory. Moreover, Sam knew first hand that many settlers saw all Indians as murdering, thieving savages beyond civilizing, beyond peaceful coexistence. Hatred, fear, contempt, and revulsion often surfaced when they met, never mind the good intentions of people like Nicholson and Custoga. Sam sighed and began to whet his sheath knife on boot leather, more to ease his frustration than to sharpen the knife.

The Indians beached their canoes and spread out, looking to see what wildlife used this land and water and if there was any sign of people. Kadomico and Tree Son unloaded enough food from their visit with Nahyssan to feed the group, but Kadomico set aside the small basket from Sayen. It contained honey-soaked bread made from tuckahoe, a wild potato-like root popular with Indian and settler alike. He intended to save it for when he was alone.

Sam smiled at the provisions and said, "Much food."

Kadomico had once seen a visiting white stranger looking for trade, but Sam Layton was the first white man to speak to him. He had also heard warriors talk of skirmishes and dealings with the whites, but this one was close-up, wearing buckskins, and a broad-brimmed hat big enough to shade his face and shed rain. He was surprised to hear Sam speak his language so easily. Hesitantly, Kadomico explained that the food was a gift from the Nahyssan.

Sam sensed Kadomico's uneasiness and spoke softly. "I am glad to know one who will speak for his people among the whites."

"I am Kadomico, son of Custoga, Chief of the Saponi."

Kadomico and Tree Son moved the last of three large stones into place and covered them with a deerskin, forming a sort of table to keep the food as safe as possible from insects. Tree Son remained silent and close to his friend.

Sam tested the cutting edge of the knife and resumed stroking the leather. "The Saponi are well known as mighty warriors and great hunters. They traded with my people, the Shawnee, long ago before the Saponi left the valley of the Ohio."

Kadomico was stunned. "You are Shawnee?"

"I am," Sam said. "You will meet other white men and women who have lived with and were even adopted by Indians.

Same as me. I never knew my white family. They were killed and I was captured. I was too young to understand or to remember."

Red Wolf stood nearby, listening and checking the arrows in his quiver, adjusting and trimming sinew bindings and the odd feather with a tiny beaver-tooth knife, hafted to a handle of pearl-white bone.

Sam liked what he saw in Kadomico—a young man eager to prove himself and probably able to meet the challenges before him. He guessed Kadomico was about the same age as he was when he left the Layton's. If he underwent what Nicholson had in mind for him, he would face many of the same experiences: conflicting religions, degrading corporal punishment, inferior treatment, strange clothing and food, and confinement in classrooms. Within his passion to prove himself would he find the strength and wisdom to endure this English experiment to civilize him? Sam hoped so.

He decided he had given Kadomico enough to think about and turned his attention to Red Wolf. "Williamsburg is less than a day's travel. We will take three in my canoe, six in the larger of the dugouts. From here on, there will be many settlers, farms, and fields. We are likely to see other canoes, rafts, and boats on the river. We will see the Chickahominy town and maybe Indians from other tribes as we travel downstream.

"We will keep our weapons out of sight, leave at first light and hold to mid-stream until we reach Jamestown Island, a half day's travel. Take only the people who are needed—the fewer our number the better. Settlers are nervous about groups of strange Indians, and some are dangerous, quick to start trouble. I will speak when speaking is necessary."

Red Wolf nodded, understanding. Deeply conscious of his obligation to bring Kadomico to Nicholson, he suppressed his seething hatred of the white strangers, and, surprisingly, grew to trust Sam Layton and willingly accept his leadership. Later, he spoke to the Indians.

"At sun-up we go. Tree Son and two Nahyssans wait here. When we reach Jamestown Island, the Nahyssans will leave us and return here with the canoe."

Slinking back to a safe place to move unseen, Kajika had posted one warrior to watch the island when he caught sight of the two canoes, barely visible and closing fast, favoring his side of the river. He watched as they drew near, the paddlers stroking the water in perfect unison: dip, pull, dip, pull until they saw Sam's signal. They immediately slowed and changed course for the island, moving away from Kajika. He counted eleven paddlers and watched as they joined Sam. The marking on the canoes were Nahyssan. He remembered then that after warring with the Tuscarora over the southern hunting grounds and trade routes, the Nahyssan had relocated to a town somewhere on the Appomattox only a few winters ago.

He suspected this whole area was under the protection of the colonial militia, and he was careful to avoid the white settler farm just the other side of a ripening brown field of maize. Kajika decided his warriors were best concealed in the place they presently occupied—densely forested with sufficient undergrowth to make a little movement safe and his kind of battlefield if attacked.

Kajika eased himself into a sitting position apart from the others and prepared to rest, his knees drawn up against the chill of the evening. He visualized the unprotected Nahyssan town. Some of their warriors would be away on this canoe trip, and the rest might be away on the first communal hunt of the season.

Even if there were no valuables in the town, a captive would bring a premium price from the badly diminished Iroquois, who were in need of people to replace those lost to disease and war. Recently both the Oneida and the Onondaga raided and massacred on the piedmont frontier, and farther north, the

Mohawk and Seneca had been making war against inland tribes of Susquehanna and Delaware. To trade captives you simply needed to get the captives and then find war parties that wanted them. Pleased with this new prospect, Kajika slept.

Kajika and his warriors camped quietly without a fire. They ate dried venison, parched maize from their food pouches, and fresh walnuts. Some of his men slept while others watched. They traded off sometime after the light of the rising moon changed from an enormous red-orange globe over the black earth to a shining white light that flooded the little openings in the forest and cast jet black tree shadows. Across the dark water, moonlight drew a silver arrow over tiny wavelets raised by the night wind.

Before first light of the eastern sky, Kadomico nudged Tree Son who was sleeping soundly on a bed of long-grass covered by a soft deerskin. Instantly alert, Tree Son growled at his friend behind a barely perceptible smile.

"I go," Kadomico spoke in a low voice. "Take this basket to Sayen. Say Kadomico will return to the Nahyssan before the leaves return."

Tree Son stood, looked into the eyes of his friend with understanding and approval and said, "It is good. I will speak to her as you say." They grasped forearms in the traditional gesture of parting friends. Both looked away. Sam Layton, working silently nearby, smiled.

Kadomico walked to a small, private, low-laying peninsula leading southward into the river where a view eastward opened to a skyline already visible to the oncoming morning. There in the darkness he stood in beaded moccasins, clothed in a soft buckskin shirt and pants with flowing fringes, clothing his mother, Tanaka, had made during the moons of snow and ice. A leather headband with connecting triangles of color fastened his coal black hair close around his young face, now turned upward, eyes closed.

> *Great Spirit, let me learn the things that will protect our people and the lands we know. Guide my way among the Strangers. Grant me strength to live without my people until I return.*

Kadomico walked back to a campsite that stirred busily in the faint light of dawn. Fresh from bathing in the cold, clear water, Red Wolf, Wapiti, and Wiwohka were resplendent in their full dress decorated buckskins. They wore headbands of colorful weaves and paints. Their heads were shaved on the side nearest the bow-draw, and each displayed one or two hard-earned feathers in their warlocks to signify their rank. Tall men, with strong chestnut brown features crowned with coal black hair and dressed in buckskin of the finest tailoring and most elaborate decorations, they made an impressive party from the western frontier.

Sam felt a surge of pride when he saw them. Williamsburg was about to be visited by six Indians representing three frontier tribes: Saponi, Tutelo, and Occaneechi. Kadomico, Hawk, and Shanda were young sons of tribal chiefs. They were to be educated and converted to Christianity at the College of William and Mary. Their escorts, Red Wolf, Wapiti, and Wiwohka, were sure to raise suspicion and caution, if not outright fear, in Williamsburg. These proud men were brave warriors, skilled hunters, no doubt deeply loyal to their own religion and their people.

Sam steered quietly toward mid-stream. Red Wolf motioned Kadomico and Hawk to their paddle positions. Tonawanda kneeled in the stern, paddle wedged in the river bottom to hold the craft steady for loading. Kadomico and Hawk stepped single file into the bow, hands on gunnels, and their feet placed dead center. They worked their way back and took up positions between Red Wolf and Tonawanda. Red Wolf shoved the canoe a little way from the bank and boarded, kneeling in the first position near the bow. Gaining speed, they followed Layton's canoe. Shanda, Wiwohka, and Wapiti paddled silently in unison, with a stroke and rhythm that would last all morning.

The fields of tobacco and wagons hauling harvested crops of maize, tobacco, and hay gave them their first look at the wheel, cart, horse, and the English farmer. Occasionally, they saw cattle, sheep, goats, pigs, chickens, and dogs. Sometimes children were at play, but sometimes they were at work in the fields. There were clothes fastened to lines flapping in the light breezes and houses of more than one room. Once they passed a ship of many sails, but Sam led them as far from its path as possible. Kadomico thought of gathering pebbles later or cutting notches in an arrow to represent the number of English he saw but soon gave up the idea. Already there were too many to count and this was the first day.

Sixty miles of steady paddling brought them within sight of the island on which the ruins of the old Jamestown fort were barely visible. Sam squinted into the distance toward Jamestown Island. A long boat made its way upstream towards them, two oarsmen on each side and armed, uniformed, red-coated guardsmen fore and aft.

7

S am back-stroked, slowing the craft to almost full stop. "Hold your position," he called to the paddlers. "This looks like Governor Nicholson's doing."

Both canoes waited.

"Sam Layton, you're a sight for sore eyes, if I do say so."

The voice was faintly familiar. Sam just couldn't place it until he pulled alongside and saw it was Jock Adams from his school days before he left the Laytons.

"Jock, you haven't lost your knack for surprises. It's been a while and you don't look any the worse for it."

"Follow me and we'll give you and your friends a proper welcome."

"Lay on. We're right behind you."

Jock led them through a maze of abandoned fish weirs and watercraft to the rotting remains of the Jamestown dock area where they beached their canoes and began to disembark. The oarsmen and two guards joined a four-man detail of the Governor's Guard, their red and white uniforms in sharp contrast to the ruins of Jamestown.

The little town had burned for the third time just two years ago. The church building of hand-hewn post-and-beam and a few of the smaller thatched roof buildings had escaped the fire, but the area look vacated. Not a single person stirred among the surviving buildings. Two black slaves were tending a trot line among the fish weirs and remains of the dock. In the distance a fire burned as if people might be at work clearing land. A three-seat buckboard drawn by a team of matched sorrels in gleaming harness rested in deep shade.

"Where are the people?" Kadomico asked Layton.

"Not much left here, Kadomico. The town burned two winters back, and most people have found better crop land and fewer mosquitoes on higher ground." Sam was pleased with the question. A healthy curiosity and wish to learn would help Kadomico to deal with the English world before him.

"He'll do," he thought, as he turned to the other Indians and motioned them to him.

"This is Jamestown, or what is left of it after many winters of struggle against attack, fires, and sicknesses. Most of the people have moved on to Williamsburg. Not far."

Jock arranged with the slaves to take care of his boat and Sam's canoe until the next day when someone would come for them, then turned to Sam. Face-to-face and satisfied with what they saw, the two men grinned and shook hands.

"What's the chance of getting six armed Indians to Williamsburg without trouble, Jock?"

"Probably better than you think, 'specially since the Governor chose to have us use the forest road from here instead of running the canoes up the creek to Williamsburg. Canoes loaded with Indians could be too much of a temptation for those opposed to the idea of inviting Indians to live and learn here," Jock said.

"And there is much of that?" Sam asked.

"Well, the arrival of Indians for the school has been the talk for weeks. They're expected, some for, some against, and a few fightin' mad about it. Some say civilizing and converting Indians to Christianity isn't worth the bother even if it can be done. It hasn't happened that we know of, not since Pocahontas married a settler and went to London years ago. Others say they're ready to try anything to stop the killing." He pulled the slipknot in the reins of a shining black horse of some fifteen hands at the shoulder with his powerful neck arched high, his mane and tail flowing thick and full in eye-catching waves of reflected light.

"Name's Cheek, and for good reason." Jock smiled, handing the reins to Sam. "He's saddled for you, compliments of the Governor."

Sam took the reins in one hand. Watching Cheek's eyes and ears, he moved up close and lightly touched the black's neck. When he was satisfied Cheek knew a stranger had the reins, Sam turned his back to the horse.

"Fine animal," he said. "A man could cross a mountain on a horse like this."

"That buckboard will seat them all," Jock said, pointing to the Indians. "I'll drive. Tell them to stay together when we get there and follow me close."

The Indians crowded close around Red Wolf.

"We leave you here," Red Wolf said to the Nahyssans. "In two moons we will return where the rivers meet and wait three suns before we return to the homeland of the Occhaneechi, Tutelo, and Saponi. If you are there, we will return to your town and speak with Yahou-Lakee before we go to our own towns."

Now six uneasy Indians watched the Nahyssans paddling away in the quiet water. Those left behind were about to put themselves in the hands of strangers, and they did not like what they saw. The land seemed unfriendly, even hostile. There were ragged black men at the river's edge and the rotting remains of the abandoned town overgrown in a sea weeds and tangles of vines. The whole scene suggested a failure, defeat, and the presence of the spirits of Indians of long ago. These English buildings, horses, warriors, and that road to more strangers and weird ways, made them uneasy. They did not understand the talk between Jock, Sam, and the guards, all of whom carried muskets and longknives. The guards stood lounging and smoking pipes by a pair of harnessed horses hitched to something with wheels.

"Red Wolf, we go. Climb into those seats," Sam said in perfect Siouan, pointing at the buckboard. "Williamsburg by sundown."

"We walk," Red Wolf replied.

Sam had not expected that, but it was not a bad idea. The Indians would feel the freedom and independence of traveling in their usual manner, and they would be right at home along the forested road. No point in arguing, no need to persuade.

"Fine. Follow me."

Sam turned to Jock who was about to climb onto the buckboard. "Jock, we'll walk," he said. "If you don't mind, would you take the black and let the guard have the buckboard? When we get close to Williamsburg, the guard can escort us on into town."

"I understand," said Jock. "We'll set the pace. Holler if you want it changed. This roadway, if you can call it that, leads straight to Williamsburg—about six miles."

As they moved about adjusting their buckskin garments and retying the laces of their moccasins, a tiny sea-going square-rigged vessel appeared on the river, making its way upstream in a gentle wind out of the east and a favorable incoming tide. To the Indians it looked like a floating island.

"It is called a pinnace," said Sam speaking in Siouan. "She's moved by the current and by the wind caught in her sails. Right now, she's headed to one of the upstream farms, probably to load tobacco. When loaded, she'll cross the great water and return with blankets, copper, beads, muskets, and other things of the white man."

"Will the pinnace bring iron tomahawks and longknives?" Red Wolf asked.

"She will, and you will see many more sails, some much larger than these. They are ships. They carry away the fur, tobacco, and the wood of the oak and pine and bring back cloth, longknives, and iron tomahawks," Sam said and stepped back to let the buckboard turn into the road, now loaded with six guards who looked pleased to be riding the six miles they had expected to march.

The Indians' interest in tomahawks and longknives lingered in Sam's mind. They wanted them more than anything and a lot more than they wanted schooling. Once, they had gladly traded the white man all the fur they had from a winter's hunt for a handful of colored beads or a copper kettle. No more. Iron weapons so shifted the odds of winning a battle, and metal tools so eased and hastened the labor of farming and building, that they now brought the highest trade prices, and Indian demand had reached troublesome heights. Not only were they eager to buy the metal products, but they were also willing to kill for them. Consequently, the black market prospered, and the Indians grew stronger and better able to wage war, but Sam knew it was futile to fight the enemy that controlled the weapons and the ammunition. He turned back to the road and fell in behind the buckboard now jolting along after Jock, comfortably mounted on the gaited black.

Sam knew that things now commonplace to tidewater natives still appeared as wonders to people from beyond the western frontier. The ship had little meaning in the minds of those who still found shelter, food, and drink in the forest. Therefore, it was not surprising to see the look of wide-eyed wonder on the faces of the Indians. However, on Kadomico's face it was an expression of confusion and curiosity. Sam approved. It was the mark of a thinker. He had seen the look before. Kadomico's inherent curiosity and struggle for understanding improved the odds he would face in just a few hours.

Now that Sam had explained it, Kadomico squinted at the spectacle and wondered at the great number of ships and the enormity of the cargoes. What would he say to the Saponi council? Could he get some of the iron tomahawks and firesticks? Where do ships stop? His mind spun with questions.

They passed by more fields of maize and tobacco and came close to a team of oxen pulling a huge tree stump in a field of trees that had been cut down to make new ground for more crops. Several brush piles smoked and blazed as men fed them from the seasoned wood felled the previous year. After a while, they emerged from the last stretch of dense forest. As they neared Williamsburg, they passed a pasture of sheep. Cattle and horses grazed in a field of knee-deep grass. Soon they came to a stately barn and an intersecting wagon road.

"I'll take the buckboard to that barn and put the horses up," said Jock. He turned Cheek toward the rear of the buckboard and tethered him there. "Join you at the school shortly. They'll be watching for you. I expect a runner left Jamestown with the news as soon as he saw us meet on the river."

The guards left their seats and assembled in ranks, got their orders, and moved into position. They filed into the tiny hamlet of Williamsburg at a fast walk, the red-coated, white-breasted guard marching in a smart formation, four in front, two behind Sam and the Indians. A few unpainted post-and-beam houses clustered near a brick building still under construction. Kadomico stared at the new building. It was facing east three and one-half stories high, as wide as three Indian longhouses and three times longer. The many windows looked like mistakes to him. What purpose were they, why so many? This unfinished building was the first planned structure of the College of William and Mary, already two years into serving the colony.

"This building is where you and others come to learn, and it is where councils meet to govern the English until another building much like this one is built. They call it their capitol building. It will be located past those two buildings you see near the path." Sam pointed east beyond the market stalls, horses, oxen, dogs, and people. Once an Indian race, it was now a well-travelled horse path named Duke of Gloucester Street.

The headmaster, fully dressed in an embroidered coat, powdered wig, and gleaming white stockings, stepped smartly from the huge building adjusting his three cornered hat. He exchanged words with the leader of the guard, acknowledged his salute, dismissed them, and turned to Sam with outstretched hand in greeting.

"We are glad to have you safely back, Sam. Please welcome the Indians and let them know the Governor of Virginia and the President of the college are pleased they have come and will meet with them tomorrow. They can use what's left of the day settling into their quarters and seeing our town. The evening meal will be announced by the bell and served over there."

Before Sam could answer the greeting, Red Wolf pointed to the headmaster and said, "Nicholson?"

"No," Sam answered. "This is Headmaster Arrington of the school, sent to welcome you. A house and food has been prepared for you and the others. Governor Nicholson sends greetings and will meet with us tomorrow."

Red Wolf moved away and summoned Wiwohka and Wapiti. Sam winced, hoping the warriors had not taken the absence of Nicholson as a slight. It reminded him that Indians put a lot of stock in the proper treatment of guests.

The Indians spoke quietly to each other, then Red Wolf returned to Sam, "We will see this house."

A small group of curious citizens, mostly women and children, had gathered. Suddenly, they parted to give way to three ragged, bad-smelling, and bewhiskered men with matted hair splashing over their necks and shoulders under misshapen broad-brimmed hats. Staring at the Indians through red-rimmed, watery eyes, and breathing cheap rum and tobacco smoke, they swaggered toward Sam. The warriors saw the threatening movements and heard the harsh voices. They motioned the younger Indians behind them. Hawk obeyed only when Wiwohka stepped directly in front of him and faced him. Words were not necessary. Hawk moved back, praying that this would become a fight. He could take those three scalps himself, but he would not challenge Wiwohka, a warrior of great stature among the Occaneechi, and one whom Hawk deeply respected. The towering Wapiti quietly moved to the front next to Sam and Red Wolf. His very presence calmed the Indians.

Sam scanned the three troublemakers for arms and measured the threat. Two half-drunk weaklings cowered well behind a scowling leader and mumbled encouragements to him. Sam turned his back to the leader of the troublemakers and spoke to the Indians softly in Siouan.

64

"Red Wolf, hold your people."

"We know all about them murderin' vermin," shouted the leader of the three. He moved forward shaking a clinched fist and growling his words like a mad dog. "They come here, live off us, and steal everything they can, then cut our throats, scalp us, and run. And the way I see it, you ain't no better'n them." He spat tobacco juice at Sam's back and took the next step into a jaw-crushing uppercut as Sam spun to his left on flexed knees, swinging from the ground.

With all his weight and power behind it, Sam delivered the right with such surprise that the jutting bearded jaw made a perfect unprotected target. Sam felt the bone collapse as the jarring impact lifted the big man a little upward and backward so that his fall to the ground looked more like a slump than a crash. He bounced only once before drawing himself into the fetal position groaning with pain and spitting blood. Sam stepped over the dazed and writhing body to meet the other two just as Jock Adams, grinning with pleasure at seeing his friend stop a troublemaker, settle a crowd, and keep three Indian warriors in check, put his hand on Sam's shoulder and spoke.

"I'd have got here sooner, Sam, but one of the horses came up lame, and it took some time before I could turn him out to the pasture. That's bad Luther Rawlings laying there at your feet spittin' blood and teeth. From the look of his two retreating friends, the fight is over."

"Not a good start, Jock," Sam said. As he turned to face his friend, Sam forced the calm within him to overcome the rush of adrenalin. The fight was over. In spite of their pleasure at what they had just seen, the Indians remained quiet. Their inability to understand the language diminished in no way the clear hostility and hate they had seen. But for Sam's quickness and Jock's quiet words and smile, they would have responded as a group.

The other citizens had reassembled a little closer to the Indians—curious, interested, and anxious—when from behind Sam came a soft feminine voice. "Master Layton, will you please

65

accept these baked breads and sweets as a gift to these gentlemen. We understand they are here to study our language and religion."

Sam turned. The sincere words of welcome came from within a light-green bonnet that shaded a smiling, freckled face surrounded by flame-red curls that flowed to the shoulders of a determined lady.

"I will, madam," said Sam, barely able to retain his composure, confused by her boldness, and uneasy at what this gentle woman had just seen. "Thank you. Can I ask who you are?"

"I am Mary Stilson, wife of Raymond Stilson, blacksmith of Williamsburg. I speak for the women of our town. Tell the Indians we welcome them in our homes, and we hope to see them often and will work to help them in this very worthwhile endeavor."

Where this angel came from Sam did not know, but what she did so pleased him and meant so much to ease the anxieties of this bad start that he felt immense relief and strangely proud of this unexpected, welcoming behavior. He turned to the Indians now restless and eager to leave.

"The man who would attack us had much firewater, is bad, and will be judged and punished by Nicholson. This basket of food is a gift from the people of this town. They welcome you. They offer you their homes. This lady speaks for them," he said.

Kadomico stepped forward and approached Mary. Taking a tail feather of a turkey wrapped in rabbit skin from his pouch, he presented it to Mary.

In Siouan, he said, "For arrow."

"This is a gift, madam, from Kadomico, the son of Custoga, Chief of the Saponi beyond the western frontier. It is a thing of value to him. Please do not misunderstand," said Sam.

Mary bowed her head, and slowly curtsied to Kadomico and said, "Thank you. Will the son of Custoga visit my home soon?"

With Sam interpreting, Kadomico accepted, and they set a time.

"Tomorrow, near sunset then," Mary said. "My family will be home, and we can give Kadomico a proper welcome and . . . ."

Sam took advantage of the pause. "It is thoughtful indeed for you to entertain Kadomico and to be concerned about the others. Give it no further thought. The others will be very busy, and there will be time for them to visit homes in Williamsburg later. It is a good start."

"Then so be it, Master Layton," Mary said as she turned to go.

"Call me Sam, if you don't mind." Sam hoped that his aversion to titles was not mistaken for familiarity. "I met your husband on another occasion and know him to be a man of great respect and importance here in Williamsburg. Please give him my best regards."

"Be assured I will."

"And if I may make a suggestion?"

"Please."

"Kadomico is not accustomed to dining in the English fashion. He will mistake a wine glass to be as strong as a pewter mug, have no understanding or use for chairs and tables, and while he is meticulously clean, you may find the odor of bear grease about him strange, possibly offensive."

"Please keep in mind, sir, that this is not the first Indian we have seen. We have been surrounded by them all our colonial lives." Mary was slightly miffed at Sam's assumption that she needed advice on how to treat guests in her home.

Sam scrambled to explain. "The difference is that these Indians are from beyond the western frontier. They are seeing much of what is here in Williamsburg for the first time. They are as different from local Indians as a panther is from a house cat,"

Then, thinking he had overstated his case, he smiled and said, "Well, maybe a friendly panther."

"I see," Mary replied. "You were about to make a suggestion."

"Well, I just thought that if you entertained and served the food outside, you both might be more comfortable, but I am certain that whatever you do will be just fine." Sam was trying to steer this awkward conversation to a friendly close.

"Thank you, Sam." Mary spoke directly to him but softly and sincerely before she turned and walked away. Sam drew a deep breath of relief and pleasure to hear her use his first name.

8

K ajika had watched carefully as Sam's party loaded their canoes and departed for Williamsburg. Two of the three canoes left the campsite. In the lead was the birch bark craft he so longed to have. He would find Sam later, and he would find a way to take that canoe. For now, he realized that the remaining Nahyssans did not intend to leave the island. Kajika guessed they waited for the return of their brothers from Williamsburg. Making deep-throated grunts like a wild boar rooting up ground for the succulent tuckahoe, he signaled his warriors to follow, and they trotted deep into the cover of the forest.

The Tuscarora filtered quietly into the trees, southward away from the river and the farm and then turned up-river in a straight line, running or walking quietly depending on the density of brush, briar, and vine. The thick canopy, formed by the great oaks, maple, and beech, and the occasional tract of pine, shielded the forest floor so well that only a few of the millions of fallen seeds germinated. As they moved westward, the land swelled with hills, their bases often defined by tiny streams of rushing water scrambling to join the Appomattox.

After the sun slipped past noon, they stopped at a serpentine stream of water that splashed over rocks and formed quiet pools in the numerous bends, then moved on to the next turn. Kajika motioned them to prepare. They strung their bows and checked their arrows.

Several carried highly valued flintlock muskets with powder, ball, wadding, and a ramrod. Kajika knew that in wet weather, it might not fire at all, but in dry weather, it delivered an awesome killing power compared to the bow and arrow. In the hands of a skilled marksman, muskets were lethal at forty or fifty paces. Beyond that, they could send killing lead balls another 150 paces, but at that range they were unlikely to score on a target as small as an enemy warrior or wild game. He had heard that the English sometimes fired in great quantities by line after line of soldiers creating a wide spray of lead, but he could not imagine such a tactic.

He understood and practiced stealth and ambush, intended each ball or arrow to find its selected mark, and could fire several arrows in the time it took a rifleman to reload. Moreover, the arrow's accuracy at forty to sixty yards was as good as or better than the musket. Kajika had been told that, for a very long time and at great cost in the lives of their soldiers, the English military regarded the ambush tactics of the savages as little better than murder on the battlefield. However, Kajika knew that the militia was made up mostly of farmers protecting their communities. These men had honed their wilderness fighting skills and had adopted many of the Indian's tactics, and they were deadly accurate with their firesticks.

The Tuscaroras washed and cleansed themselves, drank lightly, and smeared their faces with colored or blackened bear grease, rendering their appearance as fierce and frightful as their imaginations would permit: black faces with white circled eyes, some with white or red stripes drawn across their faces, foreheads, and necks. Combined with the element of surprise and blood curdling screams designed to terrorize their enemy, it often gave them an edge in battle.

They moved on into the afternoon sun. Kajika thought they might find the Nahyssan town before dark if they did not have to alter their course to avoid the settler farms. He watched carefully for hunters and other travelers. He would kill any witness or anyone who might sound the alarm of Indians on the warpath. His success depended on surprise, quick and complete destruction, and a fast retreat to cover. Once clear of the killing ground, the party would regroup briefly, check their weapons, captives, and wounded, if any, and strike a fast pace toward the Blue Mountains.

The Tuscaroras failed to find the town by the time the sun had reached the rim of the Blue Mountains. Kajika halted the war party in a cove of cedars for the night and dispatched scouts to check the river and their back trail. He also sent two hunters for food. He went on alone in search of the town and soon found trampled grass and footprints of both moccasins and bare feet in a place of soft marsh ground. Since there was no well-worn path, he stopped and scanned for higher ground where he might observe the terrain ahead and perhaps see the town.

He moved up the hillside and climbed an old oak tree. Squinting into the evening sun toward the mountains, he scanned the area where he expected the river to be. There he saw a brown field of ripe maize planted in hills, Indian fashion. Beyond, on higher ground and shielded by a thick forest of pine, he saw a thin line of rising smoke, maybe a cooking fire. This had to be the Nahyssan town. He saw no warriors and only a few women and children harvesting maize in the lowland field. He watched until darkness obscured his view.

He considered both an early morning attack to conquer the town before the start of daily routine and a mid-day raid to take captives from the field. He returned to the cedars and alerted the others.

The hunters brought in but a single rabbit, not unexpected with a town nearby. They carefully selected dry hardwood twigs and limbs and kindled a fire under a massive tree thick with branches that would disperse any accidental smoke while the rabbit roasted. Not much food for nine warriors, but augmented from their trail pouches, it was enough. Then, from an adjacent creek bed, they gathered and laid stones around the fire in a circle and prepared a small ceremony to sacrifice bits of their food to the gods for victory and protection in tomorrow's raid on the enemy Nahyssan.

9

Headmaster Arrington struggled with his nerves. It was not every day that he saw violence of the sort he had just witnessed, and tough as this colonial life was he for one, favored the dignity and grace of his beloved England and did his part to practice it daily. He swallowed, cleared his throat, and faced the Indians. He was unable to conceal the nervousness in his voice. "Let us go inside to the rooms you will be using to study."

The Indians, still uncertain, stood cautiously together and watched Sam and Jock. Sam nodded to Arrington, interpreted his words aloud and followed him inside, motioning to the others. Before joining Sam, Jock checked the vanishing crowd to be sure that Rawlings had left.

Arrington walked along the hallway past a great stairway and came to a large room of tables and chairs. Sam followed and turned around just as Red Wolf stopped. The Indians refused to enter. Red Wolf saw the large unfinished opening at the back just beyond the room and motioned the others in that direction. The room reminded Sam of the one he was given at the Laytons and the uncomfortable confinement he had felt when he first saw it. He spoke in Siouan.

"This is the place where you will be shown how to speak the English language and make the talking papers. You come here each day to study the work. It is good that you are chosen to do this for your people. Soon you will know the way of the white man. I did this when I was your age. To know these things will help your people. I will be with you until you are settled."

73

Kadomico stepped around Red Wolf and entered the room. The other students, Shanda and Hawk, followed. The warriors remained by the door eying openings to the outside, shifting positions, uneasy, murmuring among themselves. Sam saw that Arrington had moved to the customary position of the headmaster before a class. The three boys stayed close together, standing and facing Sam in uneasy silence.

Jock stepped up to Wapiti and motioned him to follow him into the room. He went to the chalkboard and drew a large circle, pointed down and said, "Here" in Algonquian, then drew a short straight line to the right and another of the York and James River coastlines speaking the words "York" and "James." Wapiti made a face of understanding, took the chalk and proudly drew lines to represent the island where they had camped. Jock then drew a long line upward across the York River, and pointed north, then to himself.

"Iroquois," he said, handing the chalk to Wapiti. They exchanged the chalk several times to show directions and places. The boys watched with interest changing to excitement as they began to understand and relax. And they laughed heartily as Jock, waving his arms wildly and making faces of astonishment and disbelief at Wapiti's drawing, clowned his way into their confidence and trust.

Arrington yielded to this unexpected turn of events and liking it, postponed his opening address to the group and suggested to Sam that they go on to the boys' quarters where food would be waiting for them.

They walked past the wheelbarrows, stacks of brick, piles of sand, scaffolding, and other neatly arranged building materials. The unpainted post-and-beam house measured twenty by forty feet with a tiny porch and two rooms separated by a hallway, each with a window overlooking the porch. The room to the right of the entrance had a brick fireplace and chimney. A shed roof of cedar shakes over the porch sheltered the entrance. The back door simply opened one step down into a bare earthen yard. Each room contained a table and chair and two single beds with mattresses of fresh straw on a web of ropes. A wool blanket covered each mattress. The tables, located by the windows, were bare except for the stub of a candle held fast to a saucer. Scrubbed floors and dust-free, bare, polished windowsills suggested severe housekeeping practices. In the hallway a large candle would burn for a while each evening to allow residents to light the smaller room candles.

The Indians nodded approval. Their house was located near the woodland behind them and aligned along the wagon road on their front. From the porch looking north and beyond the new college building, fields of tobacco and maize were visible, giving them a feeling of space. From where they stood they could see several other buildings: a smithy, a church, two ordinaries (taverns), and the grammar school. Roofs of thatch, slate, or shingle covered the buildings made of stone and brick, some of planks, and some a mixture. The buildings and activities were set among tobacco fields and patches of woods and scattered along the horse path, which marked a thriving community.

Although Kadomico was yet to learn the purpose of the places he had seen, he wondered what his grandfather would think of all this, so many buildings and horses, cows, pigs, and chickens. He could see that some of those buildings housed people and guessed that others contained maize, tobacco or food stored against the winter. The Saponi also stored food in caves and certain buildings, but here in plain sight grew vast fields of maize and tobacco in quantities beyond anything he had seen. Nor did he yet understand that the shops and stores provided a variety of services, or traded medicines, tools, food, cookware, and the guns and iron hatchets he so admired.

Kadomico did not yet know that among those buildings the blacksmith, carpenters, and wheelwrights plied a lively trade, but he did understand the rudiments of trade and commerce. The Saponi also engaged in trade, and enjoyed a vigorous exchange of goods with other tribes. They regularly used the trade routes of the rivers and wilderness trails to trade for chert, stone tools, buffalo hide, furs, and pottery. More than any other discovery or wonder, the magnitude and method of colonial commerce challenged Kadomico's imagination and fired a burning curiosity and determination to learn more.

What would Choola think?

Kadomico thought that Choola would be quick to notice that all this would be impossible to move when the game and firewood were gone, and he would see waste where the colonists worked diligently for ever larger buildings, harvests, schools, churches, and government. Choola would be pleased and maybe concerned to see all the tools of iron for harvesting and for fashioning other tools of wood and stone, and he would scoff at the clothing but not the helmets and breastplates of the English. Choola would curse the strong drink of people like the man that Sam struck down, and he would spit at the notion of so many ships, buildings, fields, horses, and cattle for so few people. But even Choola knew that the old ways were over.

"It is why I am here," Kadomico thought.

He followed Sam and the others to a kitchen building with a small dining area. There they found a smiling woman named Carrie. Dressed in a soft gray dress flowing just inches above the floor, she was retying her white apron and moving busily about as Arrington and his party entered.

"Welcome," she said, pausing and proudly gesturing toward the pork, venison, vegetables, broth, fruit, and sweets set out on tables. Her smile and welcome masked an uncompromised loathing and an abiding fear of Indians. She had lost her husband and her only two children in a raid on their frontier homestead ten years ago in the spring of 1690. Carrie was twenty-six then. The militia had found her barely alive in the smoking ruins, trapped in the root cellar beneath the house. After the burials, she remained at one of the frontier forts in a stunned silence of empty stares. She rejected food and any movement but that demanded by her body. Although the settlers nursed and cared for her with all their sympathy, love, and support during the grieving and healing time, it seemed to them she might never speak again.

One warm spring day two of the settler women of the fort made the usual visit to get Carrie's day started. They placed porridge and bread on the table, tied a fresh colorful bonnet over her thin strands of nearly white hair, and left her sitting outside her log room in the cool morning sunlight. She was quietly staring down at the interlocked fingers of her hands lying still in her lap when a boy and girl, their faces barely visible under their flop hats, came up to her holding hands. They stood there watching her, waiting. Finally the girl leaned over to the boy and whispered, "Well, ask her."

The young fellow did not really want to do it, but he knew he must since Sally had said so and Sally always seemed to know what to do. So they stood there a moment while he gathered courage, Sally's eyes never leaving his. Finally, he put his hand on Carrie's knee and said, "Will you come and play with us?"

Carrie's eyes had blinked slowly that morning, and focused on the children with a look of warmth that only a mother could give.

"Yes," she said, and after a few moments, she stood.

Three women of the fort watched this scene from a distance and hugged each other in celebration. Their devotion and care had worked. Carrie was back. Afterwards, they found her a new home in the safety of Williamsburg.

After that experience, who would not understand her fear of Indians? The loathing, however, was uncharacteristic, for Carrie was by nature a gentle, peaceful soul, eager to please and to be liked. But as time passed, and she gathered the memories of her husband and children and ordered them in her mind to be recalled regularly, the senselessness of the killing and scalping consumed her and the loathing of Indians thrived silently deep within her. But this morning brimming with pride and pleasure in her work, she suppressed the hate and fear and prepared to serve six frontier savages. Kadomico ignored her, choosing instead to examine the food.

Sam followed Arrington to the tables of food and turned to address the Indians.

"Here is where you will find food prepared for you each day. A bell will ring near sun-up, mid-day and at sun-down to let you know to come here. Before eating, just as you speak to the Great Spirit, the English give thanks to their God. Headmaster Arrington is about to speak to the English God now," Sam said.

"When the English speak to their God they call it prayer, and they often bow their heads and close their eyes. Sometimes they kneel," he added.

Arrington rose and offered thanks for the food before them, speaking for a very long time to include a request for the health and well-being of the guests and for the Lord's help to civilize and convert them to Christianity in the Anglican faith. He went on to beg forgiveness for their life of sin, they being savages fresh from the wilderness and ignorant of Christianity. Then he prayed for the Lord to help him with their education in English and the arts and sciences. He was about to include a lengthy request for divine guidance for Sam, the Governor and others, when Sam nudged him gently to bring him back to the current situation—hungry Indians, fresh from a day-long river and trail trip. Arrington took the hint and made a general plea for guidance, followed by "Amen."

With darkness descending, the Indians took their food outside, formed a convenient circle and sat down on the ground. Sam joined them and explained the custom of tables and benches or chairs, leaving the choice up to them and being careful not to characterize it as right, wrong or expected—an approach he knew the English headmaster would not likely take—though maybe Mary Stilson would.

After they had eaten, the Indians milled about the area, noticing the nearby forest and other buildings, and finally settled into their rooms and chose their beds, much to Sam's relief, a matter he took as modest progress. Arrington had a worried look when he and Jock joined Sam on the little porch of the sleeping quarters.

"I hope the Governor understands that what he has in mind will take time, if it is at all possible," Arrington said.

"I'm sure he will," Sam replied. "And we will just have to wait and see if it is possible. As far as I know, only the black-robed Catholics of the French in the north have managed to convert a few Indians to their faith. They converted those few by actually living with the Indians and being adopted by them--and especially by respecting their sovereignty, their right to their land."

Sam continued. "Now, from what I know of the English, they don't hold much with the Catholic religion and figure that rather than being converted to Catholics, the Indians would be better off left to their own heathen ways.

"It's not a simple matter, but the Governor and the three Indian chiefs of these boys are trying." Sam saw Arrington fidget uncomfortably. He clearly saw the whole business in a way he dared not discuss. After all, the governor had decreed it and the reverend had sanctioned it as a Christian duty.

"Gentlemen," said Arrington. "I thank you for your help, and bid you good night. Tomorrow we begin." As he walked away into the dark street, his lantern swung gently by his side throwing a moving circle of ghostly yellow to light his way.

Sam was glad to have this time alone with Jock. He eased down alongside one of the porch posts. "Jock, I'll be returning to the Shawnee in a few days. Could you arrange for someone to bring my canoe up from Jamestown and leave it at Capitol Landing?"

"Of course, Sam, it has been done. But listen, my friend, I've arranged with the Governor to put you up at my house over yonder," Jock said, pointing. And then looking away he continued softly. "You might remember Rebecca Shaughnessy. Well, we have three boys—Matthew, Mark and Luke—and we hope you will stay with us."

Sam's memory of Rebecca was faint. He had hardly noticed her among the youngest students in the school. He did notice Jock's hesitancy, but did not understand that it stemmed from his awareness of how different his life and Sam's had become in the twelve years since Sam had left the Laytons. Jock could see that

Sam clearly lived as a Shawnee Indian and not as the English lived. These Indians sensed it also. They accepted him, followed his lead, and seemed to admire and respect him, even in this short time. Yes, Jock concluded, the Governor had the right man for this job, but because many settlers thought of Indian sympathizers as no better than Indians, it would not be easy for Sam. And it would not be easy for the Indians.

"Jock, I thank you and your family. I will come to your house perhaps tomorrow or the next day, but the morning will bring the beginning of the Governor's notion to close the gap between Indians and English. And I want to be as sure as I can that it gets off to a good start. So, I will stay with the Indians until they are a bit more settled in these new surroundings. You know them and appreciate the situation confronting them and the school. I saw this in the way you eased the tension on the trail and here in the classroom. Much appreciated, Jock. I am glad to have your help."

Jock understood. He moved to the edge of the little porch. Darkness came early in late September and with it drifted cool air rich with the aromas of dried leaves, wood smoke, and the hint of someone baking. The faint sound of a familiar melody from a dulcimer came with the coolness and the scents of the evening. "Makes sense," he said. "I'll tell Becky. She remembers you well and is anxious to meet you again."

"There are many stories told and retold here about captives, massacres, and the war with the Indians, my own among them. But Sam, you are just about a living legend here. The Laytons themselves sent us accounts of your hunting and farming skills, your handling of farm animals, and your respect, but silent rejection of their family. And I recall your way with books when we were in school together. Some of them I couldn't even read much less understand.

"We know you have interpreted at the treaty meetings in New York and acted as go-between in many Indian-settler negotiations, but legend has it that you returned to your Shawnee people and re-adopted the Indian way. Is it true?"

Jock sat down and adjusted his position against a porch post, drew one leg up to anchor himself solidly, produced a pouch of tobacco and a pipe. He leaned forward a little, offered the pouch to Sam. They lit up.

"Not entirely true, Jock," said Sam as he settled against a post opposite his friend. "My home is with the Shawnee. I married a Shawnee woman named Star Light for her smiles and good humor, and we have a daughter five years old. Between the two of us, Jock—and only because I believe you will understand—I am neither Indian nor English. The Shawnee believe I have god-like powers because I am gifted to know where the beaver and deer are, and because I have books, understand them and can tell what other men think even though they are many miles away. The English see my Indian friends with me and look at my buckskins, bow, and arrows. They know where I live and my knowledge of Algonquian and other dialects, and they see me as Indian—more to the point, not English. But what about you? It is clear that you are English, and one I am proud to know."

"I do understand, Sam, and it raises questions. Too many for this time, but I hope there will be many occasions for them later," said Jock, suddenly deeply sorry as he sensed that this friendship could never again be what it once was.

"I work with the farmers, traders and mariners, and some of the English and Scottish firms engaged in shipping," he said. "Mostly, I collect tobacco and fur, and arrange for its shipment. It's an honest living, but between the two of us, and to borrow your words—only because I believe you will understand—I sometimes long for the way of the Iroquois, a secret longing I doubt will ever leave me but can never be met."

Kadomico lay quietly on a rope bed inside the first room listening to the tone of the exchanges between Jock and Sam. Soon he would know the words, and he was anxious to begin. He whispered words secretly sometimes just to see if his pronunciations sounded like Sam's. Already in just one day there was much to tell Custoga and Choola: ships, huge fields of tobacco, armed soldiers, Sam Layton, these tall houses of red stone—even the stones were made by the white men. Before he slept his thoughts returned longingly to Sayen. He remembered that she did not quite reach the level of his eyes, and he thought of her standing close, head tilted, waiting, yielding. He swallowed, turned over and crushed the rope web in his hands. Sleep came reluctantly.

Hawk was sound asleep. Sweating profusely, Shanda groaned aloud, kicked the blanket away, and turned fitfully. The warriors sat dozing on their blankets in the tiny hallway near the doors. Jock and Sam said goodnight. Sam stretched out comfortably into a blanket on the porch, and fell asleep instantly, unaware that Kajika was preparing to raid the town of the friendly Nahyssans who had escorted Kadomico and his party.

10

Although he slept lightly, Kajika managed a good night's rest, and woke alert before the first light of day. Without moving from the warmth of his position, he listened to the reassuring sounds of the forest: a whisper of the tallest cedars, trickling water from a determined stream nearby, the distant call of a mourning dove and the cheerful exchange of a pair of wrens. Satisfied, he turned his thoughts to the day before him.

His nine warriors wore many badges of bravery, skill, and victory in battle and were ready for the raid. If palisades surrounded the town in the overlapping coil formation, penetration would be too costly—unless, as he expected, most of the people were away on the annual communal hunt. Still, the town would have lookouts posted in strategic places to give warning of strangers in the area. It seemed unlikely that they would be warriors—more probably, boys or old men posted there to warn the gatherers working outside to return to the safety of the town. If the town had no palisades and few unprotected people, he certainly would attack, search for weapons, iron tools, blankets, fur, and other valuables. He would take selected captives, kill and scalp the remainder of the enemy Nahyssans, and head west to the safety of the high ground.

Kajika stood up in the crisp, cold air of the fall morning, stretched his arm and back muscles, and walked away from the cedars to relieve himself. The coal black outlines of the trees began to yield to the gray light of a promising sun not yet visible.

When he returned, his raiders were busy preparing knives, ammunition, bowstrings, and arrows. He dispatched two braves to check the status of defenses of the town and dispose of any outside sentries. They were to meet him on the hill at the old oak. The scouts parted in separate directions, one to the river, the other to approach the town from the south. There the ground was higher and much closer. He walked slowly toward the hill and the old oak. Six warriors followed single file just close enough to keep the man before them in sight. The seventh warrior watched their back trail for movement and sound. The wrens and the mourning doves fell silent. Only the whispering of the cedars and the rustle of late autumn leaves added to the muffled sound of the Indian footfalls.

The remaining Tuscaroras found cover in thickets of laurel. Kajika sent one man into the tree to watch for the returning scouts, then settled down to honing the cutting edges of his knife, tomahawk, and the four iron tipped arrows he carried. His hands needed the activity more than the weapons. He grew uneasy and the uneasiness troubled his concentration. He checked and rechecked. His warriors were ready, silent, focused, and eager. What then? Was it a sign from Okee, the all-powerful and ever-watchful god of man's behavior? The eastern sun came on, promising fair weather. In the west, clouds drifted broken and peaceful.

He glanced in the direction of the sound of a cricket. Seeing nothing, he looked up into the tree. The lookout was pointing. He scanned the trees, horizon, and thickets as far as he could see—still nothing. He waited several minutes before he heard the cricket again. This time an answer came from a nearby stand of crimson dogwood and sumac. One scout was back.

The scout spoke rapidly. "The town is there beyond the trees. Palisades. One entrance. Maybe sixty paces from the river on higher ground. The town is surrounded by open space and a field of maize. I go unseen in the river, shielded by the bank. There are six canoes. In one canoe, a wounded warrior, a boy, and a girl paddle downstream to tend muskrat traps. No other warriors. One old brave limped upstream. Maybe to watch. Four women carry baskets toward the maize field."

84

Cricket sounds again broke the silence. The second scout had returned.

He confirmed the location and defenses of the first scout, and added that he had seen the four women nearing the maize field and the old man hobbling upstream armed with a musket. No warriors. Kajika decided they would leave the town itself alone, take the girl and the youngest boy captive, and use their canoe to escape. Leave no enemy witness alive, take another canoe for crossing the river, and meet downstream beyond the first bend on the opposite shore. The raiders departed. Two headed for the old sentry and the musket, one went to the river to take a canoe, four would stalk and capture the trappers, and two would take out the women in the field.

In the town, the Nahyssans hustled about their morning work, unaware that the hated Tuscaroras stalked them, preparing a leave-no-witnesses attack. And although there had not been an attack on the town in the many winters since coming here, there had been on other nearby settlements, both Indian and settler. Yahou-Lakee posted the usual sentries and made his morning rounds to view areas visible from the palisade sentry stands. Sayen finished her morning chores quickly, and joined her ten-year-old brother, Tayamiti. The two of them met Sinopa, a tall, stout young warrior with a leg wound mending from a hunting accident, and started toward a small bark canoe, just long enough to seat five people.

They carried three iron muskrat traps to be set where muskrats made slides into the river near the tunnels to their nests, and in places where the muskrats left the river to take maize from the town field.

They would anchor the traps on the bottom out in the stream where there was evidence of muskrat passage. The water must be just deep enough to drown the trapped muskrat but within sight from the surface. The muskrats had been so heavily trapped near the town that the children counted themselves lucky to catch even one.

They also carried a small club of dogwood root. Rock hard and beautifully carved, it was a lethal war weapon—exactly what they needed to club a trapped muskrat if it somehow had managed to avoid drowning. The three trappers approached the canoe. Sinopa went first, hands on gunnels to balance the craft as he walked the bottom centerline to the stern paddling position. Tayamiti followed to the center thwart to be in position to tend the traps. Sayen stepped into the bow position, turned and knelt resting against the bow thwart to watch for the best path through the submerged limestone and to lend paddle strokes when needed.

Setting and running trap gave the children valuable experience, and occasionally they did bring back a muskrat, sometimes a raccoon, and rarely, the most valuable of all, a mink. The skins made an important trade item and could be exchanged for a piece of brightly colored cloth, mirrors, pieces of iron, lead, copper, pins, needles, fish hooks, sugar, salt—things of great use, beauty, or in some cases, eye-popping wonder. Yahou-Lakee made sure the young trappers received proper praise and reward for their work. This year marked the first time they had set and tended trap without the supervision of a seasoned trapper.

Inspired by the brilliant fall colors against the deep blue of the sky, Sayen and Sinopa lifted their paddles and slipped them into the clear water in silent rhythm with the morning. They watched the changing light, gentle air movements in the fall foliage and the brightly colored swirl of restless leaves over occasional pockets of deep water. Running trap alone filled the youngsters with a sense of importance, confidence and responsibility. They had become expert trappers, able to locate the best places for their traps. They had learned how to conceal and position the traps and how to club and remove the drenched animals from the spring-loaded jaws of the trap without being bitten or tipping the canoe.

Sinopa knelt in the stern position of the small dug-out, paddling and guiding the canoe downstream on the Nahyssan side of the river toward a bend that would take them to the last

86

trap in the line before losing sight of the town. A broken limb hanging a boat-length from shore pointed down toward the trap. They readied themselves to retrieve. At mid-canoe and ready to work the traps, Tayamiti laid the club close by and positioned himself, his knees firmly planted to keep his weight as evenly distributed as possible. He hoped that this trap would be loaded.

Sayen noticed the silence—no fish strikes, no birdcalls, no animal movements—and dismissed it as something they themselves caused. They could see that the trap was empty without going nearer to the shoreline and paddled on to the next den about fifty paces downstream. Four concealed Tuscaroras, bows ready but not drawn, watched the canoe pass. The paddlers neared the next muskrat den and prepared to set the last trap. The Tuscaroras nocked their arrows, and with two kneeling and two standing, all four released their arrows at Sinopa, the young warrior in the stern of the canoe.

Upstream, Nastabon, the eldest of the Nahyssan men, hobbled slowly forward, favoring a painful hip and knee on his left side, badly torn in his youth during a war with the Senecas. He smiled at the strike of a large bronze-back bass. The strike was so vicious it carried his considerable body clear of the water. At the zenith of his rise, he twisted as though to keep climbing. Flashes of light reflected from his copper sides and white belly into an explosion of sparkling droplets falling around about the big fish before he crashed back into the river, well fed. Nastabon mentally marked the spot.

"Enjoy, old fish. I will come for you when the sun hangs low." He laughed, knowing that in truth he was no match for such a magnificent fish, but he enjoyed the vision of lifting him twisting and turning into his canoe.

"The joys of old warriors are taken where they find them," he mused aloud.

As he limped clear of a willow thicket, he continued upstream and passed the two Tuscarora raiders crouched in a stand of thick sumac and honeysuckle. When he was ten paces past them, they stood silently, drew their bows the full length of the chert-tipped arrows, and released them into Nastabon's back.

Downstream nearer the town, a lone Tuscarora waded and crawled in the water along the bank with only his head exposed as he worked his way to the Nahyssan canoes. He chose a long dugout of poplar with four paddles propped in the bow and cut it loose so that, guided by the thief, it drifted slowly downstream partially concealed by the hanging brush on the river bank. Ahead lay a large downed sycamore recently dislodged from the bank by the relentless current. He could not get around it without exposing himself. He was more than half way to the bend where he expected Kajika to be waiting. He found cover in the branches of the sycamore, climbed on board, and swept himself clear of the tree. Shortly, he was on the downstream side paddling fast toward his rendezvous.

A fair distance from the riverbank, four women walked toward the entrance to the maize field carrying strong baskets made during the quiet days of winter from splits rived from straight-grained white oak trees. At the entrance, two young mothers carried their babies on their backs strapped to a cradleboard. They hung the cradleboards on a convenient low limb of a young maple tree and adjusted their clothing to prepare a place to collect the matured ears of maize.

The women left the baskets near the infants and entered the field of small hills each supporting one or two stalks of maize and yellow squash. They were laughing and teasing the youngest among them about the attention she had been getting from a junior warrior now away on his first communal hunt.

On the opposite side of the field, Kajika saw that there were too many women to kill without rousing the town. At least one of them would sound the alarm. Other than the scalps of war and the satisfaction of revenge against an enemy, there were no prizes to be taken here, babies too young to manage on the trail, women too old to make valuable captives. If they could accomplish the ambush without alerting the town, the raiders could escape before discovery. So far, they had managed to remain undetected.

Kajika could still call off the attack with a bird-call, but he had only seconds to decide.

Beneath the brown fronds of foliage from discarded stalks of harvested maize, two Tuscaroras lay flat to the ground. They gripped razor-sharp knives in their teeth to free their hands for the work of moving forward on their bellies. They were listening to the steps of the approaching women when they heard Kajika's call to retreat. Quietly, they worked their way backward until well clear of the women, then rose to a deep crouch and hastened to catch up with Kajika. By the time the women discovered the tracks in the soft ground and sounded the alarm, Kajika had reached the safety of the forest cover.

Yahou-Lakee, standing on the southeast parapet, could see beyond the maize field and the bordering thickets of briar, honeysuckle vine, wild shrubs, and saplings. As he squinted at a movement in the tangles of vegetation bordering the field, he heard Wayra shout from the parapet facing the river. She was pointing downstream. Glancing in that direction he saw the stern of one of the town's canoes disappearing downstream beyond a dense group of drooping sycamore branches and young willow trees. He picked up his musket and tomahawk, trotted over to the other side, and checked upstream. From there he could see about 100 yards to the first bend of river—nothing unusual. As he turned to step down, he saw Wayra running towards him.

"One canoe is taken. Not by Nahyssan. One brave with war paint like Tuscarora," she gasped. "Sayen, Sinopa, and Tayamiti are there working the trap line—that way." She pointed downstream.

Yahou-Lakee's blood ran cold. Because of the communal hunt, only four warriors remained with him, and he had sent them to transport the party of his Saponi friend, Chief Custoga. Although he felt he could defend their walled town with the women, children, and elders, he knew it would be foolish for them to engage an enemy of unknown strength in open-space battle. Now he feared that great harm threatened those caught outside the town.

Sayen and Tayamiti did not see the attack coming, did not have a chance to fight. They were clubbed into unconsciousness. Three of the four attackers boarded their canoe and crossed the river, depositing them still unconscious on the far bank. They tied the children's hands with fiber thongs and dragged them into the river to revive them. Sayen regained consciousness, but could not stand in the shallow water. The world spun in dizzying circles, and each time she tried to stand her captor jerked her forward so that she fell. At the water's edge, he left her lying in the shallow water groaning while he helped give the children's canoe and the Tuscarora paddler a strong push toward the opposite bank.

On the other side of the river and alone now, the remaining Tuscarora scalped and pushed Sinopa's body into low-hanging brush at the bank, then found footing to climb the bank. Glancing up he saw two canoes approaching. The nearest was the stolen dugout, the other was the captives canoe returning. At that same moment, Kajika and two other Tuscaroras burst out of the forest, splashed into the water, boarded the first canoe, and started paddling furiously toward the opposite bank. The second canoe swung in alongside the bank where the last of the Tuscaroras scrambled aboard and pushed off.

By the time they reached the opposite shore, the others had disappeared into the thick undergrowth of the forest. Tayamiti lay unconscious. Sayen had been dragged into the forest. She sat against a large tree, sick with pain and dizziness, unable to think straight. Her untreated head wound throbbed. It badly needed attention.

The two raiders who killed Nastabon had crossed and followed the river downstream until they came up on their companions and the captives.

Kajika noticed the musket they carried and that they apparently had no wounds. He motioned them into the forest with the others and then turned immediately to the business of getting away. He would avoid, at all costs, an encounter with any Nahyssans who might be returning to their town, but the real danger lay before him. He planned to take cover in the mountains as soon as possible. To do so they had to cross Monacan territory, and he knew the Monacan tribe to be warlike, strong, and unforgiving to trespassers. Maybe they could make the crossing undetected.

Kajika ordered Two Bears, his oldest warrior, to carry Tayamiti and sent them and two other warriors northwest with instructions not to cover their trail until they turned back to join him. He would go directly west. He repeated the instructions to two other warriors, but sent them southwest, then walked over to where Sayen sat dazed.

"We go. Walk or die," he said, as the drums began to beat back at the Nahyssan town.

11

Yahou-Lakee faced the people gathered at the entrance to the town. "Call the women in from the maize field. Arm yourselves. Take your positions at the entrance. Set lookouts on all the parapets. Do not go outside the palisades, and keep the drum going until I return," he said, then turned and walked toward the longhouse for his weapons.

Thoughts of defense, rescue, and retaliation flashed through his mind like a checklist and released a surge of confidence and strength not felt in many winters. This was not the work of a large war party, else they would have attacked the palisades by now—probably a party of a few raiders. He thought, find the enemy and destroy him, and it felt good to think like this. He sheathed a ten-inch steel knife and hung a tomahawk to his waist. He strapped on a quiver of arrows and strung his longbow, then primed and loaded a musket and walked out.

"I go to find Sayen and the young ones," Yahou-Lakee said as he walked past the gathered women and old men armed with spears, bow-and-arrows, and clubs. He noticed their looks of determination—not an easy force to overcome, he thought. He listened with approval to the slow beat of the huge drum from within the town as he followed the low growing stand of bayberry to the riverbank where he could observe the surrounding area.

There was a good chance the four warriors travelling with Custoga's people would return today or tomorrow, he thought as he squinted downstream, scanning the terrain for the best route to the first bend of the river. That bend hid the area where Sayen and the boys would set the last trap for the elusive muskrat.

He looked closely for footprints, disturbed grass, and investigated every place of concealment. He continued squinting downstream to locate a canoe or movement of any kind on the bank—nothing. To his left the river width spanned 100 paces to the far bank, and then there was an open field of long grass for another thirty or forty paces before it changed to forest—no movement there. Upstream he could see far beyond the flat dark water to a spread of rapids. A man could easily wade across the river there. Yahou-Lakee watched that section and the riverbank trail for several minutes hoping to see Nastabon returning to the summons of the drum, but he saw nothing, and the empty trail spoke plainly. Very likely, they had attacked Nastabon, and that accounted for at least two maybe three of the enemy.

Was the town under surveillance? If he had been seen leaving the entrance alone it was a sure give-away that there were few or no warriors protecting the town. Armed and ready for battle, he was eager to engage, but he held his position, hoping for confirmation that what he had seen was the extent of the raid. If so, Sayen and the boys ought to be within view by now. If not, they would no doubt confront the thief when they recognized the stolen canoe. They certainly could hear the drum re-call. But the empty river confirmed the dread within him and triggered a flow of adrenalin.

He turned to his right where he could see across a large expanse of grass to the maize field. The four women with the two babies were returning at the call of the drum. They did not seem alarmed; they were walking fast but not running.

Yahou-Lakee signaled for the women to come to him. Checking downstream again, he saw the canoe thief in open water, well out of musket range paddling furiously and closing fast on the bend beyond. There Sayen and the boys would be busy with the last of the trap in the line or on their way back having heard the drum. The thief disappeared into the bend of the river; no sign of the children.

The women from the maize field were more puzzled and curious than alarmed. The drumbeat meant they should return immediately to the town, but it could also be the signal of fire alarm, or the shaman could be calling a gathering to answer a vision from the god, Okee. They did not suspect an attack after many winters of peace here on the Appomattox River. They approached Yahou-Lakee silently. He motioned to Aponi, one of the women well known to give a good account of herself in risky situations, and spoke to her.

"Tuscaroras have taken a canoe, Aponi. Arm yourself. Go upstream. Remain out of sight. Find Nastabon. Do not go beyond the rapids. If he is not there, he is captured. I will wait for you."

Shortly, Aponi returned. "Nastabon is dead," she said. "Two arrows in the back, no weapons left. The tracks of two men enter the river at the rapids." She went on to tell how some of the thick white hair flowing below his shoulders had been brought back over the scalp wound as though to amend for the act. Anger overwhelmed her grief.

She shook her tomahawk and said, "Let us go! We will find and kill them."

Yahou-Lakee needed help, needed his warriors to return, needed the English militia, needed his allies, and all of these he could have, but only in time. He now knew the risk his town faced. If the Tuscaroras attacked the town, they would leave no witnesses—man, woman or child. Yet, they had not attacked; they had stolen a canoe and scalped an old warrior. As badly as he needed to be back in the town, he forced himself to continue the search for Sayen and the boys.

Then, he remembered that movement in the heavy brush beyond the maize field, and instantly he was running through a riverside field of grass on a clear trail toward Sayen and the boys. He divided his sight between the trail and the gradual exposure of the area behind the river bend. He hated the awkward ten pounds of the nearly six-foot musket, but he dared not leave it. The gun could kill a man at two hundred yards.

The view beyond the bend of the river was opening fast, but the morning sun rising above the treetops blazed blinding light directly into his face, diffusing outlines of the distant bank and river. The bare-earth trail hugged the shaded riverbank at the place where the grass field finally gave way to giant sycamores and cottonwoods. Yielding to endless erosion of the bank, they leaned toward the water. Across the trail behind them, stately oak, hickory, and ash joined branches with the riverside trees to form a thick canopy, block the sun, and sharpen Yahou-Lakee's view.

As soon as he entered the shaded coolness, he stopped. Far away, downstream on a gentle slope of the opposite bank, he saw the two canoes left half out of water, no other sign. Standing quietly in the cool shade, he eased the stock of his musket to rest on the ground and stared through the branches of the trees.

Within his vision, a red-orange leaf turned, swayed lightly in a wisp of moving air, and dropped from the stem. It drifted lightly to rest on a flame-colored blanket of other leaves, and became still again. At his feet, a group of tiny minnows broke the surface as though escaping some predator and a mourning dove called. He scanned the bank and trail before him. The signs were plain; he was too late.

Yahou-Lakee choked back the swell of grief forming within him and waited several minutes before he began a systematic search of the riverbank for evidence of the war party. After the long quiet stretch of flat water flowing eastward, the river turned almost due north where he stood. The children would have been setting trap near this bend. He checked for the most likely place. It would be on this side, shallow water, near a muskrat nest hole. He knew of two likely places a little farther along and out of sight of the town.

Yahou-Lakee became a part of the surrounding plant life, almost invisible as he moved forward and searched the leaves covering the path. He examined the weeds and wild flowers until he came to the place where a small patch of freshly scraped bare earth confirmed the recent passage of a man or a thirsty beast. A little farther, he saw other disturbed ground. Signs were now plentiful: the wrong position of a leaf, a tiny broken twig, a bent blade of grass, and in one place, moisture where he expected dryness. These travelers had been careful, moving slowly, perhaps stalking the children, but deliberately covering their trail, trying to leave no evidence of passing this way.

How many, he wanted to know. More than two, possibly four, he thought as he looked at the wide pattern of signs in the disturbed soil and plants. That would make seven altogether. Two had crossed upstream after killing Nastabon, four had been here, and the thief in the canoe made seven. It looked like ten, but no more than twelve attackers. The mouth of the first muskrat den was visible just forty paces before him, and even from this distance, he could see the torn earth bank at the water's edge and the place where the Tuscaroras had entered the river. Yahou-Lakee straightened and walked directly to that point.

There he found many moccasin prints. Just offshore, he saw the iron trap lying upside down on the bottom in knee-deep water. A mark at the bank in the clear shallow water would fit the canoe bow. He re-examined the tracks and ground and satisfied himself that three Tuscaroras had boarded one of the canoes there, probably the canoe of the thief. He looked again at the trail downstream and walked toward a point opposite the two abandoned canoes, visible across the river. Twenty paces ahead, he found the lifeless body of Sinopa, face down in shallow water, still bleeding from the arrows and scalp wounds.

It was enough. He turned toward the town, placed his cupped hands around his mouth and made a long, wailing all-clear call. Almost immediately, a group of young people came sprinting, followed by some of the older women and men. He set several to claiming Sinopa's body and called aside a boy of about twelve.

"Shoteka, you must take the small canoe and follow the river downstream. Find Tonawanda. He was to join others where the big rivers meet. Maybe all are returning now. Look for two of our dugout canoes coming upstream. If you find Tonawanda, tell him to get word to Governor Nicholson of the Tuscarora attack. Two were killed and two were captured: Sayen and Tayamiti. If you do not find Tonawanda, give this message to the first English house you see after you arrive at the place of the two rivers."

"Yahou-Lakee, I go," said Shoteka, filled with pride and excitement that he had been chosen for such an important task. He ran toward the canoes.

As Shoteka sped away, a tall man approached Yahou-Lakee. His long white hair parted in the middle and swept back tight to his head, leaving his chestnut face and huge ears projecting defiantly over a square chin held high and jutting forth under thin lips and a sea of wrinkles. His name was Tosawi.

Yahou-Lakee grasped Tosawi's forearm. Here was a man he had hunted and fought with side-by-side all his life. Five winters his senior, Tosawi had guided him through the trials of warrior status when he was but fourteen winters, and they had spent the remainder of their lives as inseparable friends.

"Yahou-Lakee, it is certain that the Tuscaroras are deep in Monacan territory and have no way to get out before the next sun. I can be at the lodge of the Monacan Chief Massaqua before dark. There I will say what has happened and alert him that Tuscarora warriors are on the warpath in his hunting grounds. It has been many winters since the Monacan attacked the Nahyssan. I will say that our own warriors are following the Tuscaroras and ask Massaqua's approval. It is possible that he will see the opportunity to profit and work with us," said Tosawi.

"Go, Tosawi. You can reach the Monacan town while the sun is still high. Tonawanda will follow, perhaps later today, possibly tomorrow. If you are taken prisoner, listen for his call," said Yahou-Lakee.

Tosawi took the first canoe available, and armed only with a tomahawk and sheath knife, he crabbed the upstream current to make his landing close to a well-known trail. He left the canoe on high ground, for the Nahyssans to recover and entered the forest while the sun was still high enough to cast only short shadows.

He carried no food or water, and no war paint. His dress consisted of a breechclout hanging from aged hips under visible ribs and over thin but strong legs, made so with a lifetime of running the hunting trails and warpaths. Now his long silver hair moved with the rhythm of his trotting steps except where an ornate headband kept it firmly in place. The headband was half the width of a man's hand, made of porcupine quills, and richly decorated in geometric designs of red, white, and black. He wore it proudly. It was an outward manifestation of war prowess, and it marked him as a leading war chief.

He ran easily, not fast, never straining, never short of breath. He felt young. He could keep it up as long as the light lasted and the trail remained clear. Tosawi had not known this feeling of strength and purpose in a long time. *Too many warm fires and soft beds*, he thought.

When he arrived at the Monacan town, he spoke to a hastily convened council presided over by Chief Massaqua and attended by Haw-Chi, senior warrior. After hearing his story, Haw-Chi escorted Tosawi to a roundhouse comfortably furnished and supplied with food. A sentry took a position outside the only door, and Haw-Chi left with a war party to investigate what Tosawi had told them. Tosawi was to remain a captive guest of the Monacans until Haw-Chi returned.

As a dark and foggy night gave way to the oncoming first light of dawn, Tonawanda, Tree Son, and the Nahyssan warriors started paddling their canoes upstream on the Appomattox River. The current was very strong against them in mid-stream. It was weaker near the bank, but navigation there was nearly impossible because of the pre-dawn darkness and fog-shrouded limbs that dipped low into the water..

Glad, however, to have this early start, they paddled on, anxious to be going home. If they paddled all day they could be there by night fall. Tree Son rode the bow of his canoe with a warrior in the stern position. Although sometimes enshrouded in the mist, it was easy to follow the sounds of Tonawanda's canoe just ahead,.

When day broke over the river, they moved into the weaker current and paddled steadily on. By noon, the river became smaller and the first riffles appeared, a sure sign of good westward progress. When the sun was past its zenith and well on its way to the crest of the Blue Mountains, Tonawanda sent his canoe into the cover of the shadows of a giant sycamore where some of its branches, still thick with yellowing leaves, dipped into the water. Tree Son looked upstream where Tonawanda was pointing. There a tiny dot appeared. As it drew closer, they could see the paddler gathering speed, and moving in a straight line.

They moved out toward midstream, and when the paddler began motioning them to stop, they recognized Shoteka and turned toward the west bank to meet him. They eased their canoes forward in quiet water among the low hanging branches of a willow, one on each side of Shoteka's canoe.

Shoteka gave a good account of the attack, and made clear Yahou-Lakee's orders to Tonawanda. He waited until the last part of his report to speak of the captives. Here Shoteka choked back a painful swelling in his throat, and the strength of his voice wavered, but his eyes remained dry and locked on Tonawanda. He spoke clearly.

"After they killed Sinopa, the Tuscaroras crossed to the other side and took Sayen and Tayamiti with them."

Tonawanda's face did not change, but an all-consuming fear for his children rose into his chest, and his throat swelled, fighting for control as he slowly realized that the children were probably alive, and the fear changed to suppressed rage. He spoke with a steady but lowered voice, almost a whisper.

"Shoteka, you have done well. Exchange places with Tree Son."

When the boys were settled, Tonawanda said, "Tree Son, you know the way. Go back to our camp of last night. If you arrive after dark, cross over to the first English house on the James River when the sun is up. Ask for English militia. Repeat the word, *mi-lish-ah*. Ask to be taken to the English chief. Repeat what Yahou-Lakee has said. Return to the Nahyssan when this is done."

Tree Son nodded his head in understanding and prepared to paddle. The group separated. In minutes they had lost sight of each other.

Tonawanda took the lead position and paddled on with renewed strength. He mentally calculated the movements of the enemy, factored in their route through Monacan territory, and continued to mentally lay out the pursuit without missing a single paddle stroke.

Shoteka had said that Yahou-Lakee believed their direction was westward, and it made sense that they would seek high ground refuge in the mountains. He glanced at the position of the sun. It would be late when they reached Yahou-Lakee, but not too late to find the trail of the Tuscarora. It was not likely that they would take the time to conceal all traces of their travel, even if they split up into many directions.

Yahou-Lakee met Tonawanda on the bank where the getaway trail started and motioned him in. Together they inspected the surrounding area for trail sign. When they were satisfied they had the right direction, Tonawanda and the three warriors entered the forest to travel as far as they could before light gave way to darkness. When the remaining light failed to confirm trail sign, they stopped beside a tiny stream fed from a nearby spring. One footprint was visible, probably a decoy, but also a welcome confirmation that they were on the right track. By the time they kindled a small fire, women from their town appeared with baskets of food.

12

Kajika, with his braves and two captives, set out at a slow trot. Sayen fought to keep her balance as she staggered along held upright between two warriors. The little branches of the dogwood, cherry, and other young saplings whipped her viciously from head to toe. She was unable to focus on anything except standing and moving on. Her head throbbed with pain and swelled grotesquely at the wound site.

They kept going, Kajika's eyes westward, keenly aware that he traveled in Monacan territory, the shortest way to the safety of the mountains, but certain war if the Monacans discovered him. The wing decoys he had sent out rejoined him without incident, confident that their work would at least delay the trackers.

After the sun passed its zenith, clouds began to gather, and the heat eased somewhat. The group had slowed to a walk because of the thick undergrowth when they heard a bird call announcing the return of a forward scout sent out earlier. He approached Kajika.

"No sign of people. A deep ravine and cave are there." He pointed ahead and to the left away from the Monacan town. "No trail," he said.

"Divide and go there," Kajika said.

They had been traveling since mid-morning leaving subtle signs for Nahyssan trackers. The tracks they left gave a message of mixed haste and caution. Obvious tracks and broken vegetation would confirm to a good tracker that this was a decoy trail. Now, reassembled, Kajika ordered more such trails. Two

101

warriors followed the back-trail to a stream they had just crossed and set about destroying all trail-sign they could find on the west side of the stream. They left all signs of the trail that entered the stream undisturbed, even added to it to suggest that even it might be a fake. They followed the stream both ways, and made exit decoy trails upstream and downstream, circled widely and moved on, careful to leave no sign of their approach to the ravine and cave.

Kajika ordered the group to move forward single file. The last man in the line double-checked to make sure they left no trail sign. The shadows of the afternoon sun had begun to lengthen and the mountains were still a full day's travel west. At their present pace, they would barely reach the cave before dark. He estimated he needed more than half of the day to clear Monacan country, so they must camp that night. The cave might work. The night would give him time to check his warriors, captives, rations, and prepare for a hard run tomorrow. He gave a concerned glance at the gathering clouds.

A half mile from the cave, Kajika gave signals and the groups dispersed in different directions. Eventually, they converged on the cave at separate times and from separate directions. Sayen and her escorts were the last to arrive, but by the time the sun touched the western rim of the mountains, all had been accounted for.

Sayen fell to the ground on a gentle slope outside the cave entrance. Exhausted from her wound and the exertions of the trip, she lay motionless on her side with her face pressed against bare ground. After a while, she stretched her tightly bound arms outward, but could not complete the turn onto her stomach. The cool earth seemed to caress her face in a healing way. She breathed the word "Tayamiti" and slipped into a deep sleep. A gentle movement of cold air lifted a pair of autumn leaves and moved on to brush a single strand of coal black hair across her face. They left her there while they attended to their packs and weapons.

Kajika squinted at the sky and sent three warriors to scout for hunters or other travelers while he decided on a defensive camp. The cave was ideally located on high ground back from a rock-strewn stream of tumbling water. The entrance to the cave was ten paces wide and formed by an enormous solid rock slab resting on another rock of similar size. The slab rock ceiling was so low at the entrance a man must be on his knees to enter, but shortly there was standing room and then easy walking into pitch-black darkness. It was good shelter against gathering clouds, if needed, but no place to be caught by an enemy. Behind the cave, huge oak, beech, and hickory trees stood on gently rising ground and cast a deep evening shade over the campsite—excellent protection, but those big trees also provided protection to an enemy. Twenty paces from the cave, a rock cliff twice the height of a man safeguarded its entrance. Two sentries behind the cave would be enough.

Kajika posted the sentries and turned toward the cave entrance. He frowned at the rolling thunder in the west. He needed the crackling leaves and snapping twigs of a dry forest floor to announce any movement toward his camp. He knew he was in Monacan territory uninvited, but he was satisfied with the natural fortification of the cave and its obscurity. Darkness was near, and they would travel at morning's first light. He shrugged at the next rumble of thunder and turned toward the cave, unaware that a Monacan warrior watched.

Tayamiti sat still, arms around his knees, waiting for his custodian, Two Bears, to return. He could see Sayen on the opposite side of the cave entrance but dared not call out. She had not moved. Turning, he could see others scattered about gathering firewood, unpacking, checking, and repairing arms.

Night fell fast. The first raindrops spattered the bare ground sending up dusty puffs at first and then formed little rivulets. As Tayamiti stared past the small cooking fire at the barely visible form of Sayen, he saw her turn on her stomach. Inch-by-inch she dragged herself up a gentle slope toward the shelter of an ancient beech. The lower limbs of the old tree were as thick as many of the trunks of smaller trees. Their branches spread like webs heavily laden with leaves still green against the call of autumn. They formed a shelter against the wind and the first drops of the oncoming rain.

In his excitement at seeing Sayen move, Tayamiti raised himself to his knees, pursed his lips and tongue, and oblivious to the fact that wren birds had gone to roost, gave three sweet sounds of the song of a wren. The withering look of the nearest warrior sent him back on his heels with his head bowed, but not before Sayen, unseen by the warriors, had turned her head in recognition.

The first raindrops brought Sayen to a cloudy consciousness. Her thoughts, jumbled at first, gradually began to clear. As she moved up the slope toward the shelter of the beech tree, the cool, clean rain helped to ease the pain of her head wound. She remembered the attack and that she had been taken captive, and she looked again and was relieved to see Tayamiti asleep near his guard. Then she lay still under the protective branches of the beech.

A warrior came, untied the bonds on her arms, and left a large portion of shelled nuts, berries, bits of dried venison, and a skin of water on an exposed root of the massive beech. Its gnarled surface made a convenient table for the food. Sayen ate and fell asleep exhausted. She slept without changing positions until the storm broke just before midnight soaking the ground beneath her. She rose and walked to the shelter of the cave and slept there alone. Outside, the warriors, unwilling to risk the confinement of the cave, huddled beneath crude shelters at the uprooted bases of trees felled by earlier storms, or inside tent-like shelters they made by bending the tops of young saplings together and covering the makeshift round frames with branches.

13

The day the Tuscarora attacked the Nahyssan, Williamsburg woke to another pleasant autumn morning. Kadomico had not slept much. His mind kept switching from Sayen to his eagerness to learn to speak the English language. Although he had only vague impressions of papers that talk, of the killing power of the musket and of iron, he was already sure that learning to speak English was the key to understanding them. It excited him to think he could learn these things. He thought of Sam Layton. Sam understood, and he said that speaking English would be a good thing.

He dozed off and on through the night. Twice he had seen Shanda leave the room. Now, almost at dawn, he noticed Shanda's bed was empty. Hawk was breathing gently in deep sleep. Kadomico slipped into his moccasins and went toward the back door. From sitting positions in the hall, Red Wolf and Wiwohka watched him go. Near the back of the building, he found Shanda sitting wrapped in a blanket shivering in the arms of Wapiti.

"Shanda is sick," Wapiti said. "Tell Layton."

Kadomico knelt next to Shanda, placed his hand on the shoulder of his trembling friend and leaned close to the blanket covering Shanda's head.

"Shanda, the sickness will be gone soon. I go for medicine," he whispered. Shanda's body was so hot it alarmed Kadomico.

He spun around ready to run for Sam Layton just as Sam stepped out the back door followed by Red Wolf and Wiwohka.

"I heard the stirring about," Sam said.

"Shanda is sick. I will find a *shaman*," said Kadomico, not at all sure where he would find an Indian medicine man or priest.

Wapiti was visibly concerned about his young charge. He stood. "We go. Come back when Shanda is well."

"Shanda looks too sick to travel," Sam said. "Give me time to get help."

The renowned warrior and great hunter Wapiti was clearly out of his element. He adjusted Shanda's blanket although it didn't need adjusting, and sat down slowly, uncertain what to do. Embracing the youth, he looked up at Sam and nodded his willingness to wait.

Sam gave Kadomico a reassuring pat on the shoulder and struck a fast pace toward Arrington's quarters just as the morning sun lighted the grounds and eased the chill left by the September night.

Arrington had been up only a few minutes. He removed his nightcap and gown, and sat down with his breeches lying across his bare thighs while he buckled a garter on to the fresh, white knee-length hose left by his manservant last night. The knock on his door caused him to look up visibly annoyed. The marks of sleep on his face had not yet been washed away; he had not shaved, and his thinly distributed hair lay plastered to his head where the nightcap had remained tightly in place all night.

"If this is that half-crazy manservant again, I'll have his skin," mumbled Arrington to no one in particular as he pulled on his breeches.

"Come," he said.

Sam entered and eased the door back under the latch. "Sorry to bother you, Headmaster, but we have a seriously ill Indian boy, and need medicine and care for him."

"Oh, it is you, Sam. Good morning," Arrington said, as he laid his shirt aside and moved toward the washbasin and water pitcher. "I am sorry to hear this. We don't have a physician in

Williamsburg right now, just an apothecary." He rubbed his face vigorously with cold water. He kept speaking as he toweled off and combed back the strands of thinning hair. He would deal with the whiskers later. "The apothecary does as much as he can, and that's a lot, actually. His quarters are just there by the church. Good man at a time like this. I'll get him."

"Well, best hurry. The Indians have quit the building and are outside on the ground talking about leaving. There'll be no stopping them if that's what they decide to do."

"If possible, get the sick boy in the room and keep him warm. I'll have Carrie bring over broth and fresh water right away." He slipped his feet into a pair of black leather shoes with polished pewter buckles that matched the buckle design of the garter straps.

"I'll let the Governor know about this. As you know, he is supposed to speak to the Indians this morning. It may be best to postpone that until we know more about the boy's illness and the Indians are at ease about it." He abandoned the effort to get his cravat exactly straight, squirmed into his waistcoat and reached for a powdered wig and a three-cornered hat.

Both men stepped into the hallway.

"Makes sense. I'll speak to the Indians," Sam said.

"Good," replied Arrington. He was still fumbling with his cravat as he hastened toward Carrie's kitchen.

As Sam walked back toward the Indians now gathered outside the building, he pondered his situation. Last night just before he fell asleep, he realized how much he wanted to return to his own country and the Shawnee. He despaired at the activity and stunning growth of the colonist occupation of Virginia. Although it had been less than two years since he had been in Jamestown, the fields of tobacco, maize, and pasture land had spread far beyond Williamsburg and Jamestown, especially along the James and York rivers. Hundreds of shiploads of immigrants from Europe, England, and slaves from Africa were already in Virginia, and Jock had said many more are on the way.

Unfortunately, even though it meant a delay for his departure, this was not a good day to start the schooling. There was much yet to be done. The Indians needed an interpreter. It would help if he could take them to see the blacksmith, wheelwright shop, and the horses, cattle, and sheep of nearby Middle Plantation. Maybe they would be interested in some of the field activities like harvesting, hauling, and plowing, and perhaps he could introduce them to some of the colonists and neighboring Indians.

He decided to discuss a postponement with the headmaster. He felt sure Governor Nicholson would agree. That would give them this day to see how Shanda progressed and would no doubt ease some of the anxieties the Indians were feeling.

The apothecary's assistant arrived just as Sam finished reassuring the Indians that someone with medicine for Shanda was on the way.

"I am David Corbett," said the assistant. He carried a wooden case of bottles filled with herbs, potions and other medications. He placed the case on the ground and began to examine Shanda. Sam and the others gave Corbett plenty of room and waited.

"It looks like a bad case of the flux. The diarrhea, vomiting, and fever can last several days, and the patient will be very weak at the end. He will need someone with him continuously to see that he takes the broth and drinks fresh water—as much as possible," the assistant said. "I will leave a potion and sassafras to make tea. The boy needs the potion four times daily. Carrie will see to it. A doctor from the hospital at Henricus will be here in a few days on business with the House of Burgesses. He will look in on the boy. Sometimes recovery takes a month. It is usually more serious for Indians. Some have died. Let's get him inside."

Sam had seen this sickness before. He knew the assistant was not exaggerating when he talked about the possibility that Shanda might die. He looked at the Indians. Except for Hawk who was still sleeping, they gathered close to him waiting to learn what the assistant had said.

Sam knelt before Wapiti and Shanda so he would be at eye level with the great warrior when he spoke. "Shanda will get worse unless we can get him back inside and keep him there until the medicine and food have a chance to work. We must do this now. Keep him warm, and keep the broth and water ready for him when he can take it. It will be many suns before he can travel."

Wapiti rose slowly, gathered the feverish boy into his arms and walked toward the back door of the building. Sam stepped ahead to open doors. He hoped Arrington had postponed the meeting with the Governor. David Corbett and the others followed Wapiti into the house. They were uncertain what to do, but stayed as close to Wapiti and Shanda as they could.

In the room, the stench of the night's sickness was overpowering in spite of the mild flow of fresh air moving across the room. David gave Sam the medicine.

"Carrie knows what to do with this and how to reach me if she needs me. I must get back to the shop." He placed the bottles in Sam's hands.

Wapiti eased Shanda down on the bedside, soiled and reeking of vomit. When Shanda sat down, he began to retch. Then, surrendering to delirium, he swung his arms and twisted his torso as though to free himself from some invisible torment. Gasping for every breath, he fought off the blanket and refused to lie down. Suddenly his eyes rolled back in a merciful faint.

Alarmed that Shanda was dying, Wapiti began to sing a slow chant-like rhythm, the sounds rumbling up through his massive chest, as he pulled a blanket over the boy, quiet now except for the gurgling sounds from his swollen air passages and congested lungs. Each breath fought to reach his lungs, but Shanda lay still in a burning fever. Wapiti continued the song in a low voice, finally positioning himself on the floor near the ailing boy. Sam looked longingly at the front door. He needed help. Hawk, roused from a deep sleep and pleasant dreams, still in his breechclout, sidled confused and embarrassed, toward the crowded doorway clutching his buckskins. Anxious to get clear of the commotion, he headed for the nearest woods.

The front door slammed behind Carrie with her basket of food and a large pitcher of water. She took one look at the room, now crowded with naked savages, and said to Sam, "Just clear this room, please. Wait outside. I will see that the other room is prepared for Hawk and Kadomico." She proudly pronounced their names just as Sam had given them to her last night. Sam translated the message, and everyone left except Wapiti. He gave way to Carrie a little, but remained close to Shanda.

Carrie looked up as she gently removed the blanket from Shanda and spread it in the middle of the floor. She took account of the scene and went to work completely absorbed in the task before her. She rolled Shanda to one side then the other as she stripped the bedding, unaware that her old fears and hatred had vanished, at least for the moment. When she looked up, she was startled to find that, other than Shanda, she was alone in the room with a savage of such awesome strength and stature. But when she saw the worried look on Wapiti's face, drawn and pale with deep concern for the youth, her alarm quickly faded. Here was a powerful man feeling pain and helplessness.

She glanced over at the door and called out. "Sam, I am going to need some help in here now. Have someone strip these beds. Pile everything on this blanket; everything, pillows, blankets, sheets. Everything. Then put them out back near the wash pot, fill it with water and start a fire. You'll see the pot. Just look."

She took the blanket from Shanda and spread it on the floor. "Tell Shanda's friend he can stay. It doesn't look like he'll have it any other way, anyhow. Tell him to be sure no one, and I mean no one, enters this room except me and the doctor when he gets here. Tell him Shanda is to remain covered and given as much water as he will take. I will be next door in the kitchen if he needs me, and I will sleep there until Shanda is well. I will also bring food for him," she said, pointing to Wapiti. "Tell me his name."

"Wa-pee-ti is his name," Sam said. He emphasized "pee" and wondered if he could remember all Carrie's instructions.

Back in the room, Sam repeated Carrie's instructions to the letter to Wapiti and urged him to stay and to give the white man's medicine a chance. He told him he had seen its power to heal. Wapiti nodded agreement, hesitantly, as though if later he chose to leave, he would.

Sam turned to Carrie. "He understands, madam. And I'd like you to know we are much obliged for your help and your concern. Thank you for coming."

"Well, why wouldn't I? The Governor himself sent me to see after this sick boy. But it is going to take some doing. I'll need boiling water and lye soap on most of the floor and this bed. Hand me two clean sheets and a pillow cover from that closet out there across from this room. As soon as I get that bed made, I want Wapiti to put Shanda there, and you can take his mattress out with the other bedding. A little fresh air and sunshine will do a lot for it. You can tell the others food is set out and waiting for them. They can get on with their morning meal, but you might suggest they put some clothes on before they come back into my dining room."

"I will tell them," said Sam, mentally trying to recall all the orders—boiling water, sheets, move Shanda, bedding, breakfast, and clothe the naked. Turning back to the hallway and linen closet, Sam translated Carrie's orders to Red Wolf and Wiwohka and asked for their help, concerned that these hunter/warriors might regard such work as beneath them. However, when he handed Carrie the clean bedclothes, stepped over to the first bed, and began to strip it, they followed quickly and soon emptied the room of bedding while Carrie scrubbed. She saved a little clean water for the washbowl.

She made the bed with the fresh sheets and motioned to Wapiti to move Shanda to the bed. There she covered him, then reached under the covering and stripped off his breechclout. Giving it to Wapiti, she motioned toward the back yard for it to be included in the wash. Wapiti's expression changed from grief to confused alarm as Carrie turned back to Shanda and began bathing him from head to waist. When Wapiti returned, she gave him the washcloth and clean dry clothes for Shanda to wear in place of his breechclout. She turned her back while Wapiti worked.

After the Indians cleared the room of soiled bedding, Sam showed them the deep free flowing spring of icy water at the back of the building, one of five spread throughout the area serving sweet, pure water to the townspeople. Nearby this spring sat a huge iron wash pot to be filled and heated. Instead, they drew cold water from the spring, filled a handy wooden tub, and enjoyed a luxurious bath, dunking their heads and splashing water like children at play. Then they filled the wash pot, stoked a well-seasoned oak and hickory fire under it, and began to grease their bodies. Finally, they reassembled on the front porch as Sam approached with a bar of lye soap and a pail of hot water from the kitchen.

When Sam returned from delivering the hot water to Carrie, Kadomico and Hawk confronted him.

"Is there a shaman here?" asked Hawk.

"It is likely there is a shaman among the Powhatan or Chickahominy people," said Sam, feeling the first touch of impatience. "However, we do not know them. I trust the English and their God to take care of Shanda, and I believe it is best that we wait."

Still uncertain, and with growing concern about Shanda, Kadomico deferred to Wapiti. "Shanda's sickness is bad. If Wapiti wishes, we will go with him and return Shanda to his people."

"I understand," said Sam. "I am sure Shanda will be better by tomorrow. Let us see if this treatment works. We will talk again tomorrow morning."

These reassurances seemed enough for the moment. Hawk and Kadomico turned away. Their shared concern for Shanda seemed to strengthen the bond between them.

Sam was still dressed in yesterday's clothing himself, but looking at the Indians and remembering his last order from

Carrie, he said, "Food is waiting. We will eat and talk more there. It will be good if you wear your buckskins."

They entered Carrie's kitchen-dining room, and sure enough, abundant food was waiting. Sam was pleased to see them follow him to the tables and benches and take seats instead of going outside. He also noticed they filled their travel pouches with dried fruit, nuts, and bread. During the meal, Arrington came in, and talked with Sam before he addressed the Indians.

"Governor Nicholson sends to Shanda his wishes for a quick recovery, and asks everyone to take this day to visit Williamsburg. I have arranged for a tailor to fit Hawk and Kadomico for clothes right after the noon meal. Their education begins today with an introduction to our church, crafts, and farms. Tomorrow we will assemble for the first day of the school. You will meet Governor Nicholson at that time. Later you will meet other leaders in our community."

Arrington gathered some fruit, cheese, bread, and a glass of milk and took a seat by Sam who translated his message. After Sam had spoken, Hawk pushed the remainder of his food away as a gesture of rejection, faced Kadomico and said, "No. It is not good that I wear the clothes of the English as though Indian clothes are bad."

Having had a momentary reservation about dressing in English clothing himself, Kadomico quickly decided his own position about the clothing and replied, "I think it is not so bad. They are gifts of the English. We are guests. I will try. It is important to learn as much as we can."

"No," said Hawk. "I will learn. I will not become English. That is not the wish of my father or my people." He spoke so softly and in such distinctly measured tones that those who heard him missed the intensity of their meaning. But, to Hawk, they were the same as a solemn oath, and he would speak no more about it.

Kadomico, however, did sense the depth of Hawk's conviction and tried to reason.

"Do you see that Sam has done this? He wears some of the English clothes. He speaks their tongue. The English trust him and work with him for the good of both Indian and English. If I can be that way, my people will be pleased, and I will bring the Saponi council the information they seek. It is why I came."

Hawk remained silent. It was as if he had not heard. Kadomico dropped the subject, knowing it was of no use at the moment. He would watch for a better time to discuss it. Sam heard only enough of the exchange to know Hawk had objected to the English clothing. What else, he wondered. First a near fight with Kajika, then a stupid drunk and his friends to spoil their arrival; then Shanda's sickness; and now possibly a rebellious youth.

<u>14</u>

S am decided the best way to get through this day was to make sure the Indians spent their time in interesting ways. Walking around town was not the answer, but what was? What were they most curious about, what would impress them? Certainly, the cutting, hauling, plowing, or the animals of the plantation would not. Nor would they understand or be impressed by the sewing, carpentry, wheelwrights and other such. Suddenly he knew.

"Headmaster," he said to Arrington, "I think the Governor has hit on exactly the right thing to do, and the sooner we get started the better. Only Kadomico has a commitment later today at the Stilson home. Can you arrange with the blacksmith shop? I'd like to go there first."

"Of course, I will alert Master Stilson. The Governor will want them also to see the church and meet the reverend," said Arrington.

Sam understood how important the church was to Arrington. Much of what was to happen in the classroom came directly from the church: morning prayers, bible readings, music, the songs, sermons about right and wrong. He also knew, given a choice, that the English church would rank low on the Indians' list of where to spend their time.

"Yes. Of course, they will see the church," Sam said. He was sure, given the plan he had in mind, that the best he could do about the church would be to mention the building when they passed it, but he also knew discussing it further would only

115

intensify Arrington's insistence. Let the day begin. What he had in mind might take up most of the day, and as the plan formed in his mind, he was anxious to get started. He was also sure that the tailor would have to postpone his fitting session, but let that happen as it may.

Arrington left the room to alert Stilson the blacksmith and the Reverend Doyle. Sam moved closer to Red Wolf and Wiwohka.

"Today we will see how iron is made into tools. The English make them here, and I will take you to see how it is done. You might see axes, tomahawks, longknives, and points of sharp iron. Bring your weapons and a good supply of arrows and tell Kadomico and Hawk to do the same."

It was no surprise to Sam that Wiwohka and Red Wolf both very much liked the notion of handling weapons of iron.

"We must see the iron tomahawks of the English," said Wiwohka.

Red Wolf said, "Yes. We will do this." Red Wolf motioned to Kadomico and Hawk to join them, and they started back to their quarters to collect their bows, arrows, and tomahawks.

Sam noticed the change in them. They were discussing weaponry, knives, and shooting, busy planning what they would do. Whatever it was, he was certain it would be impressive. As they walked along, Jock caught up with Sam, exchanged greetings, and fell in beside him.

"I heard about the Indian lad's illness. I hope he is going to be all right."

"So far, so good," replied Sam.

"We're counting on you tonight. How is your day looking? I hoped we could have some time together. A few things I want to show you."

"I look forward to this evening's visit with you and Rebecca even though this day looks pretty full. I am taking the Indians to the blacksmith shop. However, I could use your help if you have any free time, and I think I can guarantee you a day you won't soon forget, one you might even cherish if all goes well."

"I thought as much, Sam, and I've already made arrangements to remain in Williamsburg today. Just let me know what I can do," Jock said.

Sam smiled his relief and thanks to have Jock working with him and turned toward the building to look in on Wapiti and Shanda. He motioned Wapiti to the door.

"Any change in Shanda?" asked Sam.

"Shanda sleeps now, hot, restless. Sometimes he is cold and trembles in the blankets. The sickness is strong. When the woman comes, Shanda drinks," said Wapiti. "I will stay."

Both men knew it was too soon to tell, but it was comforting to Sam to know that Carrie was being vigilant in spite of all her kitchen duties. Sam explained to Wapiti where he and the Indians would be and what they would be doing today and that he would be close by throughout the day.

"Her name is Carrie. If you need me, let her know. She will send for me," said Sam. He regretted not having this magnificent warrior in his group this morning. He stood an imposing head taller than most of those about him and always carried himself with a catlike grace as though his massive frame was weightless. Wapiti was a good representative of the Indian. But so are the others, thought Sam. Smiling at what he had in mind for the day, he returned to Jock on the front porch.

While the others collected their arms and chatted, Sam explained his plan and laid out the day for Jock's part.

"No time for details, Jock. Just let your imagination be your guide and be ready for us when you hear the pistol shot right after the noon meal. We'll be on our way now to the blacksmith shop."

Jock smiled his understanding and agreement. Barely able to contain his excitement, he said, "I'll be ready. It will be a sight to see, and if I find you in the stocks tomorrow morning, I'll give the sheriff the best character reference I can."

"Well, you have a point. Maybe we ought to make him a part of it. Give it some official sanction. Let him know we would like to have him over at the blacksmith shop right after high noon. Say whatever you have to say to get him there."

"Done," said Jock. Enjoying the anticipation of the next few hours in this young town, he struck a lively pace toward the barnyards of old Middle Plantation. Once there, he sent for Matthew, his oldest son, age ten, and made arrangements with Jesse Jenkins, the farm manager, to use a forty-foot-long soft, poplar half-log. He then set one of the slaves auguring one-inch diameter holes set two feet apart. Jenkins, fully cooperative and enjoying the idea, supplied more labor and materials while Jock and Matthew went to the blacksmith shop and stepped off fifty yards on the cleared edge of the woodlands behind the shop, marked it and then set two more fifty-yard markers beyond the first. Jenkins sent two more men to the nearby canebrake to gather the cane Jock wanted.

Jock's mind was working fast as he surveyed the building materials scattered about the tool shed of the barn. He was scratching his head to complete the vision of what he needed to be ready for Sam when he saw a neat stack of ten-foot lengths of poplar bark that had dried and curled tightly from side to side into single pieces like ancient scrolls. They must have come from an old poplar, probably last spring when the sap ran heavy and loosened the bark from the tree. They looked like a stack of small logs pyramided on the ground near one of the buildings.

15

At last, Sam and his party were ready. The sun was drawing near its zenith in a clear sky when they stepped out between the caked wagon ruts of Duke of Gloucester Street. The church was in plain view on their left as they walked east, and there were a few small, well-built homes and shops of craftsmen and merchants. The new capital was attracting such tradesmen in growing numbers now. Their homes bordered future streets as though they were already cleared and ready. In fact, the surveying *was* complete and the lots and streets were marked, but little else had been done.

Sam noticed that some of the buildings sat askew to the east-west alignment of the Duke of Gloucester Street markers. He decided those were survivors of old Middle Plantation buildings. He also noticed the two brick storage buildings of Middle Plantation oddly located about thirty feet apart in the middle of the Duke of Gloucester Street markers. As though to remind the public that Williamsburg would rise in strict accordance with the approved plan, those buildings were marked for removal. The church, however, stood perfectly aligned on one of the future corners.

"That building is the place the English call church. You will go there soon and hear their reverend speak. There will be singing and ceremony and a chance to learn about their God," said Sam. Then he remembered the many Sundays he sat painfully still in hot woolen trousers and coat on the wooden benches of another English church with the Layton family.

"Every seventh sun, the English gather here to worship their God," he said, satisfied he had at least acknowledged Arrington's concern.

In spite of the tumultuous ruts and debris from a recent storm, paths to the shops and hitching rails for animals gave the scene a feeling of industry, even prosperity. The smell of fresh manure dissipated in the path of a freshening breeze. An ox-drawn cart loaded with firewood rolled toward one of the buildings. The man tending the ox walked and carried a long wooden rod that he occasionally used to touch the animal, as he murmured soft words of reassurance and direction.

Sam pointed out stakes and flags, recognizing them as marking the location of the courthouse soon to be built.

"That will be the courthouse, much like your longhouse of council meetings. It is there that the judges deal with those who break the laws of the English," he said. Then, seeing the Indians glance at it nervously, he continued, "That strange-looking contraption with three holes in it is used to fasten a man's head and two hands and hold him there for all to see—called the stocks—combines pain and humiliation—loss of face. It is a severe punishment."

Two riders mounted on large, gaited, high-stepping horses approached the group. Just as they drew near, one of the horses threw his head, fighting the bit. He tried to turn toward a field of grass, only to be reined back, but not before he pranced twice to show his objection. Red Wolf, nearest to the rider and startled by the unexpected moves of the horse, jumped aside and crouched, hand resting on his tomahawk, ready to engage. Red Wolf's sudden movement and the strange bear grease scent of the Indian was too much for the stallion. He half-reared, pawed the air ready to lunge away, but the rider held the reins just tight enough to let the animal know he understood. The horse settled, shook his head nervously, and resumed his walking gait. The rider touched the brim of his three-cornered hat to Sam and the Indians and moved on toward the college building.

120

"Easy, Red Wolf. Some horses are just naturally high strung and easy to spook. The rider meant no harm or offense," Sam said. He knew how easily innocent mistakes among strangers could explode into deadly confrontations.

"Horses are bad," snapped Red Wolf through clinched teeth and anger. Horses and riders were of no apparent use to him or his people; they made no sense to him.

"Man and horse go to the same place with six feet when only two are needed. Horses act crazy, no good off-trail, no good in the river. Horses are no good," he concluded, convinced of his case against the horse. To him a horse could no more walk in the wilderness than a fish could swim out of water. It disgusted him to see such a huge animal set to so simple a task just to save a man from walking. Angered at the near miss, he would have pulled the rider off and settled the careless insult on the spot. Only Sam's explanation and assurance that it was not intentional stayed his hand.

Sam decided not to get into a defense of the horse nor try to explain that, in the open, a warrior on foot was no match for one mounted. There would be time enough for them to learn the usefulness of the horse in work and war. Right now, he was reminded that although Red Wolf would do his best for Custoga and his people, he had made it clear he was not a willing visitor, and now, he was in no mood to hear anything good or sensible about the English.

They turned the corner and walked north into a large open area, and then on toward an open field which had been set aside for the Governor's mansion, still in the planning stages. Before they turned east again toward the blacksmith shop, Hawk tapped Kadomico on the shoulder and pointed out a field of grazing sheep. Ready for shearing, the voluminous wool on their skins made them look much larger than they actually were. Kadomico had just made a mental note to ask Sam about them when he heard the rhythmic ring of the blacksmith's hammer and caught the first faint smell of white heat on iron drifting toward them from the shop.

When the shop came into view, the Indians surged forward, eager to see what caused the ringing and to investigate the smoke and fire of the forge. The ringing stopped as they approached, and the smith turned away from the anvil to place the end of the iron bar he was working in a bed of glowing charcoal. As he set it aside, he smiled, turned toward Sam and offered his hand.

"They said you would be here this morning. Welcome. I'm Raymond Stilson. Mary said you remembered me, and though it took a while, I did recall our meeting in Annapolis. I was trying to get some of the inbound cargo from a ship that was loading your furs for the return trip to England. As I recall, we were both satisfied with trading that day."

They noticed the Indians change positions, moving closer to watch the smith strike the white-hot iron bar. With each strike, the bar had grown thinner, drawn ever closer to a menacing point, its many uses easily imagined by the Indians. Gradually, the bar lost its glow, and the smith shifted his stock from the anvil back to the fire, and began to work an enormous bellows forcing air into the burning coals. Startled, the Indians stepped back, their faces flashed white by the powerful blaze, then watched easier but fascinated as the smith returned to "drawing" the point.

Sam remembered the meeting in Annapolis. Ray Stilson had been there on behalf of the Governor to receive a shipment of Indian trade guns: long barrel, smooth-bore muskets.

"That's right," said Sam, with one eye still on the Indians. "You mentioned they were trade guns, and I wondered at the time why they weren't long rifles."

"Indians insist on the lighter, faster loading musket, and it's a sight cheaper. Believe me, the manufacturers and the government like that. As you know, the government doesn't want to let guns out to Indians in any form, but when the neighboring tribes are fighting on our side, they often do better with muskets than bows and arrows," Stilson said, as he turned toward Red Wolf and Wiwohka.

Sam placed a hand on Red Wolf's shoulder and said, "This is Red Wolf, senior warrior of the Saponi Indians." He touched each one and mentioned their name, and then in Siouan he explained to the Indians that Stilson was the man who made the iron weapons and tools for the English. The other men in the shop were his helpers, his apprentices.

"Firesticks ?" asked Wiwohka

"Not firesticks. The guns are made in England," Sam said.

"Soon we will have guns made here in the colonies," Stilson said, and then he acknowledged the Indians by smiling and pointing to a man filing a metal fork. Unlike the black bar they had seen drawn into a point, the fork had three prongs twisted into a single unit then welded to a finely polished shaft ending in a tang to be fitted into a handle of polished locust wood. Stilson demonstrated how he drew the iron into wire prongs, then welded, filed, and polished them. He then showed them how the two pieces would eventually be joined.

They examined pots, pans, knives, and several tools, with Stilson and Sam explaining the use of each, but Kadomico was fascinated by the bellows and wondered how it worked. Sam did his best with the flurry of questions, pleased to see Kadomico's intense concentration and struggle to understand. Then, after looking around, a sliver of worry climbed into his face.

Hawk was missing.

16

S am walked over to Wiwohka, who was examining a mysterious iron tool designed for use with tobacco pipes. It had several tiny arms, each attached to a peculiar disk, blade, point, or clamp for cleaning, scraping, or tamping.

"Wiwohka, where is Hawk?"

Wiwohka looked around the shop. Hawk was not there. He returned the pipe tool to the shelf and followed Sam outside to look for Hawk. They heard raucous shouts coming from their right and followed the noise.

Almost immediately they came upon Hawk, stripped to the waist and crouched in a thin ring formed by a few of the town boys. His bow, the quiver of arrows, and his buckskin shirt lay behind him at the edge of the ring. One of the boys, thin and much taller, had also stripped to the waist. He was circling Hawk, arms extended low and outward, hands open. Both boys were eager, their faces drawn with intense concentration and determination, their eyes locked on each other. Neither expressed hate, fear, or excitement, just a gut-twisting, eye-squinting determination to attack. Shouts of encouragement to both rang out from the on-lookers.

Sam had reached the edge of the circle. He saw that, as loud and enthusiastic as the ringside spectators were, it was clear they would not interfere, and he decided the contest was a voluntary wrestling match between two boys. It is what boys do. His mind more at ease, he stayed a bit back to avoid distracting the wrestlers by the presence of an adult.

Two women were hurrying toward the group, their faces deep within the protective shade of brightly colored bonnets, their skirts lifted to free their legs and feet for the running. One of them was shouting, "Stop! Stop! Tim!"

Sam turned toward them and raised his hands slowly in a gesture of friendly reassurance.

"They wrestle to compete," he said in a low respectful voice. "The young Indian is a guest of your town, here for school." The boys continued to circle each other. The women stopped, their haste interrupted by this buckskin clad, deeply tanned, long-haired stranger assuming authority over this matter involving their Tim. His smile and lingering looks from one to the other stemmed their rush forward. Besides, intuition was whispering to them that he might be right—no danger here. But still, the audacity!

The hesitation of the two ladies was enough for Sam to redirect his attention to the fight. He worked his way to the inside edge of the circle.

The boys came together, arms grasping, tugging, and pushing. They commanded their legs to trip each other, and prevented it by keeping their feet and ankles out of reach of the opponent. They broke apart and crouched low looking for an opening. Twice they clashed and broke apart. Then in a sudden charge, the young colonist's shoulder tipped Hawk back and slightly off balance, and, sensing the advantage, he dug in and pushed with all his might.

When Hawk felt the threat of falling, he threw his arm under the boy's arm and across his shoulder and clamped down hard. He twisted and fell with both arms now locked around the churning waist of his opponent. They fell together; Tim broke his fall with one hand and grasped wildly at the arm lock on his waist as he tried to turn within Hawk's powerful grip.

They hit the ground with such force that for an instant Hawk's hold loosened. It was enough. Tim timed his move to break the grip. Hawk's hold collapsed. They split apart, and both instantly regained their feet. Sam stepped between them and signaled them to approach. He whispered quickly to Hawk, "Follow me."

Leaning toward the boy and speaking in a low voice, he said, "You fight well. What is your name?"

"Tim," replied the boy.

Sam addressed the crowd, "This is Hawk and Tim. They have fought a fair and clean fight. I pronounce it even." Hawk did not understand the words, but by the crowd's applause, he knew it was over, and by Sam raising each fighter's hand, he knew that Sam was calling it a draw. But to Hawk, a fight was not over until there was a winner. There would be another day.

Hawk gathered his belongings. When he turned back, Tim was waiting with an open hand extended. Hawk had seen enough handshaking among the English in the last two days to know what was expected. He raised a limp open hand to Tim and managed a reasonable facsimile of a handshake, but, noticing the firmness of Tim's grip, he tightened his own grip to match Tim's, at the same time fastening his eyes on Tim's. Once again they locked eyes as Tim returned the motion, then both boys smiled and released. Yes. There would be another day. The crowd moved in, patted the fighters on the back, and shook their hands. Hawk, overcome with the attention and a little confused, endured the crowd until Sam motioned him to follow.

Returning to the blacksmith shop, Sam decided to let Wiwohka deal with how this had happened. Did Hawk challenge Tim, attack him, or was Tim the aggressor? He might learn about it later. For now, he decided it was not such a bad way to introduce Hawk to the town. It was past noon, and there was much left to see in the blacksmith shop. His thoughts turned to Wapiti and Shanda. He wanted to check on them, but he also needed to get on with his plan.

"Ray, could we break for a bite to eat and finish up afterwards?" Sam asked.

"Sure, it's about time for our usual break."

126

"Good," Sam said. "All we'll need is some drinking water. The Indians have food with them."

"Here's the water bucket. The spring is down the hill at the end of yonder foot path," Stilson said, handing Sam a gourd dipper and a three-gallon wooden bucket made of heart cedar staves.

Sam settled the Indians in a grove of nearby pines.

"Red Wolf, I will go to see Wapiti and Shanda. Rest here. Eat. There is drinking water in the spring there at the end of that path. I will be back soon."

The Indians ate lightly and went back inside the blacksmith shop, fascinated with the dozens of products there—so many different shapes and sizes, so many pieces.

Kadomico said to Red Wolf, "Why are there so many irons for so few men?"

Ray Stilson, prompted by Kadomico's intense curiosity and the questioning expressions, began to demonstrate the hammers, chisels, saws, and files, motioning as best he could to help his visitors understand. He thought of how easily Sam Layton managed English, Algonquian and Siouan and decided he would talk to Mary about learning one of the Indian languages. She would know what to do.

He picked up a hoe blade not yet fitted with a handle and handed it to Wiwohka. Wiwohka laughed, and pretended to use it as though he didn't know what it was, then found a pole and showed the group how it worked with a handle. They also saw a large hay fork and a shovel.

Stilson walked them into an adjoining shed and showed them long, flat bars of iron stocked in various sizes.

By the time they returned to the warm shop, an assistant had fired the coals and was slowly pumping the gigantic leather-and-wood bellows. Each time he pulled the long handle, air rushed from the point of the heart-shaped bellows into a small three-inch cast iron pipe passing through the masonry base of the forge and onto the coals. The strong blasts of fresh oxygen fueled the coals until the iron bar began to glow orange then yellow and flooded the room with the clean, strong smell of white heat over charcoal.

The smith moved the bar to the anvil. The Indians watched as he began to strike, then turn the bar, strike, turn, strike, turn. Each strike rang clear, rhythmic, musical tones and filled the dark shop with warmth of a different kind. Here meaningful work was taking place. Here a man could find ways and means to prosper in his doings, be it work, war, or play. The blacksmith shop gave them a satisfying sense of purpose and progress. They watched the iron change shape, bend, flatten, and open as the smith made square and round holes to demonstrate the versatility of iron exposed to heat and hammer.

Hawk grinned with anticipation as he visualized arrow points, spear points, knives, and tomahawks, but Kadomico was absorbed in the process, and he wanted to know more. Where did the iron bars come from? Was the charcoal the same as that used in his town? Did all English settlements have a blacksmith shop? How many furs would he need to trade for a hoe blade? With such a blade, Sayen could plant, weed, and remove stones and roots with a fraction of the effort it takes using bone, wood or stone tools. This strong hoe would be a valuable gift to his people. He would talk to Sam about it later.

Headmaster Arrington waited anxiously at the door of the unfinished college building. He beckoned to Sam as he drew near. "Sam, the tailor will be here shortly. Where are your people? There is no one here except Shanda, who is too sick to be measured and fitted, and that huge Indian Wapiti, who is plain hostile. The only one he will let in the room is Carrie."

"Well, the tour of the town is taking a little longer than expected, Headmaster, but the Governor was right. It is proving a valuable experience to the town as well as the Indians. Is there any way you can postpone the tailor until tomorrow?" Sam's patience was growing short with the headmaster and his clerks and assistants. He managed to choke back the words already in his throat, but his tone was unmistakable.

"There doesn't seem to be a choice." Arrington was visibly annoyed. "I will send him word. Can you have the Indians assemble in the classroom to meet the Governor after breakfast tomorrow morning? And this time, can you have the boys ready for the tailor after the noon meal?"

Sam didn't miss the admonishment, but he held his peace. Meeting the Governor early tomorrow in the class room would be a good time and place to let the Governor know that he would be leaving.

"I will have them there," he said.

He would see the Indians through the first day of school, meet with the new interpreter if necessary, and clean up any unfinished business, like finding a suitable present for his Shawnee wife, Star Light.

Sam found Wapiti vigilant and anxious to know if he had located a shaman. To Wapiti's mind, the English medicine was not working, and not having a shaman to deal with this sickness was defiance of the Indian way. Sam sensed his anxiety. It looked to him as though Wapiti might take matters into his own hands.

Shanda, still unable to abide food and very little water, turned and writhed as they talked.

"Wapiti, we need three full suns to know if the English medicine will work. To move Shanda now might kill him. Rest and nourishment is the most important way we can help him," said Sam.

"Two suns, we go," Wapiti answered, his face contorted with the loss of sleep and a day of prayers and worry.

Sam stopped by to see Carrie. She confirmed the seriousness of Shanda's sickness, but reminded Sam it needed three days at least before they would know what Shanda's chances were.

Stilson stopped working with the iron forge and anvil, drew a huge brightly colored handkerchief from his apron, and wiped the sweat from his face and neck. He stepped over to the cedar bucket and drank deeply of the sweet clear water from the spring.

When he looked up, he saw Sam nearing the shop. It was good to have him back. Demonstrating without talking was awkward, and it was apparent his audience had many questions. Sam stepped into the dark shop.

He spoke directly to Kadomico, but for all to hear. "Shanda is still very sick. Carrie is tending to him, and Wapiti remains with him. The apothecary has provided strong medicine, but it will take three suns at least for him to begin to get better." He held up three fingers, and hoped they would wait three more days before someone decided to abandon the visit altogether. In fact, Sam was much disturbed at what he had seen. Shanda's fever had not broken. Carrie was visibly worried. Wapiti seemed desperate. No, it would not surprise him if Wapiti took matters in his own hands, lifted Shanda to his shoulders, crossed the James River and struck the trail for Occaneechi country. He hoped not. A strange Indian unescorted and with a sick boy on his shoulder in the vicinity of the settlement was risky business. There was nothing to be done but wait.

The Indians seemed to accept the news. They avoided eye contact. There was no response. Ray Stilson was about to approach Sam when the doorway filled again shutting out much of the light that splashed across the dark shop.

"Well, I heard there was going to be something special going on over here," Deputy Sheriff Will James said. He ducked his six-foot-six-inch frame under the eaves of the shop and pulled off his great leather hat as he ground his fingers through thick waves of brown, disheveled hair and grinned at Ray Stilson.

"Master Layton. Glad to meet you. Name's James, Will James, Deputy Sheriff of the county. Two of your acquaintances, charged with creating a disturbance and being drunk in public, are guests over at what is serving as our gaol until the new one is built. Luther Rawlings, bad fellow he is, is due in a little later today. It's taking longer than usual to repair the damages. Looks like a glass jaw. You sure the hand that did that is all right?"

"I can't deny the soreness, Deputy, but the bones all seem to be in place," Sam said. He shook the out-stretched hand of the deputy. Then gesturing toward the Indians, he continued. "Glad you stopped by. These people come from the western frontier and near the Carolina border at the Governor's invitation to attend school."

Sam called the name of each Indian and introduced the deputy as the colony's man who kept the peace and added, "The sheriff and his deputies tend the house they call a gaol, where law-breakers like the drunkard you saw yesterday are held until a court of seniors, much like your own councils, decide their punishment."

"What will be the punishment?" asked Kadomico.

Sam translated for Will.

"Well, the last time the three were brought in for drunkenness, they just got the stocks for a day. The court might add some lashes on bare backs this time—slow learners," replied the deputy.

Red Wolf and Wiwohka knew about drunken behavior. They had seen it in their own towns on the western frontier. They even knew of traders who had used the rum to help them cheat the Indian fur trappers. And although they did not know that Caribbean rum was so cheap and plentiful, they did notice that it was a favored item in the trader's cargo, and they suspected it had something to do with making his trades more profitable. And if that kind of trader could, he would see that the Indian had all he wanted to drink at no cost before they struck a deal. Sometimes the drunken Indians flew into killing rages and fell victim to others or to the wilderness. If they did survive, their people usually overlooked the drunken behavior. They would not hold a member of their tribe responsible for behavior driven by the mysterious demon rum. So while they were happy to see the enemy--Luther Rawlings and his pals—punished, their people would more likely have overlooked it, especially since Rawlings had been badly hurt by Layton.

17

S am was satisfied with the Indians' reaction to English justice and proceeded to prepare the deputy for what the Indians were about to do.

"Will, what Jock talked about with you earlier today is actually a kind of demonstration of their handling of their weapons. It is something the Indians want to do in return for Ray and his apprentices showing them the shop and how the iron is worked here," Sam said.

"Fair enough," replied Will. "What, exactly, did they have in mind?"

"You can see there are two men and two boys here. Each has a tomahawk and a bow and a quiver of arrows. I told them you would likely enjoy seeing a demonstration of Indian skills with tomahawk and bow-'n-arrow."

"That I would," said Will. He turned to a smiling Ray Stilson. "You and your boys got time to watch an exhibition in your honor, Ray?"

"Of course," Ray answered. "Enoch Tarver has been having conniptions about those nearly finished singletrees over there, but I don't see how earlier or later today will change his fortune one bit. Let's get on with it. Sam, tell your friends we'd be honored to watch."

Sam looked again at the lay of the land. They were two blocks north of Duke of Gloucester Street and about that far east of the building site of the governor's mansion. From the north side of the shop and running north, a ravine split two large fields of brown, ready-to-harvest tobacco, but on the west side of the ravine a mixture of virgin hardwoods and pine had escaped the settler's ax. It occupied a space about 100 yards long from the blacksmith shop north to the tobacco field on that side of the ravine. They had taken their mid-day meal in the shade of the woodland about twenty paces from the shop. The settlement lay behind them to the south and west.

It was a clear September day. The sun warmed their skin; their sweat evaporated in the gentle waves of dry autumn air, scented with the fragrance of fallen leaves and touched by the smell of the heated iron. The light was perfect, the noon shadows still short. Sam gathered the Indians about him and told them their targets would appear when he fired his pistol. On the signal from Sam's nod, the Indians separated in different directions. All four bows were now strung. The smith, his two helpers, and the deputy watched the Indians as they moved about.

Sam stepped closer to Will and Ray. "If you stay exactly where you are, you will see all of the shots. Watch closely. It will happen fast."

The four Indians stood two arm-lengths apart facing the woodland, their bows lying on the ground at their feet. The trunk of a great poplar, straight-grained and clear of knots for well over twenty feet, stood before them. Sam stepped to their line and nodded.

Kadomico and Hawk drew their knives and threw them into the dead center of the tree on a straight line, one above the other, and four feet apart, then turned about and ran directly away from the target about twenty more feet where they dropped to their knees side-by-side and put their heads down. Red Wolf, running in the same direction, raced on past them. When he felt sure he had room for a good start, he turned, and in a sudden burst of speed let out a chilling, high-pitched war-whoop and charged the kneeling boys, then catapulted himself high above them. By the time he reached the peak of his rise, his knees were drawn to his waist, and as he unfolded them, he twisted his body in perfect timing with the throw, and buried the blade of his tomahawk in the tree, less than a hand's width below Kadomico's knife.

Watching the speed and weapon throws in wide-eyed appreciation, Ray, Will, and the others barely had time to catch their breaths when Wiwohka, in a flash of speed running at right angles to Red Wolf's path, also leaped over the boys and sent his tomahawk into the poplar among the other weapons. It embedded in the remaining space between Red Wolf's tomahawk and Hawk's knife completing a near perfect line.

The Indians, with bows and arrows ready and faces taut with concentration, assembled on a line perpendicular to the north run of the ravine. Sam made sure Will was watching , then slowly raised his pistol and fired into the sky. The Indians were expecting a target to appear. Suddenly, they put down their weapons and began to laugh.

From out of the forest, about fifty yards away, plodded a huge brownish-red mule named Kate. She was harnessed in a collar, hames, and trace chains hooked to a singletree rigged for pulling. On Kate's head rested a broad-brim straw hat held in place by two great ears poking through holes carefully cut to fit. The old hat flopped a little with each step. Jock straddled her bare back, one hand resting on a hame, the other proudly waving his hat in a salute to his audience. Young Matthew knelt behind his dad, held on to him with one hand, and waved a small British flag with the other.

Behind them, skidding smoothly on its flat side over the firm dirt path leading out of the woods, emerged a huge half log. A line of four curled bark posts as tall as a man stood in the middle of the half-log, each topped with a small yellow pumpkin above a whitewashed, tree-bark face. As though this were not enough to evoke a laugh from the shooters, long, wide tobacco leaf breechclouts hung from the wooden waists. Another line of four tall, tomato-topped canes spaced about a foot apart, stood at each end of the stickman line. Between the canes an ear of whitewashed maize hung suspended on leather thongs. Sam smiled, remembering his parting words to Jock, *Just let your imagination be your guide.*

Jock turned Kate slowly to position the array of targets for the shooters and stopped. He dismounted and gave the mule a pat on the shoulder along with a few words of approval before he uncoupled the target log and removed the trace chains and singletree. Matthew slipped snugly onto Kate's back behind the harness collar and hames. With a courtly bow and a wave of his hat, Jock walked away leading Kate back into the woods safely beyond the shooting range.

The Indians destroyed all the vegetable targets, shot through hearts painted on bark and fixed to the posts, and then gave a demonstration of the kill-range of Red Wolf's and Wiwohka's bows by hitting trees beyond the 100-yard mark. Will and Ray began to applaud in appreciation. A small crowd of settlers had gathered. They joined in the applause with genuine enthusiasm. The Indians trotted off toward the targets to retrieve their arrows.

"It is as good an exhibition of shooting as I have seen," Will said. "I think the Governor will want something like this repeated at the races next week. What do you think, Ray?"

"No doubt he will. Leave it to Jock to make it interesting," replied Ray. Then, he turned to Sam and said, "These small pieces of iron can be fashioned into a number of different things: knives, punches, scrapers, etc. Will you give these to your friends and explain they can be worked with grinders and files?"

"I will," said Sam. "They are anxious to see the muskets and rifles fired and to see the bayonets and swords demonstrated. Will, could you set up something like that?"

"Have to clear it with the sheriff, Sam, but with the Governor backing these Indians so strongly, I don't see a problem. You know where to find me."

A man to know and remember, thought Sam, as he turned to the blacksmith. "It's good to see you again, Ray" continued Sam. "Please give my regards to Mistress Stilson. As you know, she invited Kadomico to visit your home this evening. I count that to be most generous and helpful with things the Governor is trying to accomplish, and I am already in her debt for stepping forward yesterday when we arrived and making us welcome."

"Don't give it another thought, Sam. We're glad to have Kadomico meet the family. This is the first time Mary has entertained a native of the frontier, and she is determined to make it a visit he will remember with pleasure and help with a better understanding of us English. We just wish you could join us."

"Thanks, Ray, but I promised the evening to Jock and Rebecca. Years ago, we were classmates, and there is much catching up to do. Afterwards, probably tomorrow or very early the next day, I will be on my way back to my Shawnee home beyond the mountains. However, I would like to pay my respects to Mistress Stilson before I leave and thank her again—maybe tomorrow afternoon."

"Of course, please do so, but don't knock on the door thinking it will be hello, thank you, and goodbye. Better to expect a cup of tea, some penetrating questions especially about the frontier tribes, and a lively discussion before you get away," said Ray, smiling.

"Well, I thank you for the advance notice, Ray," said Sam.

As the Indians drew near, Sam noticed that Jock and Matthew had removed the remains of the target. He remembered their school days. Jock had always been able to see the light side, find a smile, or produce a laugh. He would not deny the dark or ugly truth, but he seemed always able to make it more bearable. When the Schoolmaster's paddle turned up missing, Jock was sorry and volunteered to make another. He got the job, and turned up the next day with a paddle so small the class roared with laughter. Final tests were hard, but he reminded us that they marked the beginning of a school break. And when it was clean-up time in the school room and the privies, Jock led the work laughing and clowning his way through it. It was not surprising that he would have some fun with this afternoon of target shooting.

The Indians unstrung their bows and joined Sam and Ray. The samples of iron fragments lay spread out on a table outside the shop. Sam showed them how the fragments could be made into spear or arrow points, a knife, or scrapers. Ray ground some of them on a stone wheel driven by a foot treadle. Then, he demonstrated how to use a file to shape or sharpen them. Ray then handed each a piece and Sam explained it was a gift. Each one examined it closely, touching the sides, feeling the edges, hefting its weight. They pressed the iron into their arms and hands and struck one piece against the other, excited to discover its superiority over wood, stone, and bone.

Throughout this visit, the Indians had measured every new thing they saw against its usefulness. If they saw no use for it, they dismissed it. Consequently, ships, carriages, horses and multiple-story brick buildings, although wonders to behold, were of little interest to them. On the other hand, these gifts from the blacksmith were precious treasures. They could envision the killing power and cutting strength, and some were shaped for digging, hammering, scraping, or punching. These small gifts would make big differences back home.

"We accept these gifts for our chiefs, Saponi, Occaneechi, and Tutelo," said Red Wolf. "Here is a Saponi arrow for this man you call the smith. He is welcome in our towns." With that Red Wolf presented an arrow to Ray. The others followed his lead and chose the best of their arrows for Stilson.

They returned to the building where Wapiti sat with the ailing Shanda, who still showed no improvement.

"He speaks crazy sometimes," said Wapiti. "He is hot and refuses water and food unless the woman Carrie is here. For her he drinks, but then he is sick again when she leaves. When he does sleep, he is restless."

Sam looked closely at Shanda. "Wapiti," he said, "go with us to the stream where the water is cool and clear. Wiwohka and

Hawk will stay here with Shanda. We will be only a little while. It will be good to rest there."

Wiwohka and Hawk stepped forward, ready to take Wapiti's place, and Sam led the others out. Wapiti gathered his huge frame together and stood looking down at Shanda sleeping quietly for the first time. He then strapped on his bow, sheathed his tomahawk, and followed the others to the creek, now at full tide. After they had bathed in the cool water to their content, they found places in the shade of the driftwood, sand, and pines to recline and rest.

Since leaving the blacksmith shop, Kadomico had stayed close to Sam Layton, sensing a change in him. He saw Sam stare off into the distance several times, and it made him uneasy without knowing why. After his swim, he again settled near Sam.

"How long before I will speak English?" Kadomico asked.

"You have already learned some of the language, Kadomico. You understand and can speak the words *go, come, yes, no, thank you*—even more. It is because you want this. Nothing can stop you from learning as long as you wish it so," Sam said. The two of them reclined on the sand against a huge dead fall in cool shade and reasonable comfort.

"It will take some time, but if you will also learn to read, to understand the talking papers, you will soon know what to say to the Saponi council. No doubt you will become the one who speaks for your people with the English, and you can be sure there will be plenty of occasions for that in the future."

"But I am to become a warrior. I have not yet finished my trials. Tree Son will finish his trials this hunting season. I will not be there. I cannot prove my ability as a warrior if I am here learning to read." Kadomico explained, but he was confused and uncertain.

"That is so. You cannot prove yourself on the hunt and in battle, but you can in other ways. And while it may not yet be clear to you, these other ways are more important," Sam said. "So important, that life as the Saponi know it may depend on what you learn here. Your father and grandfather are wise men, and they want to understand the English. They expect you to help them by attending this school.

"You are Shawnee, Sam," said Kadomico. "Are the Shawnee not troubled with the English and other white men?"

"The Shawnee are a great nation of people, and we live farther beyond the frontier, so we do not encounter the white man as often as those who live east of the Blue Mountains. But, Kadomico, it is just a matter of time. The white man will come, and it will be much the same there as it has been here."

Kadomico sat up in surprise. "What, then, do you say to the Shawnee council?"

Sam shifted uncomfortably. They were closing in on some dangerous and complicated ground. The white man's invasion of Indian lands and the uniting of Indian tribes into nations was not a subject Kadomico could safely discuss in an English classroom—or parlor, for that matter, especially in Williamsburg, Virginia.

"Kadomico, I will not answer that question until you speak English and have mastered the talking papers. When you have done those two things, I will come to you and help you in any way I can. For now, you must work hard and study. I do not know if Hawk and Shanda will endure the English classroom and church, but I believe you can and must. It will not be easy for you, but I can think of nothing more important to you and your people.

"I will learn to speak English and to read," said Kadomico, picking up a green twig and starting to peel the bark away in little strips. "As you have seen, I have learned many English words, and it was easy. I will visit the Nahyssan when the days grow short, but I will return and continue learning until I can read. Why do you say it will not be easy?"

"It will not be easy because the methods of the English will be strange. There will be times when you will feel insulted, but you must not fight. You may be punished with switches or paddles, but you will not resist or run. They will expect you to worship the English God on your knees and to listen to endless passages from the book of their religion. Sometimes what they read or say will make no sense to you. The clothes they expect you to wear will be strange and uncomfortable, and you will learn about manners and polite behavior. And, in the learning, never forget the way of the Saponi. I am sure you can do this."

"I have never been switched or paddled. It is an insult. Only captives are treated so," Kadomico said.

"You will see that the English treat their own this way, not so much to humiliate but to punish with pain. In the classroom, it might be for not paying attention, for being late, or for being disrespectful to the headmaster. In their courts, on board their ships, and in their tobacco fields, they often punish their own with whips. These things you may see, and you may even have to endure them, but you must continue to learn. You will not regret it."

"I do not understand these things you say, but I will learn to speak and to read. I will then return to my people, but I will go back to the Nahyssan with gifts for Yahou-Lakee," Kadomico said. He deliberately omitted mention of Sayen, who remained as vivid in his thoughts as she was on the day she handed him the basket of food for his trip down the Appomattox River.

The omission did not escape Sam. Back at the campsite where he met the group, he had overheard Kadomico give Tree Son his message for Sayen, and it left little doubt why he intended to return to the Nahyssan town.

"When will you leave, Sam?" Kadomico asked.

"As soon as I have reported to the Governor, possibly two suns."

Visibly disturbed at this news, Kadomico dropped the peeled wet twig into the sand, looked up at Sam, and said, "It would be good if you did not leave so soon."

"The Saponi, Tutelo, and Occaneechi are strong. There is not much more I can do here," Sam replied, looking away. Then, in a stronger voice, he said, "Besides, the season for trapping is very near." Kadomico heard the change in Sam's voice and watched his eyes as he momentarily slipped away to some distant place, before adding quietly, "And it is right for me to be with my people, the Shawnee."

"Where can I find you?"

Sam pointed a little north of west. "Five days travel. I trap that river. It is called Shenandoah. The Shawnee there will know where I am. They speak Algonquian."

Sam admired Kadomico's curiosity and interest in learning, and he very much wanted to fuel that interest and desire to learn. He was doing the best he could to describe what might be in store for the young Indian in an English classroom, and to assure him he could return to his home by winter.

"The sun is low. We best start back so you can go over to the Stilson home later this evening. They are expecting you. Master Stilson asked that you bring your bow and arrows to show the Stilson children. I will walk there with you, and Master Stilson will walk back with you when you return later this evening. It is best that you not be alone in the town for a while yet." They walked along in silence toward their quarters.

When they arrived back at Shanda's room, they learned that Red Wolf, Wiwohka, and Wapiti had arranged times for sitting with Shanda, and that Shanda was taking food and water. Sam left to prepare for the evening visit with Jock and Rebecca, timing it so he could escort Kadomico to the Stilson home on the way. Kadomico found a place on one end of the small porch where he could lay out his weapons. There he settled down alone and began to oil his bow and check his arrows for damage from the target shooting.

As he rubbed the hickory with animal fat from a tiny pouch, his thoughts turned to the events of the day. He searched his memory for something that would be useful to tell Custoga and the council. At the council meeting he had heard the discussion of the English threat to Saponi hunting grounds. He also knew how Red Wolf felt. Maybe that was why Red Wolf refused to discuss it with him. Red Wolf's way was simple: war. What troubled Kadomico was the threat he had heard his father and grandfather describe. It did not seem like a threat to him. He had traveled two suns in a vast wilderness of hunting grounds. There was almost no sign of English there. He had seen many farms and fields on the James River, but he had not seen great numbers of settlers waiting to go beyond the falls and claim the hunting grounds there.

Furthermore, except for the drunk, Luther Rawlings, Kadomico had found the English to be friendly—friendly but strange. He pondered their devotion to work. Whatever their task—building, growing crops, cooking, blacksmithing, trading—they seemed never satisfied. It made no sense. It looked as though they actually worked just for the sake of working.

The Saponi worked only as much as needed for food and shelter—no more. Mostly the women, old men and children did that work, but it was not much compared to what he saw among the colonists. Indian men warred and hunted or prepared to war and hunt. They lent their superior strength to prepare fields for growing food, and they helped gather the structural poles and coverings for housing when needed, but their first priorities were training for and engaging in war and the provision of food by hunting and fishing.

The English seemed to work for abundances beyond their needs. The differences were confusing. His father and grandfather saw them as dangerous differences, and believed they would know better how to deal with them when Kadomico learned to read and write the English words and see the English way. This day he had neither seen nor heard anything to help him understand, but Sam had said he would explain more when he had learned the English language. He was anxious to get started. First, however, there was this visit in the English home. He wore buckskins, beaded moccasins and smelled just slightly of bear grease. He had tossed a quiver of arrows over his shoulder as Sam approached.

"We go." Sam spoke in English.

They found ten year-old Nathan Stilson raking leaves in the front yard of the Stilson's modest home. The back part was still under construction. Nathan gladly abandoned his work to alert his mother that the visitors were arriving. As Sam and Kadomico entered the front yard, Mary, Ray, and their fourteen-year-old daughter Ann stood on the spacious front porch only three steps above the yard.

Mary summoned her children and walked directly to Kadomico, smiling.

"Welcome, Kadomico and Sam Layton, this is Ann, our daughter, and Nathan our son," she said. "Children, this is Kadomico, our guest this evening." Then, with the strange smell of bear grease and the Siouan language about to make these opening minutes awkward, she said, "Sam, speak the family's welcome to Kadomico in Siouan and translate aloud. Just say 'Welcome, to our home, Kadomico.' "

Sam did as instructed, but when Mary repeated the Siouan words, Sam could not suppress his laughter, which immediately became contagious; Kadomico, Ray, and the children joined in. Then each of them tried their hand at Siouan only to make matters funnier.

Finally, Mary challenged Kadomico to try the words in English. When he repeated after Sam almost perfectly, "*Welcome to our home, Kadomico*" they were all so astonished they applauded. Kadomico was not sure exactly what he had said, but he knew by the applause and smiling faces that his whispered practices each night had paid off.

It was enough to get the evening off to a good start. Seeing there was little more for him to do, Sam bowed his departure to Mary and shook hands with Ray, who walked him back to the rutted street, promised his support if he could be of service in the future, and bade him farewell and a safe journey home.

Because of the good-natured laughing and the obvious sincerity of the family, Kadomico felt at ease, and the strange surroundings did not bother him except to trigger his curiosity. The first thing he noticed was the size of the house. Even half finished, it overwhelmed him. Standing there among the four family members, he looked at them and back at the structure. His family was also four members, and they occupied the largest lodge in their town. His father was chief among the people. Here, the blacksmith was a worker and his home stretched beyond four Saponi lodges, and more rooms were being added.

Mary Stilson noticed immediately Kadomico's puzzled look.

She said, "Ray, please start the fire in the back. The children and I will show Kadomico our home."

Turning to Kadomico, she motioned for him to follow, and began a tour of the house, explaining the use of each room by motion, smiles, frowns, and demonstrations. She included the children's places and roles, showing their clothes and personal things, dolls, pictures, books, the bible, everything she thought he might find interesting. It was going well, and he seemed to be genuinely absorbed in what she was saying. About half way through, Mary Stilson reached for Kadomico's hand and was startled at his recoil and withdrawal. Thinking she must have somehow offended him, she faced him directly, and in a voice so reassuring that the *meaning* of the words was unnecessary, she invited him to follow her—and he did.

They found Ray Stilson tending a perfect bed of cooking coals, and they began to roast skewered meat and bake potatoes.

<u>18</u>

S am left Kadomico with the Stilsons and returned to find Jock waiting for him with two saddled horses tethered to an old peeled locust hitching rail.

"Glad you're back, Sam," Jock said. He pulled the slipknots on the horses' reins and handed Sam a pair. "Name's Buck. Mount up. We still have enough daylight for you to see the new port over on College Creek. The horse path is mostly clear now, and I thought you might enjoy a ride this evening seein's as how you had such an unusual day. Rebecca is expecting us shortly after dark. What do you say?"

"Jock, I just say thank you," Sam said, overwhelmed with Jock's versatility and unerring ability to surprise and please. He realized he was beginning to feel an unexpected closeness to Jock, a trust, and approval in spite of the difference in their lives.

Sam took his time, stroked his horse, spoke a few words to him, and checked the saddle girth. Satisfied, he gathered the reins at the saddle pommel, found a stirrup, threw his weight on to it, and swung into the saddle. It didn't surprise him when Buck turned into the source of the weight like he was trying to avoid it, but Sam's move was so swift and true that by the time he settled into the saddle, Buck had accepted the mount and swung back toward the horse path, stepping into a quick, easy gait to catch up.

The path led them south through thick growth, patches of forest, and along the occasional border of a tobacco patch until they encountered marshland bordering the creek. Fields of reeds swept away from the high ground toward the bed of the tidal creek. As they rode, Jock talked.

He explained the business he operated as a badly needed pivot point for the Virginia shipping trade, and how he organized deliveries and loading operations all along the James River. Unlike the House of Burgesses and the British government, he did not try to influence shipping or trading on the James or among the planters in Virginia. Planters were glad to let him arrange for the movement and subsequent payment of their crops. He made sure their business remained within the limits of English trade laws, and their fees were honestly paid. Jock's reputation was spotless. Government, shippers, and planters relied on him, and he enjoyed the prosperity of the times.

"Problem is, Sam, I have more work than I can handle now and the business is growing fast. I need a partner. I know it would be a monumental change for you to come back to the English life, but the rewards are also monumental, starting with your children's education and a guaranteed life of prosperity for you and your wife. The crown makes grants of enormous acreages for people who support the colony's growth and economy.

"With your knowledge of languages, your friendships throughout the colonies, I believe you could name your price and it would be gladly given. If you will join me, we will start as equal partners at no cost to you. I am not asking for an answer, but I do hope you will think about it. It would be a good thing," Jock said, and he knew immediately by Sam's respectful silence what the answer would be.

The horses kept a steady side-by-side gait over the soft ground.

Sam chuckled. "Jock, it was lucky for me we met up yesterday there on the river. Since then your advice and assistance has made this work safer and easier. Now you honor me with an

146

offer I cannot accept. My life must always be with the Shawnee. I have not changed since our school days except now I do what I can to ease the Indian and English negotiations when I am asked.

"We chose different paths many years ago, Jock," Sam continued. "Both paths offer happiness, good health, and prosperity if we manage them right, and it looks like we both have done that."

The new dock came into view. They stopped the horses in the late evening shade, dismounted, and walked on, leading their mounts down toward the water.

"I guess I'm not surprised at your answer, and I think I understand. It is just that we would do well together."

"No doubt we would," Sam said.

Both men reflected in silence for a short while, then Sam spoke again. "Jock, have you noticed the young Indian Kadomico? He is a quick learner and has the full confidence and support of his people. A lot of fur comes out of his part of the country. It is just south of the western Virginia-Carolina border near the Indian trails crossroads called the Trading Ford. Right now it is pretty deep wilderness, but it won't always be. I'd take it as a favor if you would look in on him from time to time. I believe he will soon be a leader of his people, and I expect him to become a man worth knowing."

They tethered the horses and stepped out onto the wooden dock.

"I have noticed, and I will visit him from time to time. You can be sure," Jock said. They walked out to the end of the dock. "The Governor plans somehow to regulate the James and York River shipping. Williamsburg has water access to both by Queens Creek to the York, and as you can see here, College Creek to the James. The problem is that the creeks are tidal, and while they will take shallow draft ships at full tide, low tide will limit travel to those with very light drafts."

They discussed the shipping and Williamsburg's prospects of becoming a hub for Virginia commerce. After a while, Jock pointed at the fading western light, and they remounted and galloped back to Williamsburg. An indentured servant took the horses when they entered the schoolyard. They walked over to Jock's house, two stories high and made of brick. It had been part of Middle Plantation for several years, and was one of the buildings that survived the capital surveyors.

A servant met them at the door and took their hats and coats. Jock showed Sam to a bedroom and left him to wash and rest if he chose. He and Rebecca would be in the room across the hall.

Sam looked around. The room was richly furnished with Chinese porcelain basins and pitchers, an imported poster bed with a feather-down mattress, silk coverlets, and huge pillows, a painting of an American wilderness scene, upholstered chairs, and a small desk with paper and pen. A finely woven rug of muted colors covered the floor. Alongside the bed lay a huge bearskin rug. Next to an oil-lamp on the desk was a small bible and a copy of *Socrates*. He thought how interesting it would be to have a few hours with *Socrates* when he noticed that it contained a bookmark. He opened the book to the marked page and read:

> *Force is of no use to make a friend,*
> *who is an animal never caught nor*
> *tamed but by kindness and pleasure.*

Jock and Rebecca had gone to great lengths to open the door of a new life for him, but not at the expense of his trust and friendship.

He smiled at the intensity of his feelings as he surveyed the room. It had been a long day for sure, and he was a little tired. That and his concern about the Indians mingled with several proud moments this day might account for this uncomfortable feeling, but how could such comforts and splendor make one feel uncomfortable? He walked over to a window and drew the curtains back just to have a look at the sky. It was there, vivid and reassuring, and just the scene brought ease to his mind.

He stripped his buckskins to the waist and washed away the dust of the day. Refreshed, he eased down into a chair and closed his eyes. His mind shifted immediately to the birch bark canoe waiting for him. If he could catch the tides right, he could be home in four days. A clear vision of Star Light appeared behind his closed eyes and summoned a yearning from deep within him.

Rebecca Shaughnessy Adams was far more beautiful than the pudgy young girl Sam remembered two grades behind him. She was dressed in a deep-green gown of wool flowing open over a finely embroidered, waist-fitted petticoat. Her gown reached the floor in a sea of deep folds. She was as tall as Jock and made a striking figure standing by the mantle to one side of the stone fireplace where flames threw flickering light over her gown and made endless momentary changes to the shades of green. Sam shook off an involuntary hesitation and approached her directly. Jock rose for unnecessary introductions. Rebecca opened her arms and embraced Sam in a warm greeting.

"Sam Layton, we speak of you more often than you might imagine," Rebecca said, blotting a genuine tear. "Jock brings us news of your work with the treaty negotiations in New York and Pennsylvania. So you have never been out of our minds for very long. To finally have you here with us is a long-awaited pleasure."

"I have just spent the day realizing my misfortune to have lost Jock's friendship for so long, Rebecca, and seeing you now, that regret is multiplied. Your home reflects warmth, good taste, and happiness, and after a day with Jock, I suspect there is considerable laughter here as well," Sam replied.

"There is indeed, Sam. He hasn't changed much, and, by the way, neither have you. I like your buckskins and long hair, but you would cut quite a figure dressed in English finery at the Governor's annual reception and dance," Rebecca said.

"Now, that is a scene to shun," Jock said. "According to you, he is already the talk of the ladies in this town."

"Sam, pay no attention to this banter. There are far more palatable subjects in the dining room, but first we want you to meet our boys," she said. She signaled a servant to bring the boys. Matthew, Mark, and little Luke came in, were introduced, and, except for Luke, shook hands with Sam. Five-year-old Luke missed the introduction and the handshaking entirely because he was absorbed in inspecting Sam's fringed buckskins and shoulder-length hair.

While Sam shook hands with Matthew and thanked him for his part in the day's shoot, little Luke pulled on Sam's trousers and looked up at the face far above him. "Are you a Indian?" he asked.

Rebecca was about to intervene when Sam knelt to speak to Luke, at the same time taking Mark by the hand and gently guiding him closer

"Yes, I am a Shawnee Indian. I live far away, and I have a little girl about your age." Sam released his gentle grip on Mark. Both boys drew closer.

"When we play Indians-and-militia, I always have to be the Indian," said Luke.

"Well, when you are a little older, I'm sure you will get to be militia," replied Sam. "Both Indians and militia are brave men. They often fight side-by-side to protect their families."

"This morning, they said I couldn't play anymore because I scalped a militia boy."

Rebecca took Luke by the hand. "That is enough talk, Luke. It is your bedtime." Then, addressing all three boys, "Say goodnight, children."

Rebecca explained it was time for the boys to work on their lessons. They said goodnight reluctantly, and left with the servant. Rebecca led the way into the dining room where a chandelier of glass graced a table of extraordinary food and drink.

They talked about their lives in the twelve years since they had seen each other. Jock and Rebecca recounted their good fortune to attend school in London for four of those years. Then there was Jock's immediate success in the brokerage business. They were careful to emphasize how favorably the crown and local government had treated them, once it was clear that they were here to stay.

Sam told them about the Shawnee and the treaty activities in the north. He told them about the fur trade, and about the freedom, challenges, and tranquility of his Shawnee life beyond the western frontier. So intensely engrossing were the exchanges that more time passed than Sam had noticed. He explained that, because of Shanda's illness and the language difficulty of the Indian guests, he could not stay the night. They parted with promises that so much time would not elapse before they met again.

By the time Sam arrived at the Indian's quarters, darkness had fallen, and he paused to fill his lungs with the coolness of the night air before entering. He gently opened the door to Shanda's room and saw Wiwohka sitting quietly but awake. Wiwohka signaled him that Shanda was resting. He closed the door, and went out onto the porch. He located his pack, spread a blanket and lay down. The pack made a reasonably comfortable pillow. Sam closed his eyes, listened for a moment to the distant call of an owl, and started to think about tomorrow. He was to meet Governor Nicholson and. . . . Sam settled into a light sleep.

Not far away on the northwest leg of the horse path, O'Riley's ordinary was about to close. Thadeus O'Riley's, a place of meager lodging, food, and drink, failed to attract the gentlemen of Williamsburg, but it thrived on those willing to put up with the make-do construction, cracks in the chinked log walls, see-through ceiling and month-old debris from the boots of the occasional traveler, sailor, and the colony riff-raff. Thad stood taller than most. His powerful arms, left mostly bare by torn shirtsleeves rolled to the elbows, were covered with such a mass of curly black hair and grime that it was difficult to tell which was which. Thus, he had been setting the standards of appearance and behavior at his ordinary since he gave up trading (some said swindling) with Indians on the frontier.

As twilight faded, darkness settled over the ordinary, broken here and there by the flickering flame of a one-log fire. Silhouetted against the faint light of the little flame, Augustus Crammer sat at a table across from the two Higgins brothers. He wiped away the wet clinging to his five-day whiskers, and set the wooden mug of beer down on the table of rough-sawn pine boards. His hairy cheeks screwed upwards toward squinting eyes, as he raised a clenched fist, and threw his index finger straight at the Higgins boys.

"Locked old Luther up, they did, and him doing nothing more 'n warning the town about them thievin' Indians," Gus said. He relaxed his fist long enough to take another long pull at the near-empty mug. It annoyed him that Thad had not lit the candle on their table. True enough, Thad reserved such niceties for special customers, but he was surely that.

Their table was near the fireplace, and beyond them on the other side of the room a stranger sat alone at a similar table under the only window now shuttered against the insects and cool of the night—with *his* candle burning.

Gus set aside his annoyance with the proprietor to listen to Obie Higgins' response. "Well, it'll serve 'em right over there at that high falutin' school if they wake up tomorrow mornin' with their scalps missin'." Obie batted his eyes to avoid the shifting unruly hair lying across his face, and grinned at his wit through gaps of missing teeth.

Billy Higgins lifted his mug, took a long swallow and added, "I say the only good Indian is a dead Indian, and them that think different can just take a look at wot's goin' on out there in the hill country. Indians been burnin' and killin' whole families all the way from here to New York. Y' hear about it all the time. And them over there at the school being treated like royalty. Makes a man wanna puke." He was quick to label everyone who wasn't a settler or a slave a marauding, raiding, outlaw Indian, and that included those friendly tribes closely allied with the colony militia. "Indian's a Indian," Billy said.

Dottie O'Riley served the stranger a bowl of steaming broth and meat with a half loaf of bread, some cheese and a mug of tea. It annoyed Gus to be ignored and left in the dark, him being a regular customer, and he was about to say so when Dottie crossed the room, patted him reassuringly on the back. She drew a burning splinter from the fire, and set his candle alight.

152

"Gus, what's your problem?" Dottie said. "Your face is long as that fire poker over there."

Satisfied with the attention, Gus grinned at the slender innkeeper. Dottie had been married to Thad O'Riley long enough to have five full-grown boys, three of them now serving in the militia at various forts on the frontier and the other two at sea. Gus pushed his empty mug toward the smiling Dottie and returned to his subject with the Higgins brothers.

"You're right, Billy, but you know what went on over at Stilson's today. Half the town watched 'em throwin' tomahawks and shootin' just like they'd be killin' and scalpin', and everybody just stood there, even clapped their hands like it was a show or somethin'."

"Ain't right," Obie said. "Somebody oughta do somethin'."

"Yeah, well," Gus said, warming to his subject. "Filthy, murderin', heatherns is what they are. They shot my grandpa in the back in '44, then scalped and burned him in his own house. After hundreds of English got theirselves massacred, the survivors cleared these lands of Indians, but look at what's going on now. Short memories, I say."

Gus had been ten years old when his father joined Nathanial Bacon to rebel against the colonial government and exterminate the Indians in 1675. That failed, but not before it drew an impenetrable line between the colonists and all Indians. The colonists eventually defeated, or subdued by treaty, all of the coastal and near-coastal Virginia tribes, reduced them to the equivalent of slaves or refugees, and settled them on small parcels of land, the first of the New World's Indian *reservations*. Now, in 1700, Williamsburg and the County of James City enjoyed a life free of enemy Indian threat while murderous raids continued to destroy the crops, properties, and families of their fellow citizens on the frontier.

"Oughta run them savages back to the frontier," said Billy, squatting near the fireplace and drawing deeply, but without much success, on a pipe of poorly lit tobacco. They recalled stories of Indian massacres, raids, thefts, poaching, and outrageous slaughter of settlers' cattle, sheep and hogs, and still it wasn't enough to satisfy the abiding contempt and hatred they visited on the red man.

Gus had a good paying job overseeing slaves and crops at the old Bacon plantation across the James River. He had been making monthly trips to the growing collection of crafts and shops at Middle Plantation for many years. Last year the plantation yielded over three hundred acres to Williamsburg, the new capital of Virginia.

Raised by a frontier Indian trader, the Higgins brothers lived on a fifty-acre place on the James River over near the mouth of Archer's Hope Creek, later named College Creek. The Virginia House of Burgesses had deeded the land to their grandfather, Ely Higgins, in 1632 in return for the upkeep and repair for a section of a palisade that ran right straight through Middle Plantation and reached from the York River to the James River. Long since proved impractical and gone to rot, the palisade had been made of posts set next to each other. Its purpose had been to fence the southeastern part of the peninsula against poachers and protect forty miles of open-range grazing for settler livestock and settlements. Finally, the colony abandoned the palisade altogether, but landowners like the Higgins were allowed to keep their property.

By the time Billy and Obie were born, several tobacco and maize fields, started by their grandfather Ely, were producing. Their father, George, had leased his part of the land to others and spent his time in the less strenuous and demanding fur trade. And when times were hard, he and his boys were not opposed to occasionally taking one of their neighbor's clearly earmarked hogs from the open range. Nor did they shun the more profitable but illegal trading of gunpowder and ball to the Indians when the opportunity presented itself. To those crimes against the colony, Billy and Obie added the illegal trade of rum and a variety of home-brewed spirits to the Indians. Some of their products were little better than flavored water, others were the real Caribbean rum, strong enough to wreak drunken havoc among the tribes of their unfortunate customers. It just depended on what was available and safe from detection by the Sheriff's deputies.

The discussion finally ended, and Gus bid the Higgins a good night. He made his way into the loft where he found a place to stretch out. He fell asleep without removing his boots. The Higgins brothers stepped out into the night air with an hour's walk ahead of them. They pulled their broad brim leather hats down firmly, turned up their collars, buttoned up their shirts against the chill, and set out, two black silhouettes, leaning slightly forward as they trudged toward Archer's Hope.

Williamsburg settled into another quiet evening, safe from the dangers of the frontier, the pirates, the French, the Spaniards, and the Indian tribes of Virginia. It had been a day pleasantly marked by the visiting Saponi, Occaneechi, and Tutelo boys and their warrior escorts from the frontier, but only a short march west, the Nahyssan people mourned two dead and two captured by renegade Tuscaroras.

The light of day faded unnoticed as Tree Son paddled on past last night's campsite, consumed with determination to deliver Yahou-Lakee's words to the white man's chief. Tree Son would not fail the most important mission ever assigned to him.

At the same time several miles west, Kajika sat at the entrance to the cave, watching the rain in a vanishing twilight and pondered his situation, disappointed that he had been unable to raid and plunder the Nahyssan town. As he watched a coverlet of darkness envelope his party, he found a little comfort in the two captives he had taken and the success of his attack. The smell of rain was heavy, not a good thing if you were straining to hear movement in the surrounding forest. Not a good thing when it drove his warriors inside.

He ordered three of them to set up widely separated rain shelters. Better they sleep in strategic locations where they were more likely to be alerted by the sound of snapping twigs and footfalls on dry leaves or, if it did rain, the softer sounds on a soaked forest floor. They used the abundant young ash, oak, and cedar saplings to quickly fashion the shelters. While Tuscaroras settled around the cave, the Monacan town, a day's march north, grew as quiet as the cold, white ashes of its ceremonial fires.

Back at the Nahyssan town, the people mourned the death of Sinopa and Nastabon and the capture of Tayamiti and Sayen. Chief Yahou-Lakee finished preparing his weapons and ammunition and stepped outside his roundhouse to sense the weather. In the western night sky, dark clouds moved eastward pushing a band of chill air before them. No doubt, heavy rain and wind would slow Tonawanda as he tracked the Tuscaroras, but no matter the time or sacrifice, they would eventually bring the enemy Tuscaroras back—alive, if possible—and turn them over to the family of Sinopa and Nastabon. Many suns would pass before the murderers died, and the enemy Tuscaroras would never forget the fierce vengeance of the Nahyssan—never. The best of the Nahyssan trackers guided Tonawanda. It was just a matter of time. Yahou-Lakee turned back inside.

The oldest of his three wives had prepared his bed of fur and English blankets on a cedar pole bed frame along one wall, then retreated to the fireside at the center of the spacious bark-covered roundhouse. She remained silently available for whatever Yahou-Lakee needed of her. She knew his thoughts and heart almost as well he knew them himself. She also felt his outrage against the enemy, his demand for vengeance, and his grief at the loss of Sinopa and Nastabon.

Yahou-Lakee stretched out on his bed in the flickering firelight of the room and contemplated the events of the day. Tosawi would be with Chief Massaqua clearing the way for

Tonawanda through Monacan hunting grounds. He hoped that Tree Son had delivered the news of the attack to Williamsburg. He wanted the Governor to know why the Nahyssans traveled and wore war paint. Perhaps the English would forward the news to settlers and militia, and they would not mistake the intent of the Nahyssan warriors. It was going to be a restless night. Before sleep closed in, Yahou-Lakee thought of Sayen and Tayamiti and prayed.

19

After dozing intermittently through the night, Kajika sat still alongside the cave opening just far enough back that he could see the front of the cave. He stared through the darkness at the black silhouettes of tree limbs. Beyond, the barely perceptible first light of the new day promised fair skies. He listened to the sounds of the rain-drenched forest. Seven warriors lay scattered about him beneath the branch-covered huts, napping lightly in what remained of the night. Stationed behind him, two others kept watch. Tayamiti slept deeply, his head resting on the shoulder of his guard, Two Bears. Sayen had just returned from the privacy of a laurel thicket. Suddenly he heard a swish followed by the thud of an arrow slamming into the soft green wood of a nearby tulip poplar.

"Down," said Kajika just loud enough to be heard by his men. The Tuscaroras stretched out flat to the ground and lay still, ready to engage. Kajika reasoned the arrow had not been aimed to kill. It was more likely a notice to talk. A long silence followed as the morning light gathered strength. Kajika rose gradually to his feet and turned toward the area where his sentries were supposed to be. They stood frozen at their posts, surrounded by Monacan warriors with arrows nocked and aimed at their bellies. More Monacans formed a line beyond the two sentries blocking any escape by the trespassers. Facing Kajika and the two sentries, four Monacan warriors stood behind their towering leader, Haw-Chi, his arms folded, waiting for the Tuscarora leader to advance.

Three eagle feathers, signifying Haw-Chi's leadership, dangled from a black braid on one side of his half-shaved head. The bear-claw necklace he wore announced his superior hunting and warring skills. From a waist strap above his breechclout of tanned deerskin hung a glistening steel tomahawk and a knife sheathed in deerskin covered with intricate beadwork and three scalps. Another sheathed knife similar to the first hung from his neck on a plaited thong decorated with tiny beads and colored animal hair. Across his bare back lay a decorated buckskin quiver of arrows. Beneath these ornate war materials, he had strapped on tanned deer-hide leggings covered with floral designs in beads and quillwork. In his left hand, he held a bow of Osage Orange with recurve ends. It was as long as he was tall. His right hand rested near his tomahawk. The red and black war paint on his face and chest made his mission clear.

Kajika appeared carrying a primed and cocked musket. A huge sheath knife swung from his neck, and near his free hand, the handle of a steel tomahawk moved with each step. He walked to a line between his sentries and stopped. On a signal from Haw-Chi, a Monacan warrior stepped forward and threw his lance into the ground. The Monacan message was war.

"The Tuscaroras come armed and painted for war and travel uninvited in Monacan hunting grounds. Unstring your bows and lay down your firesticks," said Haw-Chi.

"No," Kajika said. "We came with no quarrel against the mighty Monacan people, and we do not hunt your land. We are dressed for war because we have just fought a battle against your enemies, the white man and the Nahyssan, and your hunting ground is the only way of escape. We have Nahyssan captives to share with you. We now ask you to allow us to pay for our passage through your lands and remain brothers with the mighty Monacan against our common enemies."

Kajika slowly and carefully removed a peace pipe from his quiver of arrows and propped it against the lance. To die in battle and move on to the other side was a warrior's right. To become a slave was unthinkable; to surrender, cowardly, and to beg or

159

plead was betrayal of the proud, fearless Tuscaroras. Kajika had two options: negotiate or fight.

Haw-Chi knew that Kajika lied. Tosawi had reported the facts yesterday to Chief Massaqua and the Monacan council. There had been no white men and no fight, only an ambush of an old man and three children. However, the raid sounded well executed and without Tuscarora casualty, something to the credit of this bold intruder. Monacan Chief Massaqua had ordered safe passage for the Tuscaroras, but only at a price. Haw-Chi could use his judgment.

"Show your captives," said Haw-Chi.

Kajika's eyes were locked on Haw-Chi's chest no more than a tomahawk-throw from him. He motioned the captives forward. They came from the cave bound and blindfolded with a warrior behind each of them holding razor-edge knives to their throats. The beauty of the slender Sayen, standing straight with her chin held defiantly high, did not escape Haw-Chi. She was certainly a valuable captive and many would compete for her, but it was Tayamiti that Indian families would want to adopt. Tayamiti would replace a son or brother who had died of disease or had been slain in battle. Tayamiti was young enough for a successful adoption, strong and healthy enough to become a fine warrior. It was clear to Haw-Chi that if he attacked, the captives would be the first to die. He stepped forward and took up the peace pipe.

Warriors on both sides sat down where they had been standing. Haw-Chi and Kajika took positions on either side of the grounded lance. A Monacan warrior removed it, and three warriors from each side formed a circle around the chiefs. Another Monacan brought pitch-pine splinters and flint to start the fire. When the flames rose, Haw-Chi and Kajika sprinkled bits of tobacco as a sacrifice to their particular gods. The passage of time no longer mattered. Haw-Chi would leave with a war prize and the Tuscaroras would be assured of safe travel into the mountains, confident that no pursuers could follow without first dealing with the Monacans.

Silently, they took turns drawing smoke from the pipe. Haw-Chi spoke first. "It is true. The white man is our enemy. He destroys the hunting grounds, and his god is powerful. When the sickness comes, he lives, but we perish."

"It is the same with the Tuscaroras," said Kajika. He pointed south toward his homeland. "We fight the whites and remain strong, but other Indian chiefs trade with them and give up their lands. See what has happened to the Powhatan, Rappahannock, and Meherrin. Their land and hunting grounds are no more."

Kajika told of Sam Layton, and how two suns ago, on the James River, Sam had met Occaneechi, Tutelo and Saponi Indians, and warriors from the Nahyssan town that he, Kajika, had just raided. "They were on their way to visit the English chief at Williamsburg. All these are enemies of the Tuscarora."

This exchange grew quickly into a detailed discussion as the two found abundant common ground and cause to support each other. To them, the land could no more be bought and sold than the sky, water, or air. They regarded these, and themselves, as part of Mother Earth. The English destroyed the forest and fenced the land against even their own people. Haw-Chi and Kajika agreed: the tribal chiefs, who signed talking papers betrayed their people.

"They are old and afraid of the white man's firesticks that speak and the great canoes with wings that bring more and more English," Haw-Chi said.

Then he continued proudly. "But the Monacan warriors kill the English and take their firesticks and will not allow their fences and longknives on Monacan hunting grounds."

They talked on about English killing and robbing Indian towns, and about the efforts of the English to teach them their way and how they insulted Indian gods and said their god was the only true God. They discussed the white traders and explorers from Williamsburg that they trusted, named the ones they knew to be cheats. They exchanged the names of those they accepted, acknowledging that they needed the white man's iron, firesticks, powder, and ball. They discussed the best remaining hunting grounds and the fishing on the nearby James River, and eventually they accepted each other, bound by a common enemy—the white man.

Kajika thought it now safe to return to the matter at hand.

"The girl is young, strong, and healthy—granddaughter of the Nahyssan chief. She will bear many sons for the Monacan people, or you can trade her to the Iroquois or Susquehanna, who will bring muskets and knives of iron to trade for her," Kajika said. He pointed west. "Their war parties are even now raiding from those mountains."

Quick to anger at what Haw-Chi perceived to be a betrayal of this fragile new alliance; blood gorged the arteries of his neck and flushed the leathery skin of his face.

"Kajika spoke first of *captives* as gifts. Now he speaks of just one. Does Kajika have many faces?" Haw-Chi looked straight into Kajika's eyes.

"You can see we have but two captives." Kajika spoke with an equally strong voice, masking the fear that he had spoken too soon. "These two we took in battle with the Nahyssans at great risk, and I offer the more valuable of them to the Monacans. We ask only to pass over your hunting grounds, nothing else."

Kajika knew the "great risk" part of his argument was an exaggeration, but he thought it strengthened his case, especially since all he was asking of the Monacans was permission to travel across their hunting grounds.

Haw-Chi cooled and reminded Kajika that he came as an uninvited stranger wearing war paint. They finally settled on Sayen and the musket taken from Nastabon in exchange for safe passage. Kajika masked his relief as he ordered Sayen into the hands of the Monacans and raised his open hand in salute to Haw-Chi before vanishing westward into the forest with his warriors and Tayamiti.

20

When the Tuscaroras were out of sight, Haw-Chi summoned one of his youngest warriors and sent advance notice to alert Massaqua, chief of the Monacan.

"Go now. Tell Massaqua we have dealt with the Tuscaroras and we come with a captive woman, granddaughter of the Nahyssan Chief, Yahou-Lakee," Haw-Chi said.

Then he called Wahya, a warrior of great strength and good judgment. Sayen listened to his instructions to Wahya.

"Nahyssan warriors will follow the Tuscaroras. Take nine braves, find the Nahyssans, and bring them to Chief Massaqua. We will deal with them there," Haw-Chi said. The Monacans divided and prepared to leave. Wahya and his party went east to intercept the Nahyssans.

Sayen was heartened when she heard that her people would be brought to the Monacan town. She knew when they came they would learn that Tayamiti remained in the hands of the Tuscaroras.

At Haw-Chi's signal, two warriors took the point position and entered the forest, followed by Haw-Chi and the remaining party. A warrior grasped Sayen's arm, stripped off the blindfold

163

and sliced away the cords binding her hands. He pulled her abruptly forward into the middle part of the line that had formed behind Haw-Chi. Her wound still pained her, but she had regained her strength and balance so that walking was no longer so difficult. Twice Haw-Chi dropped out of the line and came near her, but he did not speak or look at her.

They entered the town in mid-afternoon to a huge welcoming celebration. Drums beat a constant rhythm. Cook fires blazed. The tribal medicine men flanked Chief Massaqua at the far end of a corridor formed by people shaking gourd rattles and blowing reed whistles. The medicine men were decorated with greenery, colorful feathers, and red, black, and white body paint. Children raced alongside the procession, careful not to touch or be in the way of the returning warriors. Hopeful young women strained to see the warriors they most admired.

Haw-Chi completed his report and presented the captured musket and Sayen to Massaqua, then retired respectfully into a nearby group of his senior warriors. Massaqua rose and addressed the crowd. "Haw-Chi has again led his warriors against the enemy and returned victorious. The size of his lodge will be doubled in keeping with his station as war chief, and no one will enter without his invitation. Haw-Chi is now Senior War Chief of the Monacan. He will decide where the captured Nahyssan woman will go."

Sayen gasped at Massaqua's words. She expected to be given to a Monacan family. It was the way of many tribes to adopt captive boys and girls to replace their own family members lost to disease and war. To be so bluntly given to Haw-Chi frightened her. He would certainly not listen to a captive, and he could send her away to another Monacan town, keep her for himself, or make her a slave.

Later, as twilight settled over the Monacans, they began to celebrate the victorious return of Haw-Chi and his war party. Sayen watched nervously as several shamans passed out masks of animal heads and gourd faces painted in grotesque images and began to dance in a circle around a fire of towering flames fed by rich tinder and driftwood. With their heads down and their shoulders shaking, they sliced the air with knives and tomahawks as though in battle. The fire threw eerie shadows and light in surreal patterns. Drums beat louder and faster. The sun passed beyond the western mountains. People crowded closer. Many joined the dancers and took up the chorus. Sayen's heart sank when she saw Haw-Chi pointing at her and talking to three of his warriors. She huddled back into darkness against the bark-covered roundhouse.

Unknown to Sayen and the old Nahyssan warrior, Tosawi, only the thin wall of the roundhouse separated them. Tosawi sat inside fuming, his patience vanishing fast. Surely Haw-Chi had confirmed the information he had given Massaqua yesterday. It was past time now to acknowledge the good turn he had paid Massaqua and the Monacans and let him return to his people. He went to the heavy fur door flap, pulled it aside enough to see beyond. The guard was two steps away from his post watching the festivities. He stepped out, tapped the sentry on the shoulder, and in his best commanding voice demanded, "Take me to Massaqua."

Disgruntled at being assigned to guard an old man while others danced and mingled with the women, the sentry turned without speaking. His eyes blazed hatred and contempt as he leveled the point of his lance on Tosawi's belly. Tosawi backed away slowly. His eyes were so intently locked on the sentry that he did not see Sayen's startled face peering from the darkness.

Sayen was elated. Tosawi! Here! Right here in this house! How could she reach him? The angry young guard stood at the only entrance. She inspected the bark walls. Hard-packed earth sealed them tight against the ground. There was no way to enter except through that small doorway hung with heavy fur, and that is where the angry young guard now stood.

Suddenly the sentry seized her arms, pulled her toward him and bound her wrists. He tethered her to a post near the entrance to the house and walked away a few steps for a better view of the celebration. Alone now, Sayen slipped a tiny beaver-tooth knife from a small sheath stitched on the inside of her skirt. She cut her bonds and moved close to the entrance.

"I am Sayen of the Nahyssan," she said, speaking loud enough to get the attention of the sentry *and* Tosawi. "My wounds are bleeding. I need help." She deliberately staggered as if she were fainting and fell inside through the heavy skin door cover, then scrambled up and crouched alongside the doorway.

The sentry jerked the door flap aside and stepped through, bent nearly to the ground to clear the small opening, his lance poised to strike. Sayen threw herself catlike on to his back and rode him to the ground fighting desperately for the sheath knife in his waist strap. As he crashed toward the floor, he dropped the lance but was too late to break his fall or rid himself of the clawing madness on his back.

Startled at the sound of Sayen's voice, Tosawi stood just in time to see Sayen's attack. He instinctively armed himself with the only weapon at hand, a smooth round stone from the fire pit, and flew into the fray. He targeted the sentry's temple and missed killing the man by half the width of his hand. However, his delivery was so powerful that the young warrior slumped unconscious beneath Tosawi and Sayen.

They scampered to their feet. Sayen avoided Tosawi's embrace. She grasped his hand and started for the entrance.

"Hurry, Tosawi. We can escape. They are celebrating. They will not see us. Hurry! The Tuscaroras still have Tayamiti," she said.

"No. Wait, Sayen. We cannot escape into this strange land in the black of night. We do not know the trails. I am old and you are wounded. Listen. Massaqua has made two mistakes. Follow me—quickly, before this one awakens and sounds the alarm." Tosawi took the sentry's weapons, and holding the trembling Sayen's hand, moved toward the entrance.

Suddenly Sayen felt relief. Tosawi would take care of her. Whatever he meant to do, it would be right, and with the relief came an overwhelming desire to stop and rest. The surges of strength she had summoned began to fade and Sayen sagged, one knee almost touching the ground.

"No," Tosawi said. "Stand straight and follow me."

Together they moved unnoticed, hand-in-hand toward a circle of people watching a well-known and practiced dance. Such was the spasmodic energy, twisting gyrations, and primitive rhythm that the onlookers paid no attention to the two captives walking among them in the thunderous sound of the drums, chorus, and rattles. Massaqua stood close by, arms folded in approval of the celebration and surrounded by several warriors. Haw-Chi sat cross-legged on the opposite side, attended by two young girls bearing food and drink.

"Stay close but behind me," Tosawi said to Sayen, as he turned toward Massaqua, slipped between the onlookers, and stepped directly in front of the Monacan chief. An almost imperceptible flicker in the change of expression on Massaqua's face betrayed his suppressed surprise. He glared into Tosawi's eyes but did not move.

"Massaqua, great chief of the Monacan people, mighty warrior and speaker of wisdom and truth, here are the weapons of the careless boy sent to guard me. It is an insult to Tosawi, Senior War Chief of the Nahyssan, here to offer friendship and help to the Monacans.

"This Nahyssan child is badly wounded and she is now a captive of your people, but she has received no care. Instead, the warrior that you sent to guard this child abandoned her as though she is unworthy. Now you know I spoke true when I warned you that Tuscaroras in war paint travel in your hunting grounds. And, even though I have remained quiet awaiting your summons, I have been ignored by you and insulted by your careless warrior while the Monacans celebrate a victory that would not have been possible without the warning I gave you.

"If we may continue as guests of the Monacans, we will remain the night and leave at first light."

Tosawi exaggerated his height a little by stretching as tall as he could. His voice was strong, confident. Not once did his eyes leave those of Massaqua, who moved only once when he lifted a hand slightly to stop Haw-Chi's rush toward them.

Massaqua, arms still folded, stood still. He had not missed the admonishment that they had mistreated the captive woman Tosawi so cleverly called a child. He admired the nerve of this old warrior. He may even have faced him in times past when the Nahyssan and Monacan exchanged occasional raids on each other's hunting grounds and towns. His eyes shifted to Haw-Chi.

"Haw-Chi, the woman is yours, but until you decide whether to keep her or offer her to a family, see that she is cared for. If you are thinking of a trial for her to become Monacan, look at her. She is wounded and sick. She will not survive it. After she has recovered you can decide," Massaqua said.

A woman named Aranck standing nearby spoke softly. "Massaqua, I will keep the girl until she is recovered. She is welcome in my family."

Dismissing Haw-Chi with a slight hand motion, Massaqua nodded his approval and turned back to Tosawi and Sayen. "Tosawi, this woman you call Sayen will be well-cared for by Aranck. Make no mistake. She belongs to the Monacans by fair trade, and here she will stay. When she is well, she will become a member of a Monacan family here or in another Monacan town. Which of these, we will know later. Haw-Chi will decide. As for you, go back to the roundhouse. Sleep. There will be no guard, but do not leave the house. Do not seek or speak to Aranck or the Nahyssan woman you call Sayen. Our warriors will bring other Nahyssans here soon. At that time, I will send for you."

"I will do as you say, Massaqua. I will wait until the morning sun moves into the western sky. Then, I will return to my people and speak to Yahou-Lakee about Sayen, child of the Nahyssan," Tosawi said. Then turning to Sayen, he continued, "Sayen, go with this family. Rest. Regain your strength. Be patient. We will find the Tuscaroras and Tayamiti, but first you must be well."

After the excitement of their encounter with the guard, blood continued to seep from her wound, and the pain returned, but she found comfort in Tosawi's words. He spoke as a visitor, not a captive. He accused the Monacans of violating traditional Indian protection of children, and although Sayen was on the border between child and woman, Tosawi insisted on referring to her as a child, and he had judged Massaqua right. Sayen had watched the face of the Monacan chief as Tosawi spoke. Massaqua did not miss the point, and even though he spoke of her as a woman, he had immediately seen to her care.

Aranck moved forward to Sayen's side and held her by the waist to offer comfort and reassurance. At last, Sayen relaxed, but with the relaxation she began to sag slowly in a merciful faint. Without Aranck, she would have fallen. Two other women stepped forward to carry her to Aranck's lodge. Tosawi started to her side but stopped. Remembering his words to Massaqua, he turned back toward his own lodge and prepared to spend the night.

Haw-Chi smoldered within, but stood straight-faced as Massaqua turned his back on him and left. "Bring the sentry that guarded the captives to me," Haw-Chi hissed, the words spoken through clenched teeth at the nearest warrior.

Before dawn at Tonawanda's campsite, the Nahyssan women kindled the campfire, sorted out dried venison, parched maize, and dried fruit for the men to store in their belt pouches. The warriors strapped on moccasins and leggings against the thorns and briars of the wilderness and, to terrify the enemy, they smeared their faces and chests with war paint, black, red and white. At the campfire, each made a small sacrifice of trail food or tobacco and prayed.

They returned to the place of the bogus footprint, ignored it, divided into pairs and circled in opposite directions for more sign. They found a tiny stone dislodged, perhaps by an animal but maybe not. The pair that found it slowed their search and carefully inspected more of the area. No more sign. An animal had not turned the stone. It was another decoy.

Tonawanda gave the call of a wren one time only to summon trackers. He had confirmed the right trail and started trotting west, certain that he was at least a half day behind the enemy Tuscarora. At the same time, far ahead and approaching him on the same track, Wahya and his nine Monacan warriors were preparing to intercept.

By mid-day, Tonawanda and his men reached a deep ravine bordered by steep banks. There they found undisguised Tuscarora tracks that confirmed the number in their party. Sayen and Tayamiti's footprints were also there, and it gave Tonawanda relief to see them. On the far side of the ravine, the land lay open. Knee-high switch-grass suggested an expanse of land formerly used for cropland. The Nahyssans, excited by the sign of Sayen and Tayamiti, rushed on.

The rain from last night had soaked the ravine banks. They slid down the first one, jumped the dead falls in the bottom of the ravine and climbed the far bank, slipping and sliding until the four of them scrambled over the edge onto level ground where ten face-blackened Monacan warriors formed a half-circle, arrows nocked.

Tonawanda, first on the level ground, recognized the war paint of the Monacan and spoke. "I am Tonawanda, senior warrior of the Nahyssan. The Tuscaroras killed two of our people, captured two of our children, and came this way. We track them to reclaim our children. Massaqua, Chief of the Monacan, has received this word."

Wahya, the Monacan leader, walked forward, flanked by two warriors. A long conversation between the two leaders followed. Tonawanda learned that the Tuscaroras had given Sayen to the Monacans in exchange for safe passage, and Tayamiti was alive but remained captive of the Tuscaroras. Relief and anger stirred deep within Tonawanda, but he gave no outward sign. Later, when alone, he would thank the Creator and pledge his life for the safe return of his children, and he would swear revenge.

"We will show you the way to our town where you will be honored guests of our people," Wahya said.

Although couched as an invitation, eight Monacan bows with nocked arrows made it plain that refusal meant a battle the four Nahyssans could not win.

"We will go with you, but we cannot abandon our pursuit of the Tuscaroras. One warrior, Kitchi, will continue to track them so that we can find them when our warriors return from the fall hunt. They have been summoned," Tonawanda said.

"No," replied Wahya. "Tuscaroras must pass safely through Monacan land."

"And they will pass safely," Tonawanda said. "We will not attack them on Monacan land, but we must track them. One of my braves will track and follow them. He will leave us a trail, and we will destroy them and bring our son home."

"Then two of my braves will go with your tracker," Wahya said. "I will show you the trail. The Tuscaroras are more than half a sun ahead of you and running hard. By dark they will be settled in high ground and well protected."

Wahya led them to the trail, and the three warriors set out, moving westward in single file.

"There is not enough sun left to arrive at Monacan town before dark. We will hunt and camp at a cave where there is good water and shelter and leave with first light of the next sun," Wahya said.

<u>21</u>

Tree Son was so intent on his Williamsburg destination that he had not noticed the growing darkness until he was well into the James River crossing to the north bank. Downstream, several canoes of Chickahominy fishermen spread out near the mouth of the Chickahominy River. Some of the canoes had small, elevated platforms where tiny bright fires burned to attract fish. Tom Singleton, well-known friend of the Chickahominy, was with the fishermen when Tree Son hailed one of the canoes. Unable to speak the Algonquian language of the Chickahominy, Tree Son used motions to describe Kajika's raid, and he kept repeating the two words "Williamsburg" and "Nicholson." Tom understood immediately.

Later at the nearby Singleton family farm, his father, who was a member of the local militia, agreed that even though no settlers appeared to have been involved, the incident must be reported; after all, the murder site was not that far away. He directed Tom to guide Tree Son the rest of the way to Williamsburg and to leave by first light.

"Tree Son, take the bed in that room across the hall. I will wake you." Tom added motions to get his meaning across.

Tree Son understood enough to know that he was expected to sleep the rest of the night there—not something he preferred. Tom noticed his hesitation, and they settled for a pallet by the living-room fire. Later when Tom walked in an hour before first light, Tree Son was standing next to the fire place refreshed and ready to go.

Although they could have traveled on by a rough overland trail, they chose to continue by water via the river and College Creek. Just past mid-morning, Tree Son, with Tom Singleton riding the bow position of the little dugout, paddled steadily up the tidal creek toward Williamsburg's unfinished dock at College Landing.

While Tree Son and Tom were paddling down the James River toward College Creek, Sam Layton was drawing a bucket of fresh water from the well in the promising light of another Williamsburg morning. The cold water he splashed over his face and neck stimulated his blood stream and chased away the last vestiges of sleep. From the light in the kitchen window, he guessed Carrie was getting the morning meal together and probably preparing hot broth and bread for Shanda.

Red Wolf and others were beginning to move about as Sam walked toward Shanda's room where he found Shanda and Wapiti still asleep. Wapiti sat near the door, his powerful legs comfortably at rest on a pallet of fur and blankets. Standing there for a while with his back to Wapiti, Sam watched Shanda. His breathing remained irregular but much quieter, and he seemed occasionally to be able to take a deeper breath. A good sign, Sam thought, but still a very sick fellow. With that, he turned his attention to the day before him. Much remained to be done. He planned to leave for the Shenandoah tomorrow morning—*leave for the Shenandoah*—the thought warmed him.

"Shanda is better." Wapiti spoke softly without moving.

Sam nodded to Wapiti and left the room thinking that if this truly were a turn-around, it would still be days before Shanda could travel. When he is strong enough, Wapiti would likely take him home, another comforting thought. Things were beginning to look a lot better.

Smoke from the breakfast fires of several houses rose steadily, confirming the start of a new day. Kadomico, Hawk, Red Wolf, and Wiwohka donned buckskins and followed Sam to Carrie's kitchen.

"This morning," Sam said, "you will meet the chief of all the people here. His name is Governor Nicholson. When you tell your fathers, they will listen and be proud. The things you will learn here will make you strong among your people, and you will be able to help them in ways that no other can. Is it not why you came?"

Kadomico stood close to Hawk and Red Wolf."We will go," he said quietly, No one else spoke, and Sam again noticed their willingness to accept Kadomico as their spokesman. They walked over to the unfinished school building and into the classroom, a rectangular room set aside for the Grammar School. Benches with narrow desks with slanted tops for writing were positioned under the windows. There Headmaster Arrington waited with his assistant, Usher Calvin Robertson, who had yet to meet the new students. Arrington and Robertson sat erect in the warm room, resplendent in their short powdered wigs, embroidered waistcoats, white linen shirts, breeches, and stockings. Their three-cornered hats and canes lay on the table before them. Neither rose nor in any way acknowledged the entry of Sam and the Indians.

Red Wolf, Wiwohka, Kadomico, and Hawk stood together just inside and as near the door as possible—hesitant and uneasy. They refused Sam's offer to be seated.

Sam approached the head table. "I'll need a little time to explain the seating arrangements, gentlemen."

"Simple," Arrington snapped. "Seats are assigned, Kadomico in the seat nearest this table, then Hawk and Shanda—when he returns. Make haste, please. The governor is expected." He dabbed at the sweat forming on his forehead under the wig, clearly anxious to get this over. Sam thought Arrington's discomfort was a worthy return for his high-handed behavior. He led Kadomico, to the first bench and explained the seating arrangement.

"While you are here this seat will always be yours, Hawk's there, and Shanda's there when he returns. Red Wolf and Wiwohka can be seated anywhere they like, or wait in the hall or outside if they prefer."

Kadomico took his seat. Hawk followed reluctantly. Red Wolf and Wiwohka remained standing near the doorway.

As soon as they were seated, Arrington rose, introduced Usher Robertson as their primary instructor, and began to speak to them about the school and the subjects. They would first learn to read and write. After that, they would study philosophy, religion, and one or more of the sciences. Although Sam interpreted as faithfully as possible, there were no Siouan words for many of the terms Arrington was using.

Realizing that he was not reaching his audience, Arrington despaired. He was relieved to see Reverend Doyle arrive and motioned for Doyle to join him. After his introduction, Doyle stood erect, his arms raised to heaven and prayed for the salvation of these savages. His voice changed from passionate pleas for forgiveness to humble murmurs of thankfulness and on to gentle praises and admiration. He emphasized each transition with an appropriate facial expression of humility, joy, or pain, accompanied by open arms, clinched fists, or his hands over his heart while tears welled in his downcast eyes.

Reverend Doyle would not rest until these savage sinners repented and accepted Christ as their savior. He told them that Jesus Christ had died on the cross for their sins, that He was the only true God and could do all things for them. Then Reverend Doyle prayed again and promised the Lord that he would not rest until these poor worshippers of satanic superstition were gathered into the folds of the Almighty. Fortunately, Doyle gave Sam no opportunity to translate for there were no words to explain sin, Satan, and Jesus in a single translation. Still, the Indians knew this man was a praying priest of the English, and they watched his every move, uneasy that the white man's God might be more powerful than all their gods.

Not far away in a small wood-frame house rented from the college, the Governor lay awake in the warm feather bed, mentally arranging the day before him. His man-servant tapped on the door and came in with a pot of steaming tea and a plate of tiny biscuits—a pleasing sight to the Governor who was feeling good this morning and anxious to get started.

"Good morning, Henry," he said. "I will be at the school first thing after breakfast to welcome the Indian students. Afterwards I will meet with the House of Burgesses. Have Cheek saddled by mid-morning. It looks like a good day for a ride, and I intend to have a look at the new port facilities down at College Landing." He inhaled the aroma of fresh tea as he sat up and reached for the cup. Henry tilted and raised the spout to stop the flow without a drip. He smiled at the Governor's eagerness.

Nicholson was pleased that the Indians were actually ready to start school today. It was no easy matter to get their families to send them, and now that they were here, he wanted to see that they were properly welcomed and cared for as he had promised. In addition to being the Christian thing to do, he thought it a worthwhile way of promoting mutual trust and friendship on the frontier. After all, it was "…a good and pious thing." King William himself had said that, and Francis Nicholson agreed. He had even given generously from his personal accounts to help the cause. His enthusiasm for the merits of this program and the benefits it promised inspired him to be personally involved. In spite of the few successes, the outright failures, and the great expense of similar programs from Canada to Florida over the past one hundred years, Francis Nicholson's confidence remained unshakeable.

As he walked toward the construction site of the new school, Nicholson paused to glance east at the new Duke of Gloucester Street markers. Within the markers, the horse path twisted around the tips of ravines that drained the terrain to the York River on the north and the James on the south. Some ravines were so deep that a horse and rider would disappear in them before making their way out at the far end. Also, two abandoned brick buildings spoiled his view to the east end of the street. Nicholson sighed. One day the street would stretch flat for a mile of unobstructed view between the college and the planned capitol building.

Now this was rough, unimproved land by any measure, but Nicholson had a vision. He imagined a mile of level, paved street with bridges over the ravines. He saw the street filled with carriages drawn by matched pairs of prancing horses. A magnificent capitol building stood at the far end of his imagined street. On either side of the street were public houses, shops and busy people. He smiled confidently at his vision as he passed a sea of construction materials and swept into the unfinished school building.

Sam was about to augment Reverend Doyle's prayer by reminding the Indian boys of the church they had seen yesterday when the sound of quick, heavy footsteps in the hall drew everyone's attention to the doorway which was suddenly filled by Governor Francis Nicholson, followed by two gentlemen attendants.

Nicholson made an imposing sight. He stood tall and military-straight, his black wig of thick curls rose another six inches above his head and showered his shoulders with gleaming folds and curls of black human hair. He wore an ornately decorated blue coat with finely embroidered cuffs and lapels over a bright red waistcoat and white linen shirt set off by a luxurious white silk tie flowing outside the waistcoat and stopping midway to the waist. His breeches were a soft cream color laced tight to his waist and joined below the knee by white stockings and buckled garters.

He walked directly over to Sam Layton, shook hands and turned to the Indians as Arrington maneuvered unsuccessfully to get near him. He addressed each Indian individually, looked him directly in the eyes, and smiled a convincing welcome. Sam joined the Governor when he returned to the head table.

Nicholson repeated his welcome to the group, and explained that they were here at the invitation of their King William III, who lived across the sea and ruled England, the mightiest of all empires. He repeated his previous pledge to provide clothing, food, shelter, medicine, and schooling, all free. He said they would learn the way of the true God and become Christians, just like proper English boys. He repeated his welcome for the last time, and started toward the door.

Sam made the translation and reached him just as he cleared the room.

"Governor, Shanda and Wapiti will leave as soon as Shanda can travel. It looks like you will have two students, Hawk and Kadomico. They are both off to a good start. I plan to leave early tomorrow morning."

"Ah, yes, Sam. Of course. Will you meet me for the evening meal at Dyer's Ordinary near sundown? I will have your stipend for this good work, and we can talk."

"I'll be there, Governor."

Young Tom singleton and Tree Son left their canoe in the reeds at College Landing and walked into Williamsburg. At the college building, the door attendant took Tom's message to the building receptionist who worked in the room across the hall from where the Indians had assembled. "There is an Indian messenger at the door for the Governor. Tom Singleton's boy is with him. Says it is a matter of great urgency."

"Have them wait," snapped the clerk, dismissing the urgency and without looking up from the papers before him. He would interrupt the Headmaster all in good time. Indians thought everything was urgent.

When the attendant returned to the doorway without the Governor, Tree Son walked back to the yard, and with all the wind power he could muster, he gave the call "*coocoocoo-chirp chirp.*"

Robertson was explaining what the students could expect and what was expected of them when Kadomico rose and walked out of the room. Red Wolf and the others followed.

"It looks like an unexpected visitor," Sam said. "Let's see what's going on."

The procession hesitated at the open door. Tree Son stood in the yard looking up at them, immensely pleased to see his friend. Young Singleton stood quietly by him, one hand resting on Tree Son's shoulder.

As he entered the courtyard, Sam ignored the surprised clerk trying to get his attention.

Kadomico and Tree Son grasped forearms.

"Yahou-Lakee, Chief of the Nahyssan, sends a message to Governor Nicholson," Tree Son said. "The Tuscarora attacked the Nahyssan. They killed two and captured Sayen and her brother Tayamiti. They travel west toward the mountains. One sun. Tonawanda follows." Tree Son pointed in the direction of the morning sun to indicate that it happened yesterday morning. "This is my friend, Tom Singleton. He guided me here from his home where two rivers meet."

Kadomico had barely taken in the surprise of seeing Tree Son when the news of Sayen's capture struck him full force. Tree Son moved very close to him, and unseen by the others, he passed the tiny basket into Kadomico's hands.

"I am sorry," he said.

Kadomico turned toward Sam, to explain that he would leave at once to go to the Nahyssans, but he stepped back as Sam approached Tree Son speaking in Siouan.

"Tree Son, you have done well. I will see that your news reaches Nicholson. Very likely he will want to speak to you. Kadomico will show you the way to a place where you can wash, take food, and rest."

Tom Singleton watched in awe as Sam spoke Siouan to Tree Son as though they were old friends of the same tribe. Then Sam turned to Tom and switched to English. "I am Sam Layton. I am the go-between, so to speak, for the Governor and the Indians."

Now Sam was speaking to him in English so perfect that he thought it better than his own speech. Sam's long brown hair and blue eyes confirmed his English heritage, but something that Tom could not put his finger on was not right about that. He took Sam's offered hand.

"I am Tom Singleton. Our fields are near the mouth of the Chickahominy River. My father told me to report this uprising to the sheriff or his deputy as soon as I arrived here. I need to go there now," said Tom.

Sam turned to Headmaster Arrington who had just appeared. "There has been an attack on the Nahyssan town up on the Appomattox. It looks like Tuscaroras. If you will send for the sheriff or his deputy, we can all get the full report here before the Governor is informed."

Arrington nodded agreement and said, "We can use the classroom. Will you join me for a bite to eat and tea while we wait? I need your advice."

"That satisfy you, Tom?" Sam asked.

"It does."

"Then go with Kadomico and Tree Son. When finished, all of you come back here. We will join you in the classroom. The sheriff will also be here by then."

Arrington ordered lunches of light fare sent over from Carrie's kitchen, and he, Sam and Robertson settled down for some serious talk about Hawk and Kadomico.

"From what we have seen so far, we don't have much hope of making progress with these boys, Sam. They lack any semblance of discipline, they seem ready to settle issues with violence rather than reason, and there is not the slightest evidence of respect for authority," Arrington said.

Robertson nodded agreement at every point.

Sam despaired. The gulf between teacher and student here loomed larger than he had expected. When he had attended English school for the first time, it had been after a while on an English farm with English parents and under the force of their very strict discipline. His adopted brother and sister of similar ages had accompanied him. In addition, although he refused to speak English, at least he had understood it. More important, Sam was only eight years old at the time. These boys, well into their teen years, were just short of their tribal transition to manhood, the traditional huskanaw. Little wonder that the teachers felt hopelessness. What could he say to them?

"Gentlemen, I believe you are facing a challenge of such enormous weight that, if accomplished, it could enrich English and Indian life as well. Through you, this could be a beginning of understanding and acceptance between all people of Virginia. If you are able to teach them English and learn to speak their language, it is a true beginning. I believe this is the challenge, and important above all else," Sam said.

"Surely you do not place this above conversion of these savages to Christianity, Sam?"

Knowing the passion of these Anglican churchmen to convert the heathens to the true God and Christianity, Sam avoided argument.

"No, I do not place the importance of one above the other, but you can see how difficult it will be to make progress in any area until you can understand each other. Kadomico is an eager student and has already started learning English. Hawk will require more patience, but he is equally important to what the Governor is trying to accomplish with these boys," Sam said.

The scholars seemed to accept Sam's response and continued to discuss objectives for these first classes. They had serious reservations about discipline and dress, which Sam acknowledged, but reminded them that it would be a commendable accomplishment in this first trial if the boys learned to speak and understand English. Sam was pleased to hear that a Siouan-speaking interpreter had been located among the Chickahominy people and would arrive tomorrow. Still, he was becoming uneasy about his chances of departure. The matter of the Nahyssan attack and the meeting with Nicholson was troublesome.

Sam looked up to see Deputy Will James standing in the doorway. "Gentlemen," he said, "forgive the intrusion, but am I in the right place?"

"That you are, Deputy, and glad we are to have you," Arrington replied. He rose to greet Will properly. "The others will be here shortly to discuss the uprising over on the Appomattox. No white people involved that we know of—maybe just another senseless Indian raid, Indian-on-Indian."

Sam cringed. These days, most Virginia colonists not engaged in government did not see the tribes as the tribes saw themselves: independent sovereign entities, apt to disagree, form alliances, seek vengeance, join in communal hunts, and conquer each other as nations often do. They thought of them as primitive heathens, some good, most bad, no longer a serious threat, just a nuisance over there on the ever-expanding frontier.

When Tree Son and Kadomico returned with Hawk and the others, Tree Son gave a fair account of the attack. When he finished, Headmaster Arrington rose and addressed the deputy.

"Deputy James, please notify the sheriff and send word immediately to the relevant militia and settlers. The sheriff will report to the Governor. No other actions are necessary at this time, no cause for alarm. Sam, assemble the boys here in an hour, please," Arrington said as he nodded dismissal of the group.

While listening to Sam's interpretations and watching the white men's reactions, the Indians had remained silent. Sam waited by the door as the room emptied, but no one approached him. Even Kadomico looked away when he passed.

Sam called Arrington aside. "Headmaster, Red Wolf and the others are taking this raid much more seriously than we are. While the Nahyssan warriors were away from their town guiding and helping Red Wolf and the others, the Tuscaroras, Kajika probably, attacked, murdered, and captured members of the Nahyssan people. I think Red Wolf has decided to respond."

"Well, Sam, I can see you are concerned about this. Pay it no mind. I assure you it has no serious significance here. Let Red Wolf do what he will. We hear of these fights between the tribes all the time. It is only when the settlers are involved that we rally the militia. Let us get on with our work. Please be here in an hour. You will help us get off to a good start." Arrington brushed powder from his wig off the embroidered shoulders of his blue coat.

Faced with Arrington's indifference, Sam nodded and left. He pondered the situation as he walked toward the Indian quarters. Unfortunately, Arrington's attitude was typical of most of the colony. Nor did they see that here was an opportunity to demonstrate the strength and justice of colonial law enforcement to an allied tribe. Sam knew that the Nahyssan chief had sent notification forward hoping the English would help, or, if not, at least cause no interference. The reaction of the headmaster and the deputy did not surprise Sam, but he hoped that Nicholson would see it differently. Perhaps he could convince the governor of the need to respond when they met for dinner this evening.

He had planned to carry his canoe, presently located at College Landing, over to Capitol Landing for his departure tomorrow morning via Queen's Creek and the York River. He decided to postpone it for the time being.

When Sam stepped over the little porch of the small building where the Indians bunked , it was just past noon. All four of them were out back tying on leggings and moccasins and checking their weapons. He walked out and sat down on the little porch leaning back on a locust post at the top of the steps supporting the roof and the banisters. A splinter of pitch pine lay next to him. He admired the shades of gold color and rich veins of resin that would blaze instantly if given a spark. He picked it up and drew his sheath knife, laying the edge on the splinter and drawing it to him. He concentrated on the tiny curls of pitch-soaked pine forming in front of the blade. Be a snap to start a fire with this one, he thought.

The Indians, intent on their preparations to travel, continued without speaking. Sam, intent on the pine splinter, continued whittling silently. Finally, Kadomico slammed his buckskin roll to the ground, picked up his quiver of arrows and walked over to face Sam.

"We go. The Nahyssan are our brothers. There is no other way," Kadomico said.

"I know," Sam said. "I wish you many victories." Red Wolf now stood beside Kadomico.

"We will need another canoe to cross the James. It is very wide," Red Wolf said.

"You're welcome to mine, Red Wolf. I will need it back before sundown so I can move it overland to Queen's Creek. If you leave it at College Creek, it will be great help. I see there are five of you. You plan to travel by land, I reckon."

"The dugout is for but two, three at the most," Tree Son said.

"We can make two trips and carry all to the other shore. We need only the one canoe for that." Kadomico said.

"Be about sundown by then," said Sam, looking away. "At least sundown."

Sam paused. Emotion permeated the space among the Indians. To Red Wolf and Wiwohka, the call to assist the Nahyssans rang clear: it was a full day's travel, another half-day at most. They would go at once, report to Yahou-Lakee, and follow his commands.

Sam doubted that Yahou-Lakee would even be there. More likely he would be on the trail of the attackers. He also realized that Kadomico's unspoken concern for Sayen lay heavy on his mind. What a waste to abandon the schooling after reaching this point, and to do it without good reason.

"The Schoolmaster is expecting you in a little while. I'll just tell him you had to leave," Sam said.

"Yes, tell him that," Kadomico replied, counting his arrows and positioning them for strategic withdrawal. He could not clear his mind of the image of the young Nahyssan woman, Sayen, standing knee deep in the Appomattox River holding her buckskin skirt clear of the water, her eyes locked on him as his canoe slipped into midstream. Until he finished the huskanaw, he was just a boy in the eyes of his people. Nevertheless, after only a glance at this child of Tonawanda, something new and not understood had stirred within him. This image would not go away. He grasped every available moment to think of ways to see her again, and he rehearsed what he would say to her.

"Do you think he might be insulted? I mean, leaving without speaking to him?" Sam suggested.

"It is not to insult the English, Sam We go to join our friends in the search for the enemy who killed and captured their people. If you will tell them that, he will not be insulted."

"I will, but it won't be the same as hearing it from the warriors of the Saponi and Occaneechi," Sam said. "What do you think your father or grandfather would do?"

The question hit the target. Kadomico knew instantly what Custoga and Choola would do. They would honor their agreement with the Governor. They would send Red Wolf and Wiwohka to Yahou-Lakee, but he and Hawk would finish what they came for. But to not go—how could he not go? How could he lay down his weapons and submit to the schooling when Sayen was a captive? The thought loomed unbearable.

Sam had not yet broken the rhythm of whittling, but he continued to observe as Kadomico hesitated, grew pale with the dilemma and sagged slowly to his knees alongside his quiver of arrows. Sam stopped, eased himself down alongside Kadomico. After a while he spoke softly.

"Maybe the best way you and Hawk can help is to stay here and keep your friend Tree Son here as well. That would leave Red Wolf and Wiwohka free to take the canoe. If they travel tonight, they will reach Yahou-Lakee by sun-up. Red Wolf can say that Kadomico, Tree Son, and Hawk will come if called."

A long silence followed, and then Kadomico said, "It will be as you say. I will stay. Wiwohka and Red Wolf will go. Tree Son will guide them to the canoe that he and Tom left at College Landing."

Red Wolf heard the exchange between Sam and Kadomico. It made sense to him. He and Wiwohka could reach the Nahyssans by early morning. He turned back to Wiwohka, explained the arrangement and moved away while Wiwohka spoke to Hawk who was waiting by the trail, packed, ready, and eager. Hawk would not go with them. He would continue at the school. Sam watched from a distance. Hawk listened then turned his back on Wiwohka without speaking, and remained so until Wiwohka left. His anger was all-consuming, but he seethed in silence and resolved to join the hunt for the Nahyssan enemy alone.

22

S am escorted Hawk and Kadomico back to the classroom.
There Kadomico began his first lesson in the English
school. Hawk refused to participate. He sat cross-legged on
the floor beside Kadomico, upright, alert, and defiant, refusing
every effort of the schoolmaster to work with him. He neither
spoke nor acknowledged Sam. Kadomico respected his silence,
aware of Hawk's disappointment at being refused to accompany
Wiwohka on the warpath. He also began to realize that Hawk's
dislike of the English was growing toward hatred.

Hawk remained silent, his heart gripped in disappointment.
His head spun, searching for ways to get into the fight against the
Nahyssan enemy. He could leave now, just get up and walk out,
defy anyone to stop him. He had learned enough to assure the
council of his people that the English number more than the
stars and would stop at nothing to take their hunting grounds.
But for his father's sake, he could not risk a fight with the
governor's people. Better that he wait for the town to sleep, then
leave quietly, follow the path to the creek and the creek to the
river, and from there, join the Nahyssans, prove himself in battle,
earn the feather of bravery, become a warrior. That settled, his
rebellious effrontery eased, and he relaxed until Kadomico
finished his session, then followed Kadomico and Sam back to
the sleeping quarters where they found Tree Son waiting on the
front porch.

"The creek-water tide is just past high. The current sweeps Red Wolf and Wiwohka fast toward the river," Tree Son reported.

Sam acknowledged that and left to pay a final visit to Mary Stilson. He wanted to acknowledge her help and encourage her efforts to bridge the Indian/English gap.

When the three of them were alone, Tree Son said, "Before Wapiti left, he asked me to go to the Tutelos and bring back Shanda's family.

"Will you go?" asked Kadomico.

"Yes. Wapiti said it is two suns travel. Because Red Wolf is away, I will return here and be with you if you wish. Your father, Chief Custoga, spoke of this."

"I wish it," said Kadomico.

Hearing this, a perfect solution formed in the mind of Hawk. His dark, heavily lidded eyes smiled as he placed a hand lightly on Tree Son's shoulder and faced him. His chest heaved with excitement. "Tree Son, I will go to the Tutelo and bring back Shanda's family. I know the trail and many of the Tutelo people. Chief Magotha is friend of the Occaneechi and hunts with my father."

"I am glad of your offer, Hawk. I want to be here. The chief of the Saponi spoke to me and said that Red Wolf or I would stay with Kadomico as long as he desired. But you have been chosen to be in the English school. You are expected by the English."

"We will speak with Sam Layton. He will tell the English. He will know what to say. It is best that I go and best that you remain. Is it not so, Kadomico?"

Kadomico knew instinctively that Hawk had seized this trip to the Tutelo as an opportunity to quit the school and Williamsburg. He not only saw it as a convenience to Hawk, but also a great help to Wapiti who surely wanted to join Red Wolf and Wiwohka in the search for the enemy of the Nahyssan. Tree Son had been sincere in his choice to remain here. Maybe Tree Son would join him in school. They could help each other learn faster, and when school is over, they could travel together back to the Nahyssan and the Saponi. Yes. He would speak to Sam.

"It is best. We will ask Sam to take us to the place of the deputy and find Tree Son's friend, Tom Singleton. He will help Hawk find a way to cross the river quickly and bring Shanda's family across when the time is right," Kadomico said.

Hawk wasted no time gathering the few possessions he had packed earlier for the trail. Then he joined Tree Son, Kadomico, and Sam at Carrie's kitchen where Carrie insisted on packing Hawk's food pouch before he left.

They found young Singleton near the powder magazine on Duke of Gloucester Street. He drew a map on a bit of paper that showed the Chickahominy River and his family plantation. Tom gave the paper to Hawk and pointed to the location of the Chickahominy tribe. Sam explained that the Chickahominy were friendly and would help him cross the James River.

Shortly after they left the deputy's building, Hawk broke away from the group and trotted toward a rail fence beyond which Tim, the boy he had wrestled, was busy clearing brush in new ground. Without breaking his pace, Hawk placed one hand on the top rail and vaulted over the fence. Kadomico followed. Tim, hatless and stripped to the waist, noticed them approaching. He laid the scythe aside, drew a bandana from his pocket and wiped the sweat from his brow as he turned to meet them. Hawk slowed to a walk and moved directly in front of Tim. Kadomico made a sign of peace by folding his arms and bowing his head, and then began to speak in English.

"Hawk go," Kadomico said, hesitantly at his attempt to speak English with a stranger.

Hearing his name and the English word, Hawk stopped motioning and speaking. Tim smiled understanding.

"Hawk come," said Kadomico, pointing to the sun and motioning several sun trips from horizon to horizon.

Tim said, "Yes."

"Yes, Yes, Yes. Goodbye," Kadomico said.

Tim responded, "Goodbye."

Tim and Hawk grasped hands in an arm-wrestling grip, locked eyes and lightly tested each other's strength before breaking apart.

Kadomico turned and walked slowly away to leave Tim and Hawk to their own interpretation of each other. He understood that whether Hawk ever saw Tim again or not, he *had* to leave the impression that he would be back to finish their fight. After a short while Hawk passed Kadomico running hard and leaped the fence without breaking stride.

Hawk, Tree Son, and Kadomico moved on to the trail head that led southwest before turning west to the confluence of the James and Chickahominy. There, Hawk adjusted his quiver of arrows and the roll of buckskins strapped to his back, and nodded his appreciation to his friends. They watched him blend into the forest, moving silently at an even trot.

Hawk felt the muscles in his legs welcome the action and had to restrain himself from lengthening his stride into a run. Freedom from the strangeness and confusions of the past three days settled over him. He reveled in the familiar sounds, silences, and striking scents of pollens, blossoms, and dry leaves mixed with decaying wood and the wet banks of creeks. The shadows were growing long. He threw back his head and ran on unaware of the trouble that lay ahead.

The Higgins brothers had left their home near Archer's Hope for another evening at O'Riley's. Each carried a long hunting knife and an unprimed flintlock pistol. They walked at a leisurely pace. Following a night of drinking at O'Riley's, they had slept most of the day, and now they were hungry. They talked about O'Riley's food and brew as they walked along. Ahead of them just beyond the sharp turn in the trail Hawk had eased his run back to a smooth steady pace. He was filled with the joy and relief of being in a world he knew and understood after four days of exposure to infuriating strangers and incomprehensible confusion.

They were apart by only a few of Hawk's running strides when Obie shouted, "It's one of them school Indians. Get 'im!"

Obie and Billy Higgins separated to cover both sides of the wide trail. No time to prime the pistols, they drew their knives and crouched, ready to trip their running quarry and pounce on him. Running smoothly over the well-traveled trail, Hawk saw them and snapped out of his revelry into cold readiness without breaking stride. Time slowed, turning movement into slow motion for him. In the few strides he had left before contact he chose the man on his right, Billy Higgins. Right-handed and knowing nothing of fighting with a knife, Billy was bending at the waist and leaning so far forward he was almost off-balance. He raised his knife to strike downward and flailed his left arm to maintain balance, but his knife-arm stretched outward and up, leaving his right shoulder and neck exposed. To Hawk's left, Obie grinned and crouched low with a hunting knife in one hand and his unprimed pistol in the other.

Without breaking stride, Hawk shifted the direction and rushed Obie, forcing him to scurry backward. Then he wheeled sharply back toward Billy, and in two strides, he had the wrist of Billy's knife-hand in a vise-like grip. He clamped down even more and threw a right hammer-fist into Billy's fragile collarbone crushing it and disabling Billy's right arm. The big steel knife fell free.

Hawk planted his feet firmly to check his forward momentum and turned to face Obie. He drew his bone knife with one hand and picked up Billy's steel knife with the other without taking his eyes off Obie. Billy fell clear of Hawk and rolled, clutching his right arm and groaning. Hawk came up with Billy's knife held low, cutting edge up ready to slice or stab the man rushing him from across the trail.

Obie stopped, frozen at the sight of the savage bending low, seething with hate and eager to kill him. He had seen the lightning speed and fearless attack on Billy, and it was enough to replace his own hatred with fear. Obie checked his rush. From the murderous look of this savage's face, he suddenly realized that he was about to die.

Hawk saw that the odds were now even. Billy lay moaning and gripping his right arm, unable to rise. Obie was lowering his weapons and backing off. Something warned Hawk to stop the attack. His people had not sent him here to kill the English, and he thought of the friends he had left in Williamsburg at peace with the English. Slowly, the instincts of combat gave way to more mindful thought, and the fight was over. Hawk turned, slipped Billy's steel knife in his waistband, and resumed his run.

As they returned to their quarters, Tree Son and Tom Singleton walked a little ahead, leaving Kadomico with his thoughts. He admired Hawk's determination and his offer to take this task from Tree Son. His friend had strength and courage, warrior qualities to be respected and honored. For just a moment, it made him doubt himself. Would he ever take such matters into his own hands? Set aside instructions from his elders? Was he getting "strength and courage" confused with "defiance and rashness"? Choola's words came back to him, "*Kadomico will learn the way of the English and help us find the best way for the Saponi to protect their people and hunting grounds. In doing this, he will not depart from the way of the Saponi, forget his people, or bow to the English. It must be done, else we face the fate of others before us—death by war, disease, or starvation. We will wait for Kadomico to return.*"

The thought was reassuring He had done the right thing and was eager to get on with his work at the school.

23

The evening shadows were growing long when Sam walked over to Dyer's Ordinary. He stopped outside to wait for the Governor. Two saddled horses stood at the hitching rail shaded by a large sycamore shedding its rust colored leaves. Filtered sunlight formed intricate patterns of light and shade over the horses and the leaf-covered ground. By the look of the sweat around the saddles, the riders had come a long way. They might be planters from out of town.

Sam had arrived early and, leaning against the sycamore, was preparing to light up a pipe when the Governor's carriage swung in close to him and Nicholson stepped out.

The Governor shook hands with Sam for the third time that day. "Sam, I like a man who's on time. I hope you've not been waiting long."

"Just got here, Governor."

They ascended the four steps to the front door. There they were met by the owner, escorted to a small private room, and immediately served beer along with plates of cheese, salted nuts, toast, and fresh apple slices.

"Before we get started, Sam, here is my draft for twenty pounds and a letter that will assure you of fair trade for your furs wherever you might go in Virginia. We appreciate your services. Now, tell me what you think about these Indians being here. Is it not a good thing for them as well as for Virginia?" Nicholson settled back and drank deeply from his cool mug.

Sam evaded the question. "Well, we are down to one student. As you know, we lost one of them to sickness, and this afternoon, Hawk left to bring back Shanda's family. I expect Shanda will leave with them as soon as he is strong enough to travel. That leaves only Kadomico to begin the schooling, but I must tell you that Kadomico is your best chance of making progress with this project. Kadomico is bright, committed, and for one so young, shows signs of good judgment and leadership."

Nicholson nodded. "Be it only one student, I know you realize that what we will do here at the school can have great benefit, short and long term."

"I believe so," Sam said. "And the results could be far reaching as well. Word travels fast, and others are watching. Eventually, Kadomico may be chosen to represent his people. It is a start."

Nicholson leaned forward. His eyes flashed excitement. "I knew it," he said. He rapped his clenched fist on the heavy oak table, sending ripples over the two beers. "I have told them over and over. This land is big enough for all, hunting grounds for Indians and farms for the English. It is just a matter of organizing our common interests and applying it."

Yes, Sam thought, now that the Indians have been greatly reduced by disease and war while the English have multiplied to thousands—this land probably *is* big enough for all. There are not many Indians left in Virginia between the mountains and the sea, and beyond the western frontier, there are not many English—*yet*.

Sam saw no benefit in expressing his thoughts to the Governor. Instead, he said, "We have another young Indian, a friend of Kadomico, who appears to be a good candidate to replace Shanda. I have worked with him some, and I believe that he not only will be a good student, but by studying with Kadomico, both will progress faster. His name is Tree Son, a Saponi. He is the messenger that came this morning and. brought us news about the Indian attack on the Nahyssan. Kadomico has asked that Tree Son attend the school with him, and I recommend that you authorize it."

"By all means, I will have the schoolmaster include this Tree Son," Nicholson said. "Now, Sam let me turn to another matter. I know that Jock Adams offered you a position. I have great respect for him and Rebecca. They'll go far in our colony. Jock has a good business head; he's well liked by all, and he has the well wishes of the King himself. Certainly, he has my support. You would make an important addition to the work he does and to the colony. I want you to give this opportunity serious consideration, Sam. We need you here in His Majesty's most promising enterprise, and we can give you and your family the best life our colony has to offer. Will you think about it?"

"Thank you, Governor. I am honored by your and Jock's offer, but I must decline. I made my choice many years ago when I left the Laytons and returned to the Shawnee. I will remain Shawnee. It is not a choice. It is what I am."

The Governor did not like what he heard, but Sam's tone left no doubt of his conviction. "Very well, I respect your decision, but I do not understand. Why would you decline such an opportunity to lead the work and meet the challenges of building Virginia? Sam, this rich country is destined to make England the greatest power ever known. You could be a major part of it. At least, keep this in mind, it is a standing offer."

"Governor, with the deepest respect, I can no more explain to an Englishman why I prefer my life as a Shawnee to that of a colonist than an Englishman can explain to me why his Christian God did not make the Shawnee like the English or the English like the Shawnee. I cannot explain it, but I know the Shawnee life is the only way for me."

Nicholson suppressed a sigh of resignation. He truly did not understand. It was bad enough, he thought, that dozens, maybe hundreds, of Europeans refuse repatriation from Indian captivity. It happened all the time, probably destitute people of one sort or another. But Sam? And to refuse this offer of practically guaranteed riches and power, and to do it so quickly and resolutely, made no sense. Did he not understand that, whatever his goals, he could come nearer achieving them as a prominent member in His Majesty's realm than he could trapping beaver on the frontier? Made no sense at all, the Governor thought, but there it was. Sadly, there it was.

"The offer stands, Sam. Keep it in mind. Who knows what the future holds."

"I'll do that, Governor. Thank you again. How else can I be of service before I leave?"

"Deputy James mentioned the Indian attack over on the Appomattox. How do you see that?"

Sam replied, "I suspect Kajika, the Tuscarora, and his party. I encountered them the day I met Kadomico and his friends. They were moving about on the far shore of the James River. I think Yahou-Lakee would welcome help from the militia. But with or without it, you can be sure that he will pursue the raiders."

Nicholson did not miss Sam's implied support of English assistance to the Nahyssan. It annoyed him that Sam did not understand that these Indian squabbles were endless and wholly the business of the Indians, but to dismiss the matter, he said, "Well, the militia has been notified. They will know how to handle it. It is not likely that English militia will put themselves at risk unless English life or property is involved."

Sam persisted. "If it is Kajika, English life and property *are* at risk, Governor. The Tuscarora have no treaty with Virginia, and when Tuscaroras are in their area, I read that as a risk to Virginians. And does this raid not present an opportunity to work together with the Nahyssan against a common enemy?"

"You make a good point, Sam. It is little wonder you are in demand as a go-between." Nicholson smiled at his concession but gave no indication that he intended to do anything about it.

"Being a go-between is not always rewarding, Governor. Treaties are instruments of the white man and treaty negotiations are rarely a fair match between the European and the Indian. Only one side has the laws, rules, paper, ink and education to devise a treaty. Very often, even when I try to explain it, the other side does not fully understand. Many Indian leaders seek only relief from hunger, disease, and the devastating raids by militia or stronger Indian tribes, and making their sign on mysterious papers seems reasonable and promising."

"That is why we are serious about opening our school to the tribes," Nicholson said. "Education will bring understanding and enlightenment."

Sam knew the Governor was thinking of the Indian's understanding of the white man, not the other way around— typical white man's attitude. Even so, there was much to be said for the school. Therein lay hope and the beginning of the power of the English language, spoken and written.

"True enough, Governor, but in the gaining of understanding and enlightenment, I hope it will work both ways. I hope it, but I doubt it."

The two talked on through their evening meal, speculating on the Nahyssan fight, trade in the colonies, the college, and construction of the new capital building. At one point, Nicholson complained that with so many small tribes moving about and scattered over so much unbounded territory it was almost impossible to draw up contracts, agreements, or treaties. In the north, the Iroquois had organized five huge Indian nations into a single confederacy. They discussed the advantages and likelihood of other tribes uniting in a similar manner.

Sam declined the offer of a carriage ride back to his quarters, and they shook hands. Ever determined that Sam would eventually see the good sense of it, the Governor said, "Since you will be leaving early tomorrow, Sam, may your trip be a safe one, and your homecoming all that you wish. Return to us as often as you can. Our offer remains open."

Kadomico was waiting for Sam on the front porch under a clear night sky. The moon was not yet up, but the starlight over Williamsburg was enough to distinguish the black forms of structures and the pathway. Crickets in the trees called back and forth, and an owl called from deep within the forest. The air moved so gently over his bare skin that Kadomico hardly noticed it. Finally, Sam's form emerged on the path. Kadomico spoke unseen from the shadows of the porch.

"Hel—lo, Sam. I speak wel—come. Good night."

Speaking slowly and pronouncing each syllable as though it was a word itself, it took almost all of his new English vocabulary, but it pleased him to surprise Sam.

"Good evening, Kadomico. That is very good English. I am glad to see you." Sam pronounced the words slowly and clearly in English. Then he switched to Siouan. "When I am finished packing here, I am going over to Capitol Landing and check on the canoe. Walk along with me. We can talk."

Sam began to gather his belongings stashed along the wall of the porch. His bow, arrows, rifle, and pistol, which he would bring with him in the morning, were inside in the linen closet. Standing at the edge of the porch and using it as a workbench, he and Kadomico sorted out powder and musket ball, some buckskin clothing, leggings and extra moccasins. They made up small packs of food.

"The Governor likes the idea of Tree Son attending the school, and I think that, together, the two of you will learn fast," Sam said.

"It is a good thing," Kadomico replied. "I will tell Tree Son. He will be glad."

"Good. The opportunity to learn is so great that you must come back many times until you have mastered the language *and* the other subjects that they offer."

"I understand, Sam. It will be whatever my father decides, but unless the school demands more than I can give, I will ask to return. Thank you for speaking to the Governor."

Sam stopped tying a pack and looked at the tall young Indian standing beside him. His mind flashed back to when, at the same age, he rejected the white man and faced the wilderness alone looking for the Shawnee. Now he was encouraging this boy to take up some of the ways of the white man. He knew it would lead to better understanding, but he did not know where better understanding would lead.

They started walking northeast toward Capitol Landing with packs to be left in the canoe overnight. Duke of Gloucester Street was quiet. The soft light of a few candle-lit windows was barely enough to draw their attention. Nearby, over in front of Page's Ordinary, two horses shifted their weight and dozed, while inside their riders enjoyed a late supper.

"Will you travel alone?" Kadomico asked.

"Yes," Sam replied, "and it is a good way to travel. Fishing is very good. There are always many geese on the water, and sometimes turkey, bear, or deer on the banks. If there are enemies, I will see them. The air over the water is warm, and the way is always clear, except for the rapids when I go inland. Where the water falls, I will spend two suns carrying around them," Sam said.

"If I come for you, I must come by land, following the trails north or northeast from my home."

"Two suns west of your Carolina home is a trail that follows the crest of the mountains north and south. Many Indians use it," Sam said, "but also many war parties. Once on that trail, maybe two or three suns from your town, the north trail will bring you close to the Shawnee town where I live. When you are four suns on the trail, you will look west and see the river of eight bends. It will look like a huge snake from that trail. It flows north along the base of a long ridge. The Shawnee town is on the far side of that ridge. My people will know of Kadomico, son of Custoga, Chief of the Saponi, and you will be welcome."

"I am glad to know this, Sam. Soon my people will decide if they will remain, or where they might go if they must leave. There are enemy tribes north and south, and although they have not yet attacked the Saponi, it is possible. For now, we still do not know the English, but I was surprised how close they are to our town. I walked but two suns before I came to their houses. Soon it will be just one sun. My people are waiting for me to tell them what I have seen and learned, and I don't yet know what to say."

"What you have just said is what you must say to your people, Kadomico. In addition, tell them all that you have seen and learned."

"Yes. Yes, I see," said Kadomico, beginning to get some idea of what he could say to the council. "There are many things to speak of—the Stilsons, the blacksmith shop, the Nahyssans, the school—many things. Still, I am the least among my people—not even a warrior yet, and there will be the words of Red Wolf when he returns. His words will be different."

"Your father is a wise man and your council is strong," Sam said. "I am sure you can trust them to choose the right path. Unless the Saponi plan and act now, they will have very little to say about what happens to them." Sam remembered the Governor's complaint:

> ...so many small tribes moving about and scattered over so much unbounded territory made it almost impossible to draw up contracts, agreements, or treaties. In the north, the Iroquois had organized five huge Indian nations into a single confederacy.

Sam pondered the governor's words as they walked along in silence for a while. Capitol Landing lay just ahead. Kadomico stopped and confronted Sam. "Will you come with me to the Saponi council?"

"It is something I have done many times, but only at the request of the council or chief of the tribe," Sam said. "Perhaps it is better that you bring your father to spend a few days with me. We can hunt and take beaver pelts. We can talk about the English and the frontier. Later, we can meet with your council if your father wishes."

"We can do that. We will come when the snows are gone, the first moon after the hickory buds, my father and me."

"I'll expect you, Kadomico. It is a good thing. Tell your father that one way to strengthen his position for dealing with the

English is for the Siouan tribes to join together in a single alliance. I can help him with that. There is strength in numbers."

They located the canoe and stowed the packs, and Sam checked the paddles, small stone-anchor, and lines. Satisfied that the craft was ready for the trip, they returned to their quarters.

The next morning, as the first rays of the morning sun announced the new day, Sam was already turning out of the mouth of Queen's Creek into the York River, every muscle working in rhythm with the forward glide of the canoe. Each stroke, thought Sam, is one less than is needed to bring me back to the Shawnee and to Starlight.

At the town of the Nahyssan, Yahou-Lakee woke earlier than usual. In a dream, he had seen Sayen blindfolded and bound to a tree in a dark forest. Black wolves circled her, but it was as though they were protecting rather than threatening. He took it as a sign that the god of the animals would take care of her. He would talk to the shaman about this when he returned from the hunt. In the meantime, Yahou-Lakee took comfort from his dream and proceeded to see that the bodies of Nastabon and Sinopa were being properly prepared. There would be ceremonial sacrifices, prayers, and songs. Many would speak of the skills and deeds of their elder brother, Nastabon, and of the promise shown in their young warrior, Sinopa.

Although it was not yet dawn, he smelled the smoke of cook-fires and noticed movement among the roundhouses. He also noticed that the sentries on the east and west watch stations were alert and scanning the terrain. He went straight to the third lodge on his right and called out the family of a renowned hunter.

"Six warriors must return from the hunt to find and follow Tonawanda and punish the Tuscaroras. Two messengers will go where the Blackwater and Roanoke meet and call them," Yahou-Lakee said. The eldest daughter of the family stepped forward.

"I will go. I know where my father is hunting," she said.

"Then find another able to travel fast to go with you. The message must be delivered. Leave immediately."

Satisfied with his messenger, Yahou-Lakee walked the palisade, inspected the surrounding area before he returned to his wife's cooking fire, sat down before it, and sprinkled sacrificial tobacco and maize kernels into the coals before praying for the souls of Nastabon and Sinopa and for strength in the coming days. His wife handed him a bowl steaming with thin venison soup liberally laced with wild onions and herbs. It sent strength and vigor surging through his limbs.

He drew himself up to full height, belted on his knife and tomahawk, strapped on a quiver of arrows, took up his bow, stooped at the door of the roundhouse, and walked away to re-inspect the murder sites and reclaim and examine the canoes.

This took most of his morning. Inspecting the ground closely, he recovered an arrow and a moccasin stuck in the mud of the bank. He made his way past the scene where he had found Sinopa's body. It was about mid-day when he knelt alongside a moccasin print to examine the peculiar indentation on the instep. Movement in his peripheral vision caused him to look up.

Downstream, rounding the distant bend in the Appomattox River, a canoe approached, moving too fast to be on a routine trip. Yahou-Lakee straightened up from the moccasin print. As the canoe drew nearer, he saw that it was his own dugout, the one Shoteka had chosen yesterday for his trip to bring Tonawanda back to the town. An instant later he recognized Red Wolf and Wiwohka. One look at them, and he knew they had paddled all night. His greeting was genuine as he turned toward the town, waving them to follow. They paddled alongside until they reached the shallow water of the landing area, then waded ashore, beached the canoe, clasped forearms with the aging chief, and committed themselves to his service.

24

Kajika emerged from the forest and stopped There before him lay the safety he sought. Just across a clearing of switch grass and a small stream running along the base, the Blue Mountains stretched north and south majestically but not too steep to climb. The eastern slope rose gently at first with many places to set up camp and watch the trailhead. After that, it became more precipitous, eventually forming occasional rock cliffs. Kajika breathed deeply. Here on this high ground was the perfect place to engage the Nahyssans if they followed, and he was sure they would.

He sent two warriors back to make a visible trail across the open meadow of tall grass, across the shallow stream to the point where the trail forked running north and south along the west bank. After crossing the creek, his warriors were careful to remove any trail sign they'd made. In most places, they were able to step on stones, sometimes in the creek itself. They left the barest of sign on the north trail: scraped lichen on a rock, pebbles or driftwood recently turned out of place, enough of a single footprint to indicate direction. Finding these signs, an alert tracker might conclude he had found a deliberately hidden trail, but seeing no other footprints or evidence in the damp path along the creek, he was more likely to suspect it for what it was, a decoy, and turn his attention south toward the trap Kajika was already planning.

Kajika chose a location well above the south trail.

He called Two Bears. "Take the boy south along this slope. When you see the trail leading toward that low point on the ridge, take it. Keep climbing until you reach the crest there," said Kajika, pointing to a place where two mountain ridges crossed each other forming a saddle on the ridgeline. "Wait for us there. If the Iroquois are traveling the trail, make the trade. We want firesticks and steel tomahawks only. Let them take the boy now. Before the leaves fall again we will come to the Iroquois town in the north to collect what you have traded for."

Kajika turned his attention to ambush preparations. The land was steep with many large outcroppings of limestone in a thin forest of hardwood trees. The wild azaleas, dogwoods, and laurel made walking difficult, but provided a convenient handhold on the steep terrain and provided cover. It was good protection against a siege, but he needed a way to draw the enemy upward and inward between his men into a crossfire. He sent scouts north and south to look, but they were soon back. There was no such place. The base of this mountain swept gently away from the little stream for a few steps, then rose gradually to terrain so steep that only a strong, experienced climber could ascend it. One misstep on the highest part of those formidable slopes could tumble a man to death. A little past half way to the top, Kajika could see three shale slides the size of a large field of maize. It was impossible to cross them without starting an avalanche, easily visible and heard from a distance.

Kajika did not want to engage the enemy in open ground, but this was high ground, safely below the shale, and he could see the trailhead where the enemy would appear. Facing east, the little creek below splashed around boulders and over its rock-strewn bottom. On the far bank, willows and sycamores leaned in toward the water. South of his vantage point, he sometimes lost sight of the serpentine creek among their branches, but occasionally at one of the bends an opening in the trees revealed a small segment of water where sunlight glanced off the turbulence and marked the creek. But as he looked east over the tops of the trees, the forest merged into a gray-green canopy, shielding the activity beneath.

To the north, the terrain became more rugged, and visibility was slightly limited by nearby brush and trees, but he was satisfied that he could not be surprised from that direction. He scanned the region for smoke, open spaces, anything that might help him detect the movement of a search party.

Kajika decided to draw the enemy upward into a place where the slope flattened out a little but was still surrounded by precipitous terrain. He would conceal three warriors to the left above that point and keep the rest hidden below on his right until the enemy had passed. Then he would spring the trap.

He turned to scan the steep terrain behind him. Looking upward, there were three large boulders, enough cover to hide several men among them. The scrub oaks and brush in front of the boulders were thinner than in most places on the slope, and the boulders could be seen by anyone exiting the forest at the trailhead, but that view worked both ways. Still, he had the advantage of first-rate cover from his location. He had no idea how many Nahyssans would come, only that they would surely come. Let them. He could use more captured weapons and scalps.

By the time Kajika had settled on a camp site, this eastern slope had darkened under the evening shadow of the mountain. He was satisfied with the preparations, but he would double-check all the critical places again in the first light of the next sun. They found grass-covered ground and settled down for the night.

At the same time, the Nayhssan tracker, Kitchi, and his two Monacan escorts came to a tiny stream, made a smokeless camp, and waited out the night taking turns at watch. The next morning they picked up the trail and moved forward. About mid-morning, they stopped just before the trail left the woodlands and crossed the open ground to the stream. They could see that the trail forked there, running north and south along the far bank of stream.

From where they stood, the trail led straight through knee-high switch grass. Peering from the cover of brush and shrubs, Kitchi saw plenty of places high on the slope where the Tuscaroras could make a stand, but the trails north and south along the stream also looked easy for fast travel if the enemy preferred to continue fleeing. Kitchi wanted to inspect those trails and to locate the Tuscarora camp, if one existed, but he was uneasy about all the open space.

Something was amiss—Kitchi saw no bird life or movement of any kind, though there might have been a thin wisp of vanishing white smoke in the area of three huge boulders. His Monacan escorts had also noticed the smoke. Neither was certain whether it was smoke or just late morning mist, but it was enough to stop them from entering the open space before them. Still concealed by a thicket of young maple, ash, and cedar undergrowth at the forest border, they scanned the slope several times—nothing. They separated and took positions to cover the north and south terrain of the slope before them and settled down to watch.

There was no more smoke, but while they watched, a covey of quail flushed and sailed over a cleared space of crushed stone beneath the three great boulders. The wing-beat noise of a dozen birds thundering up from cover was out of hearing range of Kitchi but so close to Kajika that he jumped instinctively. Quickly recovering, he grinned at his good luck. Those spooked birds were better than a wisp of smoke for attracting the enemy. He watched them disappear in the streamside grass below him.

Kitchi moved his party back, left the trail and found a shallow ravine well hidden from the trail. One of the Monacans left to report their location to Haw Chi. Even though he moved out at a fast pace, it would be dark before he reached the Monacan town. Kitchi settled down with the other Monacan and began watching the trail, the mountain slope, and meadow.

Far back at the eastern end of the trail, Red Wolf and Wiwohka were traveling west, eager to join Tonawanda, and unaware that he had been intercepted by the Monacans.

In the Monacan town, in Aranck's lodge, Sayen awoke early from a long sleep, alert and anxious. But when she sat upright on her bed in the dim light of dawn, weakness and dizziness overcame her, and she settled back. The rustle of her movement woke Aranck who rose quietly, kindled the fire, and picked up a bowl of fresh water. She stepped over to Sayen and began gently to tend to her bandages.

Sayen stiffened without resisting, but it was clear to Aranck that her patient, however defiant, was confused, frightened, and weak. Aranck continued working, bathing Sayen gently while her ten-year-old daughter, Namid, and eight-year-old son, Misae, slept. Sayen avoided looking at her. In a little while she grew tired, dropped her head on Aranck's shoulder, and fell asleep.

Three roundhouses away, Tosawi awoke still annoyed with Massaqua for treating him like a captive. True, Massaqua was nervous about the intrusions in Monacan hunting grounds, and according to Haw-Chi, he could expect more Nahyssans shortly, but Tosawi had come in peace with valuable information. Where was traditional Indian hospitality, especially to a Senior Warrior from a neighboring tribe!

A woman came in with kindling and firewood, stirred the coals, laid a fire, and placed a bowl of steaming stew alongside the fire before leaving. Well, that was better, thought Tosawi. Yesterday, he had spent the day alone without attention of any kind except that poor excuse for a sentry. He would take his time, wash, eat and prepare himself for the council, and while he waited he would walk about the town, take the fresh air of morning and be seen. Maybe Massaqua had not realized it, but he was on the verge of war with people who had offered him a brotherly alliance. Tosawi grew anxious for the arrival of Tonawanda.

Tonawanda and his two warriors had followed the Monacans to the cave without resistance. He now knew that Sayen was at the Monacan town and that Tayamiti was still captive of the Tuscaroras. That evening after reaching the cave, both parties hunted together for the evening supper and talked into the night. Rising with the dawn, they'd arrived at the Monacan town at midday. Tosawi watched them parade through the town and stop at Haw-Chi's lodge. Bending to clear the door beam, Haw-Chi stepped out and faced Tonawanda.

"I am Haw-Chi, Senior War Chief of the Monacan."

"I am Tonawanda, Senior Warrior of the Nahyssan. I come in peace. The great Chief Yahou-Lakee of the Nahyssan sends greetings to Massaqua, the powerful and well-known warrior and chief of the Monacan."

"Massaqua will see you after this war party speaks," Haw-Chi said.

Haw-Chi pointed to the roundhouse where Tosawi stood, arms folded, at the entrance. "Go there. Tosawi waits. Rest. Food is being prepared for you. When Massaqua is ready, I will send for you."

Without waiting for a response, Haw-Chi walked away and motioned to a warrior standing nearby. "Find Aranck and tell her that Sayen is to remain inside the lodge and must not know that the Nahyssan warriors are here."

Tonawanda and his two warriors walked over to Tosawi and locked forearms with him in greeting. Tosawi nodded toward four young, armed Monacan warriors spaced equally apart at sentry positions facing the roundhouse.

"Four?" Tonawanda asked.

"Yes, four alert sentries. After last night, they remember what happens to careless sentries."

"Last night?"

"Yes, last night. Come inside. I will tell you."

"Have you seen Sayen?" Tonawanda asked as they passed inside.

"Yes, I was with her last night. She is wounded but in good care three lodges from here." Tosawi continued giving an account of last night's encounter with Massaqua. He grew more excited with each scene, and when he reached the part about Sayen's attack on the sentry, he stood reverently for a moment of silence then began.

"She sprang like a panther onto the back of the sentry, threw him to the floor right there, and wrested his own knife from him before I could reach them." Tosawi leapt toward the door and acted out Sayen's attack. His words and gestures gave a vivid account of the scenes. Then, he turned slowly and faced Tonawanda. His voice dropped to a whisper. "And while her wounds bled, she wanted to escape. Flee or fight, she was ready."

Near bursting with pride in Sayen, Tosawi continued, "The woman Aranck will see after Sayen. For now she is safe, but Massaqua says I cannot approach her or the woman Aranck. He said she belongs to the Monacans by trade with the Tuscaroras, and, if Haw-Chi so wishes, she will become the wife of a Monacan brave."

"It is so, but for the time being, you feel she is safe?"

"Yes, as long as she is in the lodge of Aranck."

"Then we must leave it there and join Kitchi as soon as possible. Since Massaqua does not know that Sayen is my daughter, it will be easier to deal with him when we meet."

Tonawanda understood the rules of adopted captives. Where they were clearly the booty of a raid or outright war, the captor had the right to treat them like a member of the tribe or subject them to slavery—it happened all the time. He realized his choices came down to barter, escape, or war. Barter was out of the question. There probably were not enough trade items in the whole town of the Nahyssan to buy back Sayen. Escape was too risky, and if caught, instead of being adopted she could be tortured and enslaved.. Tonawanda despaired. He would set it aside for now, collect a war party and find Tayamiti and the Tuscaroras.

Tosawi said, "I did deliver Yahou-Lakee's message of peace to Massaqua, and I told him you were following the Tuscaroras and needed his permission to travel across his hunting grounds. I do not know why he brought you here."

"He wants to avoid a war with the Tuscarora. We cannot depend on the Monacans to join us against them," Tonawanda said. "We have done well if they will allow us to pursue the Tuscaroras and return, but we need to leave immediately."

"Yes, and if we leave soon, I can be home by nightfall."

"And I can join Kitchi by night fall, if he is camped," Tonawanda said, rising to look outside and anxious to get started. Before he reached the door, Haw-Chi swept aside the skin covering the doorway and announced that the council was ready for Tosawi and Tonawanda.

They followed Haw-Chi to the council longhouse. There, guarding the door, an old woman wrapped in a scarlet coverlet stood tall and straight as any youth. Her thick white hair was combed back in two equal parts, and banded just above her shoulders so that it fell nearly to her waist over the coverlet. She motioned Haw-Chi inside and turned, arms folded, to stop Tonawanda and Tosawi. Then, with the council alerted and Haw-Chi seated, she motioned them to follow.

Inside the long room, men and women council members aligned themselves on either side of a small fire. Along the walls, hanging skins, blankets, masks, and weapons were barely visible in the dim light.

The old woman motioned them to places reserved for them in the circle. It looked as though the council had been in session for some time. Tonawanda and Tosawi exchanged greetings with Massaqua and took their seats. A peace pipe passed among them.

210

Tosawi, still offended that they had been kept waiting but anxious to get this over with, took the pipe without comment.

After food and water was passed around, Massaqua said, "The Monacan people welcome the warriors of the Nahyssan. We are glad that you have brought us notice of the Tuscarora in our hunting grounds, and it is good that you ask our permission to follow them. We would do the same if we sent warriors into your land."

Massaqua paused to let his words register. "Even so, we are not pleased that the Nahyssan bring their war with the Tuscarora to us. We are at peace with the Tuscarora. And we are not pleased that Tosawi joined our captive woman and attacked one of our young braves in training to become a warrior. Chief Yahou-Lakee of the Nahyssan sends Tosawi to us to ask permission to travel in Monacan hunting grounds. They want to track the Tuscaroras who attacked, killed, and captured Nahyssans. Let him return to Yahou-Lakee and say yes, the Nahyssans may travel the trails to the western mountains, but Monacan does not war against Tuscarora. A Monacan warrior will escort Tosawi. They may leave immediately."

It was Tosawi's time to speak. He let the silence hold until he was certain he had every person's attention. Tonawanda stiffened. It was not likely that the feisty old warrior would let matters rest where Massaqua had left them.

Tosawi sat upright, his hands on the knees of his folded legs, eyes focused straight ahead, past Massaqua as though he didn't exist. "Tosawi will deliver Massaqua's message to Yahou-Lakee," he said, and fell silent, much to the relief of Tonawanda.

Haw-Chi spoke to the council. He explained how he had surrounded the Tuscaroras and received gifts in exchange for passage. Then pointing to Tonawanda, he gave an account of stopping him and three other warriors on the trail east of the cave, without a fight. He had assigned two Monacan escorts to one of Tonawanda's warriors and allowed them to continue tracking their enemy. He'd brought the remaining three here to be told how to proceed while they were in Monacan territory.

Tonawanda addressed the council. "I am Tonawanda, Senior Warrior of the Nahyssan. I travel the Monacan trails to find the Tuscaroras who kill old men and children, and smash the heads of children and drag them away into unknown lands. Have no fear. We will not kill them in your territory. We intend not to kill them at all. We will return them to the families of those they have murdered and captured." There was a murmur of approval among the council—justice. Such treatment of children was not the Indian way, and Tonawanda's words planted the first seeds of sympathy and friendship with the Monacan, a friendship that would eventually prove beneficial to both tribes.

Tonawanda continued, "I ask only to be granted immediate passage over the same trail that the Tuscaroras used. If I leave now, it is possible we will meet with our tracker and find the enemy."

One of the council spoke. "It is right that the Nahyssan have their vengeance. Let them find the enemy and face him in battle. It is a good thing to grant this passage."

There were more murmurs of approval before Massaqua spoke. "Two Monacan warriors will accompany you, Tonawanda, Senior Warrior of the Nahyssan, but see that you do not attack the Tuscaroras in Monacan lands."

The council dissolved and moved away. Tonawanda and Tosawi walked back to their roundhouse. "We must move fast, Tosawi. If Sayen learns we are here, she will fight to join us. It is much better that she learn of this after we are long on the trail."

"I am ready, Tonawanda. Our warriors are also ready. We go."

They left the town, careful to avoid the lodge where Sayen had fallen into a long restful sleep. The five men strung out between their Monacan escorts, running easily over the well-worn trail. They would maintain this pace as long as Tosawi's old body could hold out, but Tonawanda could see that Tosawi would die before he would slow the group. Nor would he listen to any kind of reason for slowing down. Tonawanda moved up to the lead Monacan, but before he could speak, the Monacan stopped and motioned for a half-circle to be formed. A runner was approaching. It turned out to be one of the Monacans who had been deployed with the Nahyssan trackers.

He told them that it was very likely the Tuscaroras had stopped in the foothills and that Kitchi was waiting for instructions or reinforcement.

Tonawanda spoke to the Monacan leader of his group. "We go. Is there a faster way to get to the western end of the trail without going back to the cave?"

"Yes, it is less used but faster. I will lead you."

Tonawanda turned to Tosawi. "We leave you here. Tell Yahou-Lakee we will wait for more warriors, and we will have the Tuscaroras located by the time they arrive."

"I will tell him that and also that Massaqua has granted our passage and that the Tuscaroras are probably located. I will guide our warriors to you. We may arrive at night, so listen for my signal." As he spoke, Tosawi's eyes flashed excitement and his breath came easily, as though it had the benefit of a pair of young lungs. He turned away, motioning the young escort to overtake him and assume the lead, but the young escort was on his knees gathering his arrows. Tonawanda had quietly removed them from the quiver on the young escort's back and dropped them on the ground. Now he knelt beside the escort and spoke softly, "You will keep the pace slower, even if you have to claim injury to your foot."

"I understand," said the Monacan youth, as he gathered the wayward arrows.

Tonawanda watched Tosawi's easy stride as he returned to the trail. Free of dress except for the breech clout circling his waist and three eagle feathers fastened to the braided scalp lock brushing his shoulders, the old warrior's arms and legs moved in a graceful rhythm, his chin up as though to capture as much as possible of the cool forest air moving across his face. Tonawanda remembered the times when Tosawi strode into the town with great harvests of deer and turkey for his people. Tall, muscular, and brave with a proud heart of loyalty to the tribe, he was the envy of every Nahyssan boy, including Tonawanda. He watched until Tosawi passed out of sight on a bend in the trail, followed by the young Monacan, running fast to catch up.

In the dwindling light of evening, Tosawi met Red Wolf and Wiwohka on their way to join the trackers. They exchanged greetings and spent only enough time to inform each other of their destinations and what they knew about the Tuscaroras. Reassured of their direction and the trail, Red Wolf and Wiwohka continued, aware now that the Nahyssans waited for reinforcements near the mountain. Tosawi continued but soon saw that he would have to camp or travel in darkness. He chose to camp and meet Yahou-Lakee when the sun returned.

Tonawanda and his two warriors followed the Monacans through the dense forest using animal trails and clearings when they could, but the fading light added to the difficulty of travel. They moved on south and west, expecting to cross the west trail at every clearing they entered; but the clearings proved to be small openings where trees had fallen, or a little piece of the great forest that had yielded to insects or disease.

They soon came to a place the Monacans seemed to know. Beyond a tangle of briar and vine, the land rose as a shallow hill under a warm beckoning sea of tall grass, the tops moving gently with the occasional draft crossing from the north in the deepening twilight. The long grass reminded Tonawanda of the stories the tribe elders told of buffalo grazing lands. He had not actually seen a buffalo, but the Nahyssan shaman wore a preserved buffalo head and horns at their dances and ceremonies; there were several buffalo skins in the roundhouses, and he had also seen weapons and tools of buffalo bone used by some of his people. If there were any buffalo left, the grass here would reach their knees. On the highest part of the grassland stood three giant sycamores forming a triangle, the floor of which remained nearly bare. The Monacans explained how they burned this grass annually and hunted birds, deer, and small game here. They camped there, taking turns at watch.

By mid morning, Tonawanda and his three warriors had joined Kitchi. Shortly thereafter Red Wolf and Wiwohka arrived and the Nahyssan strength came to six warriors. He expected Tosawi soon would bring five or six more. He could not count on the two Monacan escorts; they had strict instructions: observe only, and at the end of each day, send a messenger back to report their location to Haw-Chi. Tonawanda summoned his warriors and decided to wait for the reinforcements but also to risk an inspection of the trails at the creek.

Across the creek to the west of them, Kajika stood on high ground in a thicket of laurel. He shaded his eyes against the rising sun and squinted toward the eastern forest. Was there movement there along the edge—smoke, birds, spooked deer, anything to indicate the presence of the enemy? Nothing. Neither had his backtrackers found anything to indicate that they were being trailed, but he wondered if they had gone back far enough? The silence and stillness made him nervous. He reasoned that when he attacked the town, there were no warriors there. If there had been, they would have made a fight of it, but he thought it likely that someone from the Nahyssan town would have followed him. If so, that someone would be nearby. He motioned to two of his men.

"Follow this high ground south beyond that first bend in the creek. Cross over and turn back toward the east-west trail. If they are not there, divide, one on each side, and follow the east-west trail back until you meet them. Leave no one alive. Return by sundown."

Now standing just south of where he had observed the enemy trackers, Kajika turned his attention to the ground he had chosen to trap and destroy the enemy. From where he stood, a small animal path twisted back and forth around small trees and boulders and through thick brush about a hundred paces down that slope to the creek, an unmistakable opportunity to climb the slope. Concealed warriors would have the advantages of surprise and crossfire. They had only to lure the enemy into the trap.

The two Tuscaroras crossed the creek south of the bend, doubled back deep in the woods beyond the stream, and moved on north toward the trail where the Nahyssan trackers might be. They separated but stayed in sight of each other and moved forward silently, their soft moccasins touching only places where no twig would break or leaf would rustle. Avoiding thickets of wild azalea and laurel they made good time. There was nothing they could do to stop the flutter of an occasional song-bird or the rustle of a fleeing rabbit or squirrel from announcing their uninvited presence.

Trailing the man on his right by a few paces, the Tuscarora nearest the forest edge froze when his companion gurgled in agony and dropped to his knees, one hand grasping the arrow that had pierced his neck. The surviving Tuscarora instinctively fell flat to the ground, lay still, and waited for the second arrow to find him; but it did not come, nor did the shooter disclose his location.

Now it was one-on-one, both concealed and each intent on killing the other. Beyond him, his wounded brother warrior writhed in agony, his hand still clutching the arrow, his wind passage traumatized and shutting down. Blood flowed freely from his mouth and nose until he strangled in the throes of death.

It was now a matter of who moved first. The remaining Tuscarora lay still and scanned all he could without risking a move that might expose his location. He saw that the arrow had struck downward and from the right leaving half of the arrow shaft gripped in the victim's right hand. The shooter would be there, among those trees, probably in one of them. A huge old beech tree stood not far to his right, its branches still in full foliage, and its leaves showing only the first tinges of fading green. He might be able to circle that tree and get a shot, but there wasn't enough cover to avoid exposing himself.

He could outwait the shooter and engage him when he exposed himself, or he could charge the shooter now and certainly die if he had chosen the wrong tree. It also occurred to him that there might be more than one shooter out there. He gradually worked his body backward, sliding deeper into the cover of forest undergrowth. When he was out of view, he turned and dragged himself forward another ten paces and waited, listening. After awhile he rose and slipped away, careful to use all the cover available until he judged it safe to break into a run south, back to the place where they had crossed the creek. He found Kajika and the others busy stacking debris into crude barricades.

Tonawanda followed his warrior to the slain Tuscarora. The arrow and bow markings exactly matched those Yahou-Lakee had shown him. The shooter had seen both the Tuscaroras. The one he killed was nearest him. The other one had fled the scene and, no doubt, would warn the rest. He recalled that Yahou-Lakee had estimated between ten but not more than twelve warriors in the Tuscarora attack.

Tonawanda considered his battlefield. The tracks showed the enemy had crossed the creek. There was no way to be certain they were not still running and these two were simply scouting the back trail. On the other hand, they could have turned back and were even now surrounding him. Not likely, but he sent one of his men south to check anyhow. They could be entrenched somewhere on the high ground. If so, Tonawanda figured he could control a long section of the ground on his side of the creek until they located them, then pin them down and hold them there until the rest of his warriors arrived.

The problem with that strategy was that, holding to the high ground until they crested the mountain, the enemy might escape. Two of his people had been working the trail north, but they found no evidence of travel in that direction. He'd called them back as soon as he learned about these two Tuscaroras coming so close. They had come from the south. The wisp of smoke he had been told about was also south of the westward trail, about even with the place they now stood. He walked over to the edge of the forest and scanned that area of the foothills and the mountainside.

Whether they were running or waiting, the Tuscaroras would soon know a Nahyssan war party was close by, but they did not know its strength. To his advantage, Tonawanda did know the approximate strength of the Tuscaroras—one down and maybe nine to go. As he gazed across the meadow and over the slope, his thoughts came back to the question: are they running or waiting?

"Bring the Tuscarora," he ordered. There about half way to the stream, stood an old, lone sycamore; its wind-driven branches almost bare of leaves formed grotesque white shapes reaching outward and downward as though in desperation. "Hang him there," said Tonawanda. "Let the enemy see what awaits them."

He summoned his five warriors. "The Tuscaroras are somewhere on that slope." He pointed toward the mountainside. "Red Wolf and Wiwohka, go north. Cross the creek and see that they do not escape in that direction. If the wind is right, fire the mountain. I will go south and climb to high ground on the trail that leads toward the overpass. The rest of you guard the southbound trail by the creek."

From his vantage point high on the slope, Kajika watched the two Nahyssans hang his warrior from the old tree while the one that had escaped told him what had happened. It was an invitation to fight. No matter how many Nahyssans were out there, he had two advantages: they did not know his exact location, and he knew exactly where they were.

He ordered his men into a triangle configuration around the animal path and settled down to watch from his place on the high ground. If he could draw them into attacking him here, he would control the fight. When his warriors settled down, he struck a spark into a handful of dry shavings built under the branches of a cedar tree thick with foliage. The smoke filtered upward, almost invisible. As soon as some of the white smoke had escaped, enough to be seen by a curious enemy, he extinguished the fire and eased down on his heels, watching.

Surely there could not be very many Nahyssans here in so short a time. If there were many, they would have stormed this mountainside by now. More likely, it was a small advance party, in which case he could attack them now before others came. But no matter how few they might be, he could not cross that open meadow without serious losses.

He began counting what he had seen of the enemy; two of them had appeared and examined the trail, two more, not likely the same, had hanged his man from that old tree. That made four for certain, and then there was the shooter. He estimated six or eight, and concluded that time was on the side of his enemy. If they did not show themselves soon, he would attack, kill these few, and move on to the crest of the mountain, leaving the dead as a warning for any who followed. He squinted hard at the distant tree line, searching carefully for sign: movement, more taunting near the hanging tree, a war cry, bird or animal calls, signals among them. He saw nothing.

As Kajika watched he grew restless, and just as he decided to attack the areas of the hanging tree and the trail, he smelled the smoke and heard the first faint sounds of the crackling fire. He leaped atop a stone outcropping for a clear view in all directions. To the north the mountainside was burning under a growing grass and brush fire, vigorously fanned by a strong north wind. Surrounding him stood massive thickets of laurel, briar, sumac, and other plants that had shed their foliage. Many small deciduous trees stood with limbs stretching over leaf-strewn ground.

The only escape was to the south. Now the fire had reached the tall dry grass in the little strip of flat land bordering the stream, sending flames skyward as the intense heat ignited more plant life in front of the moving flames and cut off all northern passage from the Tuscarora position. Kajika's warriors left their barricades and gathered about him, eager to move out. North and high above, Kajika could see more flame and smoke rising in places isolated from the main burn. He still could not see the enemy, but it was clear that he could not pass above the fire in that direction. An escape north was blocked.

With one Tuscarora warrior dead and one with Tayamiti on the high trail, the Tuscaroras were down to eight warriors, still more than enough to handle whatever resistance lay south if they could gain and hold the high ground there. Kajika sent two warriors climbing to take positions above them. He formed a V with himself and the remaining five, and started to move slowly upward and south, but the fire forced them to move south faster into the firing range of three-barricaded Nahyssans waiting for them.

Unseen by the Tuscaroras, Tonawanda had left the three warriors at the barricade and had started working his way upward toward a stand of pine and cedar from which he would have a protected view of the fire and fight scene.

The two Tuscaroras holding to the highest ground fell first. Under a hail of musket fire and arrows from the barricaded Nahyssans, they dropped and tumbled downward until the trees and shrubbery blocked their fall. The others spread out and moved toward the thick vegetation where the firing originated, attempting to encircle the three Nahyssans.

High above them, Tonawanda rested the muzzle of his musket on a low tree branch and nicked the thigh of the first Tuscarora to show himself. The Tuscaroras scrambled for better cover and the Nahyssans seized the opportunity to fall back and regroup for the next encounter. The oncoming fire blazed unopposed across the mountainside, greedily absorbing the north wind to make fires so hot that vegetation was exploding in front of it.

Tonawanda watched the movements below, eager for some sign of his son, Tayamiti. He reloaded and fired again. Again two more Tuscaroras fell. He estimated seven remaining enemies. Where was Tayamiti? How much time did he have before the fire reached him? Were there more Tuscarora where he had taken the two, or did they divide? The trees and brush provided too much cover to tell. Then he realized they could have spotted him by the smoke from his musket. He looked about warily and reloaded as he started toward a new position.

Far below him, the Tuscaroras tried to follow the retreating Nahyssans, but the musket fire from Tonawanda forced them under cover and slowed their progress. Barely able to stay ahead of the burning grass, the gap widened between them and the Nahyssans. Kajika now had just four men left, and the smoke and heat from the burning mountainside was driving them ever closer into enemy crossfire.

Tonawanda crossed a deep ravine to escape the fire. He was now in good position to watch the movements below. Three of his Nahyssan warriors had reached the cover of more grass and shrubs near the creek well ahead of the fire and the Tuscaroras. They were now separating to form a line to intercept the enemy that was driving southward to escape the heat and smoke. He could also see Red Wolf and Wiwohka on the east bank of the creek running south to join the fight.

The Tuscarora were still in firing range of his musket, but tree and brush cover was too thick for musket fire, and they were too far away for bow and arrow. On their present course, they would soon be above the line his warriors were forming. As he pondered giving up the high ground and coming down on the enemy flank, he noticed the north wind had died and he felt the air movement on his back out of the west. Within a few minutes, the fire began to settle, burn itself out, and slow its southward movement.

Below him, the vegetation gave way to isolated slides of crushed limestone and shale deposits. He could occasionally see three Tuscaroras running south between him and his warriors. They were well out of musket range and about to escape. Only three Tuscaroras! Where were the others? Had his estimate been wrong?

Uneasy with the possibility of being surprised, he checked his surroundings. It would make sense for the enemy to try to stop his lethal musket fire there on the high ground, but he saw nothing. Below him, it looked as though his three Nahyssan warriors had stopped moving and had taken positions from which they could intercept the Tuscaroras.

With the fire easing and the smoke reversing direction, Red Wolf and Wiwohka were able to get behind the Tuscaroras. The odds now favored the Nahyssans, but the Tuscaroras might choose to run, and if they climbed, they could avoid the Nahyssan line and escape. Tonawanda primed and loaded his musket and left the cover of the great stone outcropping and wild laurel.

Facing him, not fifty paces away in open ground, stood black-faced Kajika, bow drawn and arrow sighted on his heart. Tonawanda dived to his right, firing from the hip, and heard the arrow slam into a tree behind him. He rolled and came up crouched to present as small a target as possible; but the charging Kajika, screaming war crimes, was almost upon him, his blackened face smeared with red and white bear grease.

Crazed with hatred and determined to kill, Kajika swung his tomahawk and missed, but his body slammed into Tonawanda and sent him crashing into a thicket of briars and honeysuckle. Tonawanda let the momentum of his backward fall carry him on through a backward somersault. He landed again on his feet, bleeding over most of his back and arms from the snake-like saw briars.

Each armed with a knife and a tomahawk, the two warriors faced each other a few paces apart across the patch of briars and honeysuckle. Both tall, muscular figures wore only loincloths, moccasins, and leggings laced to the knees. Neither spoke the other's language. Tonawanda wanted his enemy alive at least long enough to lead him to his son. Kajika's task was simpler: kill this hated Nahyssan.

They moved to a small clearing where the slope was not so steep and began to circle each other looking for an opening to strike. Neither risked a throw of tomahawk or knife, knowing that a miss would leave them at a deadly disadvantage. Each kept one hand near his body ready to sacrifice it if necessary to shield his neck and vital organs from a thrust or slash. The other hand held a long-bladed steel knife gripped butt down, blade up so that either end of the knife became a weapon. This hammer-grip was the first thing each noticed as he sized up the other. It signaled experience. With that grip the knife fighter could thrust, slash, hammer or chop. Both were strong, seasoned warriors. Both held their knives ready to thrust, slash, or block the knife of the other. They circled, moving for position to attack.

It was becoming a matter of endurance and patience until one careless move would create the kill opportunity for the other. Tonawanda kept to a tactic of defensive moves. Holding his knife close to his waist and balanced on his toes, he kept moving, his side with the knife-arm facing Kajika, presenting the smallest target. Constantly alert for an opening, he used his free hand to balance his quick changes in position. He wanted to cut the knife hand of the enemy, however slightly. Finally, he saw the opening he wanted. Kajika charged with his knife-arm raised. Tonawanda stooped under the strike, stabbed upward toward the descending forearm, and slammed into Kajika enough to send him stumbling to regain his balance.

Tonawanda had drawn first blood when he slashed across Kajika's raised knife-arm. There was no time for a deep cut. He had cut and retreated before Kajika recovered to strike again, and Kajika bled from the forearm of his knife-hand. Tonawanda's confidence surged when he saw Kajika's bleeding knife arm. He summoned his patience and continued watching for opportunities to cut the arms and hands of his enemy, trying to stay as clear of his knife as he could.

Determined to finish off his enemy, Kajika struck hard in a flurry of attacks.

Tonawanda answered the attacks with evasion and patience. He managed small cuts on Kajika's unprotected free hand and arm. Trying to conserve strength and avoid serious injury, he focused on staying clear of Kajika's knife, and watched the glaring eyes behind the devilish mask of black grease for a sign of tiring.

Kajika withdrew, hesitated and poised for another strike, but instead he drew several breaths. Maybe this was the sign. Was Kajika easing his attacks and waiting for renewed strength? Tonawanda charged. He would not allow this enemy to rest. Surprised at this change to aggressive attack, Kajika side-stepped and backed away, but Tonawanda, denying him any respite, made a vicious backhanded swing of his knife just touching the shoulder of Kajika's free arm but enough to again draw blood.

Enraged, Kajika played into Tonawanda's strategy and began another flurry of attacks. Soon, the evidence of his tiring showed. His glaring eyes lost their passion, and he looked away from Tonawanda, hoping to see a better way. Seizing the moment, Tonawanda lunged past the murderous blade and drove his knife at his enemy's chest; but with his free hand, Kajika saved his life by taking most of the thrust, allowing only a small penetration of the chest. But the back of his free hand had taken the huge blade dead center rendering it useless.

Kajika knew it was over. Charging Tonawanda, he exposed his unprotected side to take the death thrust, his own knife driving toward Tonawanda's middle.

Tonawanda side-stepped and kicked Kajika's feet from under him sending him sprawling with the knife still gripped and extended. Tonawanda dived toward the knife arm and slashed. Kajika's hand opened and the knife fell free.

Dazed, Kajika tried to raise himself enough to get one knee under him, just as Tonawanda swung the steel butt of his knife into his head. The blow flattened him again. Bleeding from several cuts, his strength gone, he slowly rolled on his side and offered his neck to Tonawanda's knife.

Instead, Tonawanda delivered a vicious kick to his head, bound the hands and feet of his unconscious enemy with raw hide lacing from one of Kajika's leggings and dragged him to a grassy glade. He tied Kajika to a small tree and fashioned a crude poultice from leaves and the juice of over-ripe persimmons lying beneath a nearby tree. He applied crude compression packs to the more severe wounds on Kajika's arms, ignoring the glaring eyes, contempt, and weak resistance.

He looked at the cuts on his own body. They had stopped bleeding except for a deep cut below the elbow of his left arm. There, the blood flowed heavily. He stripped a legging from Kajika's leg, packed it with leaves and persimmons and laced it tightly to his wounded arm, then grasped his right shoulder to elevate the wound and slow the bleeding.

The brush fire had eased, and the smoke was drifting northeast. Earlier, Tonawanda had noticed a spring near the ravine. There, near the water, were more medicinal plants and proper leaves for poultices. When Tonawanda returned, he found Kajika had managed to keep one of his arm wounds open and bleeding. He faced the man who could lead him to his son. The desire to kill was powerful, but he looked again at the bleeding. The flow had eased leaving the man weakened but conscious.

He adjusted the poultice on his own wound as his thoughts turned to the fight below. Had the other Tuscaroras escaped? Had Red Wolf and Wiwohka rejoined the Nahyssans? If the enemy was running, his warriors would be chasing them. They would not wait for Chief Yahou-Lakee with reinforcements. From where he stood on the little shelf of flat ground, the trees and brush blocked his vision of the battle scene below. There could be wounded or dead scattered about down there. Where was his son? And what about this captured Tuscarora who wanted so badly to die?

Wanted so badly to die? That was the answer! He went back to Kajika. Standing feet apart and arms folded, he glared down at his trussed captive. He would offer him a way to take his own life, or if he so chose, to escape and live until the two met again. And for the sake of vengeance, they would meet again.

The deep ravine had stopped the southward movement of the dying fire and the smoke was slowly reversing direction. The mountain now shielded the late afternoon sun leaving the eastern slope in its shadow under an overcast sky. The air was almost still and unusually damp. Insects had found Kajika and were feasting on the blood. Mosquitoes swarmed and a colony of insects was busy working the abundant blood and torn flesh. Gnats formed clusters and flew at Kajika's eyes and ears biting into the skin and crawling into the ears and nostrils of the helpless murderer. Kajika welcomed the pain without showing the slightest discomfort. Let the enemy know that he would die with honor, unbowed and without help.

Tonawanda made the motions that the Tuscaroras were defeated. He stretched to his full stature over his captive and raised the two steel knives above him to signal his victory and the superiority of the Nahyssans. Kajika spat at him. Tonawanda laid Kajika's knife on the ground and drew a small figure of a boy opposite and motioned that the boy was his and the knife was Kajika's and made it plain that he would exchange the knife for the boy, but the boy first. Kajika raised his shoulder several times, and when Tonawanda cut one arm free, Kajika pointed to the crest of the mountain and indicated the number two.

As he re-bound Kajika's arm, Tonawanda noticed an amulet of polished white bone carved in the shape of a fish hanging from Kajika's neck. He cut the trophy clear and put it in his pouch. He picked up the promised knife, motioned that he would come back, and walked away.

He found his musket, but the weight and length were too much for his wounded arm. Without the musket, and unable to draw his bow with the wounded arm, he could not be much help to his warriors. He hid the two weapons under a rotted chestnut tree trunk marked by the pattern of nearby stone outcroppings and a large clearing. Still holding his right shoulder high to elevate and protect the wound, he started climbing.

Far below Tonawanda, the Tuscarora fighters heard the shot Tonawanda fired at Kajika, and started running down the slope toward denser cover, away from the threat of the high-ground weapon. The waiting Nahyssans saw them and met them with a flurry of arrows. They fired so quickly that the arrows seemed to come from many shooters. Two of the arrows struck their targets, but only one warrior fell.

The three Tuscaroras, two of them wounded, took cover and began a stealth movement meant to engage the enemy from different directions and fight to the death. They abandoned their heavy muskets and took positions for the ambush. While one moved higher and forward, the wounded men concealed themselves in brush thickets. One crouched next to an old chestnut tree, his tomahawk and war club ready. The third was stripping a dead companion of weapons when Red Wolf and Wiwohka burst onto the scene and fired four arrows, killing him instantly.

The other wounded Tuscarora stepped from behind an old chestnut tree and threw his knife at Wiwohka; it hit him under the arm and lodged there in muscle and tissue. The impact spun him around, and he dropped to one knee, clutching the knife. Red Wolf clubbed the Tuscarora unconscious. Wiwohka slipped the knife out of his arm and bandaged the wound with a piece from his buckskin breechclout, lacing it tight with leather thongs from his leggings .

Red Wolf forced the arms of the unconscious Tuscarora around a young maple tree trunk and tied his hands together with the man's own bowstring. He and Wiwohka gathered all the weapons and stored them for later retrieval.

They heard a war cry just above them and reached their companions in time to see them capture the last Tuscarora alive. If the wounded warriors lived, the Nahyssans now had two captives.

Tonawanda reached the crest of the first ridge driven on by the thought of finding Tayamiti. But the loss of blood, exertions of the fight, and the subsequent trials of dealing with Kajika had left him weaker than he realized.

At the top of the ridgeline, he struck the well-traveled trail. There, he leaned against a chestnut tree, breathing heavily. As soon as he caught his breath, he gave the call of the wolf to alert Tayamiti in case he might be near. He tried to gather his thoughts, but the strain of the climb robbed him of clear thinking, and he slid down into a sitting position and closed his eyes.

When he awoke, he found he had slumped over and rolled onto his back. He lay still, opened his eyes and listened. The afternoon weather had passed and the black night sky sparkled with starlight. He heard the far-off call of an owl.

By the time the Tuscaroras fell defeated and the Nahyssans had taken their two prisoners and gathered the scattered weapons, darkness was closing in. They chose an open place in the grass meadow near the stream and made a huge signal fire for Tonawanda.

By dark, they settled into a camp and bound their captives, but tended only to their own wounds. Then, they refreshed themselves from the stream. Aware that at least one Tuscarora was still unaccounted for, they set two widely separated sentry posts. They would begin a search for Tonawanda at first light.

25

In the little house of clapboard siding near the unfinished William and Mary College building, Shanda's strength gradually returned thanks to Carrie's hot broths, soft food and expert attention. One day Wapiti, the tall, muscular Tutelo warrior escorting Shanda, disappeared and returned with a young deer. He hung it outside Carrie's kitchen and butchered it for cooking. Carrie passed several times while he was skinning and cleaning the venison but appeared to pay no notice. Finally, he placed the venison in a small wooden tub he found near the spring, covered it with some evergreen boughs and left it at the back door to the kitchen.

Several hours later, Carrie came into the room where Wapiti was watching Shanda bend and stretch to test his returning strength. His breechclout hung comically over protruding hip bones under his visible rib cage. The effort exhausted him, and he retreated to the bed. Carrie gave him a disapproving frown, and approached with her tray covered by a bright, checkered cloth. Wapiti had caught the wafting scent of roasted venison the instant she opened the door letting the air of the hallway flow past her toward the window where he stood clad in buckskins. Carrie had made it plain from the start that she would not tolerate naked men in her sick room or kitchen.

She placed the tray on the little table under the window and removed the cloth, taking more time than necessary, but with the appearance of being very busy with straightening, arranging, folding, re-straightening, and rearranging. Wapiti moved away, as usual, waiting for her instructions. It was Carrie's way. She brooked no interference when she was about her work, and used facial expressions and motions to order Wapiti to do her bidding. The two had achieved a high level of communications by Carrie expressing urgency, impatience, silence, and dismay or frustration when something was misplaced, missing, or soiled. Carrie never smiled or looked at Wapiti, not even when she beckoned him for assistance, but after a while, it required effort to ignore him, so gentle, quiet, and respectful was this huge savage. Once he handed her a basin of water and supported it an instant longer than necessary, watching her face, but he was hopelessly incapable of expressing his gratitude for her care of Shanda. She ignored him and turned away. Wapiti withdrew like a leaf adrift on quiet water. Another time, he approached her as if to speak, but she raised her voice in anger making her rejection clear, and after that, he was careful not to approach her unless she motioned.

Now she stood near him, serving broiled venison cut into bites and skewered on green, hickory-flavored splinters. The meat lay on a large platter surrounded by squash and beans she had gathered from the kitchen garden that morning. It was closer to Indian cooking than anything Wapiti had eaten for several days, and he was pleased with this special attention. Her back still to Wapiti, Carrie stepped away and motioned him to the food. Hesitantly, he lifted the platter and let the aromas flood his nostrils. When he raised his head and turned, he was looking straight into Carrie's smiling eyes. She must have misread the look of surprise on his face—she turned away and left the room. None of this escaped Shanda, who sat on the edge of his bed ignored by Carrie for the first time.

"Eat," Wapiti said. Confused by the woman's behavior and glad to have something to do, he removed the skewer and held the platter of food for Shanda to choose what appealed to him. Shanda declined. His appetite had deserted him, and the food looked threatening to his sensitive stomach.

"I will wait a little while," he said. "I think the food is a gift to you, yet you did not speak your thanks, Wapiti. Carrie is good."

"It is not a matter for young warriors to concern themselves about. Rest. Kadomico and Tree Son will be here soon."

Wapiti settled down on the floor and cleaned the plate. The food reminded him of his people and how the English seemed to treat daily dining like a feast rather than just to satisfy hunger. He was accustomed to eating anytime he was hungry or when celebrating a special time. Then there were special occasions when his family sat down to a meal much like the English. They washed their hands and prayed before each meal, but the English did this at a small feast three times daily: morning, mid-day, and sundown. The Indian women in Wapiti's world kept pots of cooked food available: dried meat, fish, and plenty of nuts and berries. For the most part, the family took it when they were hungry.

Kadomico and Tree Son, dressed in coats, shirts, pants, stockings, and leather shoes with buckles, stood in the open doorway waiting for Wapiti to motion them in.

"Stop," Wapiti said, recoiling at the sight of these young Indians dressed as English. Shanda rose up on his elbow and gasped at the sight.

Clothing these young Indians had not been easy, but after a few days the clothing had been delivered and the schoolmaster insisted that they dress for their learning sessions. The schoolmaster was oblivious to how education and the clothing were often rejected by the tribes. The clothing screamed "different" at brother and sister Indians and "different" meant suspicious, therefore, a threat. At best, a member of the tribe that appeared clothed in English garb, might be treated as a guest, but, more likely, would be rejected outright. And if he had been rumored to be a traitor to his people he would be marked an enemy and rejected by his own people, sometimes executed. The boys might deny the education or hide it, but, to many of their people, the clothing screamed English, suspicion, threat, or betrayal.

"Take off the English before you come," Wapiti snapped as he pointed at them. The muscles of his outstretched arm bulged, and except for the accusing finger, his hand coiled into a fist of anger. "Here you are Indian. You cover yourself like all Indians. It will be the same when you return to your tribe. Leave English things with the English," he said. "Come back when you are Indian again, and we will speak more of this."

Shanda wanted to laugh, but hearing the anger in Wapiti's tone choked it back before it was too late.

Kadomico wanted to explain, but the truth was he was relieved to see Wapiti's reaction. It was reassurance that the Indian dress was a good thing and important, and therefore, the right dress for him. Hereafter, he and Tree Son would dress English only when under instruction in class, church, or in Carrie's kitchen. And they would wear buckskins as much as they could without offending their English hosts—breechclouts, if they were ever allowed to hunt or fish the nearby forests and streams.

They went into their room next door to Shanda to change into breechclouts.

"As for me, I am glad to be rid of the scratchy, stinging, hot fur of the English," Tree Son said, slinging the clothing wildly into the corner. "Wapiti is right."

"Easy, Tree Son. It is only until we return to the headmaster."

"Not so, Kadomico. Wapiti has spoken. We are Indian. I hate these things."

"Yes, Wapiti did speak, but were you asleep when he said '*Here*', meaning in this place. He did not mean among the English. There, we dress like the English. It is part of why we are here."

Tree Son didn't argue, but his mornings in the classroom and the last hour in the English clothing had ruined his enthusiastic attitude about remaining with Kadomico. There were still at least three moons before he would be free of that incomprehensible headmaster and those English wraps that seemed alive with stinging demons and suffocating heat.

"Let us go and speak with Wapiti and Shanda," Tree Son said, anxious to be with his own kind.

They returned to a friendly welcome by Wapiti and a mischievous grin from Shanda. After a few words of understanding about the times and places for English clothing, Kadomico and Tree Son talked about the slate boards and primer reading books they had seen that morning. They were excited about these discoveries, but Kadomico could see that their listeners were neither interested nor did they approve of what was happening over in the college building. This reaction was disturbing to Kadomico, but he quickly dismissed it and changed the subject.

"Jock Adams came to the school. Tree Son and I will go with him after school to see the trading at Capitol Landing. He said a *pinnace* will be there. That is a great canoe with wings like we saw on the river when we came."

There was no response to this news.

Shanda said, "Wapiti killed a deer and the woman, Carrie, cooked it for him. She was pleased to see what a great hunter is Wapiti."

Kadomico and Tree Son immediately forgot the school and pressed Wapiti for information.

"How could you find a deer here? There are so many people and so few animals left in the forest that even the English have to travel toward our hunting grounds in the west for deer and bear," Kadomico said with deep respect for this great hunter.

"The few deer left here know their enemy well, and remain invisible. They move only at night, but they leave sign when they move about and when they take the marsh grass and tender shoots of young trees preparing for the cold times of winter. The English hunt with howling dogs, shoot firesticks like thunder, yell, talk, and stomp through the forest. Animals have only to listen and disappear as though the forest is empty."

"Wapiti, will you show us?" Tree Son asked.

"No." Wapiti paused to let his answer sink in. "You must do what you are here to do."

"I was not sent here for school. I will not go back to the school. I will go with Wapiti."

"Go back to the school, Tree Son. There is plenty of meat now. When more is needed, we will see." Again, Wapiti's point was clear and final—at least to Kadomico. To Tree Son, hunting was superior to reading and writing, but for the time being, the school was also important. Tree Son was about to argue when he felt Kadomico nudge him. He caught the protest in his throat before it reached his lips. The subject was closed, and they turned to speculating on Hawk's return with Shanda's family.

At the other end of Duke of Gloucester beyond where the ruts and scattered lot-markers of the street crossed two deep ravines, Will James was cleaning muskets in the tiny office of the gaol just to the north of the capitol building site. He pondered the story Obie Higgins had told him about the attack on him and his brother, Billy, last evening. Obie had reported a surprise attack by Indians, not giving the number. They retreated after he fired his pistol, but by then they had wounded Billy. He wanted Will to gather the militia and pursue the murdering savages right then, but knowing the Higgins boys and looking at the time and place, it was clear to Will that they had encountered Hawk and there had been a fight. Billy got the worst of it and no one else was injured. He'd decided to let it rest there, but he doubted that the Higgins boys would. He thought of alerting the Indians over at the school, but then decided it would only make matters worse. Hawk would be back in a few days, and then he would get the other side of the story. Leave it rest.

Unknown to Will, Hawk would never be back. The day after his encounter with the Higgins brothers, he had reached the Tutelo town, and two days later had returned to the Chickahominy town near Williamsburg with two Tutelo warriors and two young women. Until they decided what to do about moving Shanda, the Tutelos would remain as guests of the Chickahominy. Tom Singleton, from the plantation neighboring the Chickahominy town, had offered to escort them on to Williamsburg when they were ready.

Hawk's plan was working exactly as he expected. As soon as he was free of the Tutelos, he struck the trail running hard toward the Nahyssan town of Yahou-Lakee, avoiding the odd wilderness farm, hunting party, and occasional canoe on the Appomattox River. Yahou-Lakee would show him the way to Red Wolf and Wiwohka, and Hawk would again, finally, hunt, fight the enemy, grow in the wilderness way—be an Indian.

Jock Adams had visited Tree Son and Kadomico and invited them to come and stay with him, Rebecca, and their three boys. He explained that Rebecca had insisted, certain that Kadomico and Tree Son would learn faster in the company of the Adams family. Besides, she wanted her family to learn the Siouan language and more about the way of the Saponi. The boys declined, doing their best to explain with motions, expressions, and proudly, with a few words of English they had learned, that they were unwilling to leave Shanda and Wapiti.

The following day, Jock returned with the interpreter and explained that Rebecca had prepared a place for them in their home. They could stay there after Shanda and Wapiti departed. In the meantime, they were to come often, visit with their boys, take food with them, and get help with their lessons. Jock, remembering his promise to Sam Layton and looking forward to the developing frontier trade, anticipated making many extraordinary opportunities for Kadomico to learn about colony commerce.

Tree Son was glad to be excused from Kadomico's excursions with Jock to the plantations, ports, and ships that plied the rivers loading and unloading. He preferred to remain in Williamsburg with the Adams family, showing off his bow and arrows and hunting skills to the Adams boys and learning the games and sports of the English.

Five-year-old Luke came to idolize Tree Son, and when Jock took them hunting, camping, or fishing, Tree Son abandoned all else for the care of Luke. He made sure he and Luke participated in all the doings of the trip. They caught fish, set snares for small animals, and tramped the trails just like the rest. On the overnight occasions, Luke roasted meat alongside Tree Son, slept close to him under Tree Son's bearskin, and straddled his back when they struck the trail and the others got ahead of them.

26

Kajika was barely conscious when the Nahyssans found him with his arms and legs around the young pine, his hands and feet swollen over the rawhide thongs. To hasten a merciful death rather than face the Nahyssans as a captive, he had managed to keep some of the knife wounds open and bleeding by scraping them against the bark of the young tree. Insects swarmed around his helpless form. Their poisonous bites had left his eyes barely distinguishable on his swollen face.

He made no sound when the two Nahyssans approached, but silently, he prayed for death. They cut him free and jerked him to his feet. Barely coherent and speaking in the strange language of the Tuscarora, he cursed Tonawanda as a lying demon of the worst kind, and as he did so, he flailed his blood-streaked arms in the direction of the crest of the mountain.

During the fight, the bindings and feathers of his warlock had fallen away and the long black hair, matted with blood, partially covered his grotesque face. With a mighty effort, he motioned toward their knives and threw his fist at his chest, then dragged the hair away from his swollen lips and spit at the Nahyssans. By reading the signs of the fight and locating Tonawanda's weapons, the Nahyssans had a clear picture of what had happened. They rebound Kajika's hands and pushed him staggering forward and upward toward the crest.

Above them, Tonawanda searched the trail in vain for a sign of Tayamiti or his captor. He followed it first north, then doubled back and searched south along the crest of the mountain range. Toward mid-morning, he heard the traditional call of the

Nahyssan, returned it, and met them on the trail. Kajika lay bound at their feet, half-conscious.

Kitchi stood nearest Tonawanda and spoke first. "The Tuscarora are defeated. Red Wolf, Wiwohka, and our brother are returning two Tuscarora prisoners to Yahou-Lakee. This one is near death. He was their leader. His name is Kajika, Walks Without Sound. We know of him from his past Tuscarora attacks on small towns in the south and near the great water. We collected many weapons of the Tuscarora and found the ones you buried near Kajika. The Monacans have returned to their town."

Tonawanda nodded his recognition of the name. "You have done well, Kitchi. After I promised him a knife and his freedom, Kajika motioned to me that I would find Tayamiti here with one Tuscarora, but I have looked both ways. There is no sign of them.

"One of you, go farther north, one south on this trail. Run until nightfall. I will keep Kajika here and wait for you until the next sun. I will not let him die. He will live with one foot and one hand, and he will be slave to our people until Tayamiti returns."

Tonawanda began to prepare food and compresses of herbs and leaves. Kajika, completely naked and with his hands and feet bound, was on the border of delirium. Too weak to fight off the hands holding his jaws shut, he swallowed the nourishment forced into his mouth. Afterwards, he fell into an involuntary sleep, one that would enable him to begin an unwanted recovery and journey to the Nahyssan town.

The next morning before the sun reached its zenith, the warriors came back to Tonawanda and Kajika without Tayamiti. The warrior who followed the south trail had overtaken a small band of friendly Cherokee women and children returning from a fall hunting party. They had seen a tall warrior and a small boy, had given them some of the meat they carried, and watched them leave the trail traveling in a southeast direction.

Tonawanda looked southeastward over the tree tops of vast woodlands toward North Carolina. His throat swelled with the thought that it might be too late. His whispered words were barely audible. "That is the direction of the Tuscarora homeland. Now two suns on the trail, they are well on their way, almost there."

Tonawanda straightened and called Kitchi to him. "Take Kajika to Yahou-Lakee. Say we have captured many muskets, powder and ball, steel knives, tomahawks, bows, and arrows. See that Kajika and the two warriors live.

"I go to find Tayamiti and his captor before they reach the Tuscarora hunting grounds, but if I am too late, I will go on to the Tuscarora town and face the chief of the Tuscarora."

Before Kitchi could respond, Tonawanda turned and started his run down the mountain. Kitchi wanted to protest, to go with him, but his orders were clear. He must return the captives to Yahou-Lakee. Reluctantly, he checked the bindings of the captives and motioned his party forward. Red Wolf led. Kitchi and the other Nahyssans followed with the captives, and Wiwohka guarded the back trail.

They arrived at the Nahyssan town the next day. To Wiwohka's surprise, Hawk was there, standing alongside Yahou-Lakee. After Kitchi finished his report to Yahou-Lakee, Hawk approached the frowning Wiwohka to explain his absence from the school.

"Wapiti said we needed to notify the Tutelos about Shanda's illness, and because I know the Tutelos and the trails to their town, he and Kadomico agreed I could best do that, and I have done so. Tree Son has replaced me in the school. I came here to find you." Hawk did not exactly lie but he snuggled very close to it.

Wiwohka growled his disapproval at Hawk's abandonment of the school and suppressed the pride he felt in the boy's good deed, accomplished alone over the wilderness trails.

Hawk was fascinated with the captives and yearned to hear the details about the fight, but Wiwohka's raised hand silenced him quickly as he spoke. "We go—one night on the trail to the Occaneechi, then we will see what is next."

Yahou-Lakee motioned Red Wolf and Wiwohka toward the longhouse. Inside the longhouse, he pointed to their seats and said, "We are grateful for your part in the brave defeat of our enemy. When Tonawanda returns we will celebrate this victory and your great skills in war. I will send messengers to your chiefs. They will know of our gratitude and of the battles where you risked your lives for the sake of the Nahyssan. We hope you will come back."

"The Nahyssan are our brothers. It is enough," Red Wolf replied.

"Red Wolf speaks true," Wiwohka said.

Turning to Red Wolf, Yahou-Lakee said, "Custoga has led the great nation of Saponi for many years. We who know him admire and trust him, and we are anxious to know how the English have treated the young Indians in Williamsburg. We want Custoga to know that he may depend on the Nahyssan."

Red Wolf grasped Yahou-Lakee's forearm. "I will go back to the school at Williamsburg, to see if Kadomico and Tree Son are well. Then I will return to the Saponi and speak of these matters to Custoga and the Saponi council. If, the Nahyssan decide to make war on our common enemy the Tuscarora, I will fight for you, and I will urge Custoga and the Saponi council to join you.

"And I will say these same things to the Occaneechi," Wiwohka added.

Yahou-Lakee said to Red Wolf, "Take one of our canoes. Tonawanda will be here soon and when you return, we can talk."

"I will return, Great Chief. There is still the matter of Tonawanda's daughter, Sayen, captive to the Monacans. Also, Tonawanda had us bury many muskets, steel knives, spears, war clubs, and steel tomahawks, also powder and ball. Tonawanda spoke of using them to free Sayen. He said that Haw-Chi would not be seen by his warriors as preferring a woman more than the English weapons."

Yahou-Lakee nodded understanding. "Yes, I will go with Tosawi to speak with Massaqua of the Monacan. We are old

240

enemies, but times have changed. We now face others who would take our way of life and our land. It is time we stand together."

Red Wolf caught his breath. Yahou-Lakee was right. Together they could raise as many warriors as there are stars in the night. Together they could drive the English into the sea, along with the Tuscarora, Iroquois and any other enemy. The thought of such a force filled Red Wolf with eagerness to get started. Now he had something to say that would make the Saponi council pay attention. Combine the warriors of the Occaneechi, Saponi, Tutelo, Nahyssan, maybe even the Monacan into a powerful war party.

Wiwohka waited for a long silence before he spoke. "The Occaneechi have hunted with the Saponi and fought side by side with them. Our combined strength is one reason the Tuscarora avoid attacking us. I will remain there until Tonawanda returns. Then I will return to the Occaneechi, and speak to the council. I will tell them of the Nahyssan victory and say that we are brothers in battle."

Red Wolf was thrilled at the prospect of a mighty alliance of warriors. His mind leaped forward. Slaughter the English. Drive them back into the sea. Recover the land. He reveled in the thoughts but he remained silent. Soon, he would stand before the Saponi council again. Then he would show the way to deal with the white man.

As soon as the council with Yahou-Lakee was over, Red Wolf left for Williamsburg in one of the Nahyssan canoes. One of the women led Wiwohka and Hawk to an empty roundhouse equipped with bedding, food, and water. There they would prepare for their return to their Occaneechi town.

Tonawanda ran until nightfall, swimming rivers, slogging through marshes, and cutting his way through brush and briar. To keep a straight course from his starting point he sighted certain hilltops, used the sun, and watched the moss growing on the north side of the hardwoods when the wilderness became thick and sunless. His objective was to reach the Meherrin River ahead of Tayamiti. Back on the mountain, when he had a panoramic view of the vast hills and flatlands to the south, he had observed a straight line from about where the Indian women saw Tayamiti on the high trail, and he intended to watch the river where he estimated that line would intersect. The knowledge that he must not fail his son kept him moving through most of the night. After the stars faded, depriving him of bearings, he slept, and when the sun rose, he began running again—straight to the enemy Tuscarora homeland.

He knew he was passing through the lands of the Tutelo, Occaneechi, Saponi, Nottoway, and others. All of these were enemies, or at best fragile allies, of the fierce Tuscarora. They needed to hunt and trade with as little trouble as possible from the Tuscaroras, who were strong in number, rich in weaponry, and ruthless slayers of trespassers and trade competition. Many of these Tuscarora neighbors were friendly to Tonawanda and spoke Siouan, but did not spare the time to contact anyone until he neared the Meherrin River that would lead him into Tuscarora territory.

When he arrived at the river, he asked for information from many of the people he found there along the bank. Finally, a band of Occaneechi warriors told him they had seen the campfire of one man and one boy near the headwaters of the Meherrin. Further along the well-populated river, a woman washing clothes in the river told him she had sighted their canoe. Tonawanda's heart sank as he slowly accepted that his son and his son's captor had taken a path to the nearest place where they had the advantage of the downstream current of the Meherrin to speed them on their way. They were well ahead of him.

He now knew that Tayamiti was in the hands of the chief of the Tuscaroras, and he kept moving until he saw canoes on the far bank. He swam the river and found Tayamiti's footprints where he had left the river, and, not far away he saw the palisade wall of the Tuscarora town. He reached the edge of the forest facing the gateway to the town, hesitated long enough to bring himself to his full height, adjusted his breechclout, weapon belt, and quiver of arrows, and walked straight into the town, eyes focused on the longest of the longhouses. There he expected to find the Tuscarora chief.

Three women working near the entrance saw the lone stranger striding across the open field toward them. His swim across the Meherrin had reopened some of the knife wounds on his face and body, and blood trickled across his face and arms. Frightened, they ran into the town plaza surrounded by bark-covered roundhouses, murmuring and pointing back at the entrance.

By the time Tonawanda reached the entrance, a crowd lined the pathway to the longest of the longhouses. Four warriors armed with spears and tomahawks blocked his advance. He stopped, spoke his name and tribe, and pointed to the northwest, hate and threat blazing from his eyes. His feathered warlock made his rank and seniority plain. One warrior stepped forward, threw his spear into the ground and motioned the other three to seize Tonawanda. Emboldened now with their warriors in control, the crowd cheered.

Tonawanda stood motionless, staring at the leader and said, "Kajika."

The crowd fell silent. The leader motioned the warriors to stop. Suddenly there was a commotion in the crowd. Tayamiti and Two Bears emerged from one of the roundhouses, and when Tayamiti heard Tonawanda's voice, he lunged into the crowd yelling, "My father! My father is here!"

Two Bears caught him and dragged him back to one of the roundhouses. Tonawanda, smiled. The crowd opened, and the four warriors escorted him to the longest of the longhouses.

243

There he found the chief of the Tuscarora sitting straight, arms folded, face flushed with anger. A Tuscarora priest sat to his right in all his regalia except for the buffalo mask resting by his side. An aged woman of obvious stature sat on the left of the chief.

The priest spoke in Siouan, "Who is this enemy of the Tuscarora that comes speaking the name Kajika?"

"I am Tonawanda, Senior Warrior of the Nahyssan. I speak for Yahou-Lakee, Chief of the Nahyssan. A band of Tuscarora under Kajika killed an old, old man and a young boy and captured two Nahyssan children from our town. The Tuscaroras ran like rabbits, but we found them; they are either dead or captives of the Nahyssan. Kajika is my captive. One of his warriors escaped with a Nahyssan boy and came here."

Tonawanda let the silence fall and linger until he was certain that his message had been absorbed.

"Kajika for the boy." Tonawanda raised his voice only slightly but the message was unmistakably clear

Gasping at this claim that their greatest warrior and maybe others were captives set the Tuscaroras talking among themselves. They ignored Tonawanda. He let it continue, watching the chief's expressionless reaction. It was clear that they did not know whether to believe him or not.

The chief silenced the murmuring with a wave of his hand. "You and the boy Nahyssan are captives of the Tuscarora. If the Nahyssan bring their Tuscarora captives here, a trade may be possible."

Tonawanda lifted Kajika's fish-shaped bone amulet from his pouch, tossed it into the lap of the woman and said, "To the west and south, the Cherokee and many other Carolina tribes are your enemies. Yesterday the Tuscarora fought Nahyssan, Saponi, and Occaneechi and lost. Before that, they violated Monacan hunting grounds. These tribes are friendly one with the other and are speakers of Siouan. The work of Kajika and his band is now well known by your enemies and by the English militia. If I do not return to the Nahyssan by sundown tomorrow, they will destroy this place and all within it." Tonawanda drew sixteen acorns from his waist pouch and placed them on the ground, then looked directly at the chief. "In this many days when the moon is full, I will stand on the bank of the river with Kajika. If a woman and the boy, and no other, comes to the middle of the river, I will bring Kajika there."

Tonawanda turned his back on the Tuscarora chief and his company and walked past warriors on either side of him. No one moved. The warriors waited for a signal from the chief. It did not come. The crowd dispersed. There was no sign of Tayamiti. The warriors followed Tonawanda to the river and watched through hate-filled eyes as he waded in and swam toward the other shore.

27

I was a very cool fall morning in Williamsburg. The leaves had settled under the outstretched limbs of the hardwoods around the buildings of the college. Tom Singleton knocked softly on the door of Shanda's sick room. With Tom were two Tutelo warriors and two young Tutelo women from Shanda's family. Wapiti smiled a welcome and swung the door wide for them to enter.

Shanda had just slipped into buckskin pants, and feeling the renewed strength in his legs, was preparing to walk with Wapiti, as he had been doing recently. The sight of his people brought a yelp of delight. He grasped the forearms of the men and embraced the young women. Energy surged through his thin arms and legs as they churned within the generous folds of soft buckskin. Wapiti, watching the excitement, moved into the group with his own welcomes, put his arms around Shanda's waist, and settled him down, slowing the activities, but not interrupting.

Tom Singleton watched the reunion and thought how strange it seemed—six Siouan-speaking, buckskin-clad Tutelo Indians in this small room sparsely furnished with bed, table, and chairs none of which was familiar or of use to the visitors. He was about to leave to find Deputy Will James when the deputy rode up on a bay mare. He laid the reins on the hitching rail and started up the steps to the building just as Tom appeared on the porch.

"They told me you were here, Tom," he said. "Thought I'd better see if I could help. As you know, Layton left several days ago, but they have an interpreter over at the school if you need him. They'll be letting out for lunch shortly, and the two other boys will be here soon."

"That would be Kadomico and Tree Son?"

"Yes, and Carrie will have food ready. She wasn't expecting this, but knowing Carrie, I think she will find a way to feed them."

Tom motioned toward the porch and the deputy followed him, leaving the visitors to their reunion. As they walked toward Carrie's kitchen, Tom asked about Kadomico and Tree Son.

"Well, they're dressed in English clothes and they do show up for the school work, but it must be hard for them. You watch. They move slowly, like their joints are stiff until they change back to their buckskins or breechclouts," Deputy James said.

"My father says they'll never change, and he doesn't put much faith in the government and the church trying to teach them our language and religion."

"Well, Tom, I don't know much about what goes on in the government and such, but I know that most of the people I see every day trust only their guns and swords in the presence of Indians, no matter what the government says."

"And he says these are Saponi, Occaneechi, and Tutelo, frontier Indians; proud, dangerous, and often at war with other tribes, but they seem peaceful and friendly to me."

"It's hard to tell. Wapiti caused quite a stir the other day when he brought in a small deer. The citizens were for and against it but mostly against," Deputy James replied.

They walked along in silence for a few steps, then James tried to sum it up. "They don't talk much, these boys, Tree Son and Kadomico, but they already know some English, maybe a lot. The Adams family has sorta adopted them, but the town has not. It is a good thing that Kadomico, Tree Son, and Wapiti stay close to the school, and it will be a lot easier when Wapiti and Shanda leave Williamsburg, especially Wapiti. He looks as wild as the wilderness itself and he is surely one of great strength. I'd hate to see him riled."

"Yes, I see that, and he also guards the sick boy with a great care and concern."

"That he does," replied James, and then told Tom about the Higgins brothers tangling with Hawk on the trail, pointing out that they were pure poison and bound to cause trouble. "It's just a matter of time," he said.

"By the way, Tom," James continued. "Have you heard any more news of the Nahyssan/Tuscarora fight that Tree Son told us about.?"

"No. We have wondered about it and my father has alerted our neighbors. We saw Hawk a few days ago when he brought Shanda's family to the Chickahominy. We think he headed back upstream toward the Nahyssan town on the trail by the Appomattox River. It could be he has gone looking for Red Wolf and Wiwohka. As I recall, they left Williamsburg right after Tree Son brought that news."

When they returned to Shanda's room, Kadomico and Tree Son, dressed in their English clothing, had met the Tutelos and joined Shanda and Wapiti in answering the barrage of questions. So many blankets? How many sleep here? Where are the cooking fires? Are the guns here? Where is the steel? The warriors? The chief person? What is the school? As they talked and laughed at the strangeness, Shanda and Wapiti prepared their possessions for travel.

"Tom, wait here," Will James said. "This is going to take some help from the interpreter."

While Will and Tom talked, Kadomico stood nearby listening, hoping for news of the Nahyssan. Although he had trouble following the quick exchanges, he did recognize key words. When Will left, he approached Tom and said, "Nahyssan? Tonawanda? Yahou-Lakee?"

"No. Nothing," replied Tom.

By the time Will returned with the interpreter, it was clear that Shanda and Wapiti were leaving to be guests of the Chickahominy until Shanda was able to make the long trip home. Wapiti and Tom would carry Shanda to College Creek Landing and use one of the local militia canoes. Will offered an escort to the Tutelos for the return trip to the Chickahominy town.

One of the Tutelo warriors responded to Will's offer, "It is good that we walk with the English warriors. We are ready."

"Soon then. I will arrange it. A canoe will be waiting at College Landing for Wapiti and Tom," Will said, then spoke to the interpreter. "Tell them that Carrie will have food prepared, and if they go to her kitchen, you had better go with them. They and Carrie will need your help."

As Will moved toward the door, Wapiti stepped up to him and spoke in English, "We go with the next sun."

Kadomico's heart swelled with pride. Wapiti, had spoken English! Kadomico smiled; so he had not been the only one silently practicing the English language, and if speaking it was important to Wapiti, it certainly would be good for him. He would redouble his efforts to learn more English words.

Will gathered the reins and stepped into the saddle. He turned the little mare toward Capitol Landing to make the necessary arrangements for escorts and the canoe. Afterwards he located Sheriff Cowles, and, together, they went to the college to report to the Governor.

They could hear Governor Nicholson shouting and pounding the lectern long before they entered the building. They approached the door of the room where his words flew like bullets into his audience. Sitting before him around the huge oak table, were several prominent Virginia landholders and planters. They made up the council, a powerful element of the colonial government appointed, not by the Governor nor by the House of Burgesses, but by the Crown. He needed their support to convince the House of Burgesses to fund a new fort on the southeast border of Virginia. He had called this meeting much to the chagrin of the members, some of which had to travel great distances. They also took umbrage at having no say about when and where such meetings were to be held. They sat respectfully but indifferent to words they had heard him say before.

With a wave of his hand, Nicholson motioned the sheriff and his deputy to seats along the wall.

"We piously nurture our indifference to our Christian duty to convert, educate and civilize the Indians. We point to a hundred years of failure, shrug our shoulders and say we have tried. Then we turn back to the comfort and security of all the riches the colony and the Crown have to offer while our frontier citizens fight for their very lives and what meager possessions they have been able to assemble." Nicholson pounded the lectern for emphasis and pointed an accusing finger.

"And there with them on the frontier are friendly Indians who, given the support and encouragement of our government, are willing to join them against the Tuscarora and other enemy tribes," he continued, his anger rising with each word.

"The frontiersmen are the reason the Indians, French, and even the Spanish dare not attack us. They are our buffer. What is theirs? None! They are our first line of defense. What is theirs? They are their own first line of defense!

"The Indians *and* the settlers deserve government support. They need forts, militia, and supplies."

A few council members shifted in their seats.

Nicholson stepped out from the lectern and raised his voice even louder. "The land they defend is Crown land, British soil, by the grace of Almighty God and British sovereignty. They struggle on without benefit of a single government gun, sword, or militiaman while we worry about the price of tobacco and sip wine on the porches of our brick and mortar homes in the peace of the evenings.

"This land is entrusted to us, to you the council, you who speak for the Crown, you who can provide the leadership and demand the resources from the colony government to strengthen our borders. This matter deserves your concerned support before the House of Burgesses. The brave British frontier people must have guns, forts, and militia support to continue to expand and develop this rich country. I believe it, England expects it, and you, the council, must demand it."

After he paused for effect, the Governor went on to explain his plan. The surprise and dismay on the faces of the council members was evident. He wanted to offer Siouan tribes of the southwest—Saponi, Occaneechi, Tutelo, and Nottoway—military protection from their enemies in return for their service as a peacekeeping frontier buffer. Secondly, he proposed to build a pentagonal fort seventy-five miles south of Williamsburg with five bastions each equipped with cannon. He would take the cannon from Williamsburg where they were no longer needed. Thirdly, he would set up a trade monopoly for the Virginia Indian Company and encourage the Saponi to settle in or near the fort for preferential trading treatment. Finally, he would continue establishing a system of education and Christian conversion for Indian children. He would also give high praise and other rewards to the families of those whose children succeeded in Virginia schools.

The Governor's eloquence was lost in a passion of impatience and anger, and he further alienated his audience when he shouted and threatened the one or two who ventured a different point of view. All the council members were engaged in planting and timber in one way or another. Most were tobacco planters. The Governor's proposal meant levying yet another tax on tobacco or timber or both.

The planters in this Virginia Council already faced a seriously declining economy caused by far-away British Board of Trade restrictions and the growing impact of French and Spanish piracy on colonial markets and shipping. England maintained a tight control on colony trade. Consequently, in such a limited market, prices of colony products were at the whim of the buyer, usually England. Tobacco prices were off so badly that many Virginia and Maryland growers were facing bankruptcy. The easily harvested coastal timbers had been depleted, driving woodsmen farther inland and forcing more labor, wagons, and skids to get the timber to market.

When Nicholson finished his summary of actions, a representative from the William Byrd land holdings in the southwest of Virginia stood and broke the strained silence. "My Lord, you give us much to consider. And we are fortunate to have your leadership in these military matters, costly yet important, possibly urgently important matters. However, we have been in session for three hours. May I suggest an intermission for some refreshments and reconvene at your pleasure?"

Nicholson's disgust was apparent in his agreement, but he did agree.

Will James had noticed the Governor's reference to the Saponi and thought of Kadomico, whose father was chief of the Saponi tribe. He made a mental note to talk to Jock Adams about the Governor's proposals. True enough, Kadomico had a long way to go before he could grasp the concepts the Governor described, but he could be an effective messenger. In any case, Jock ought to know about this interest in an alliance with the Saponi and possibly others. He joined the sheriff who was speaking to the Governor.

"All right, we have just two Indian students left," the Governor was saying. "One of them is promising, and I tell you, if we have a single success that we can hold up as an example to others, it is proof that our school is the right way. We can begin to civilize and convert the Indians to the true God where others have failed," Nicholson said.

28

Kadomico and Tree Son, at first hesitant about the classroom and their instructor, soon found ways to adjust to the demanding schoolmaster, uncomfortable English clothing, and the strange, often disagreeable, food. The regimens of ordinary English life—daily church, prayers, mealtimes, classes, housekeeping, and work—were more difficult to follow, but they tried, determined to represent their people in the best possible way.

They had moved in with the Adams family as soon as Shanda and Wapiti left Williamsburg. They quickly learned that the Adams children worked daily in the home; they gathered and cut firewood, took out ashes, weeded the yards, and worked in the kitchen garden, along with other tasks their parents assigned to them. Even young Luke, always in a hurry to get outside, was reluctantly learning to dress himself, button all the buttons, tuck in his shirt, and fold his clothes. Kadomico and Tree Son observed and cautiously joined in the work, glad that the boys in their town could not see them doing women's work.

They learned the English ways by following Matthew and Mark's example, gradually relaxed and became comfortable with their role as guests in the Adams home. There was almost no time for fishing or hunting, but when Jock arranged it, the boys soaked up the familiar freedom of field and stream. Those trips reminded them of life back at their Saponi town on the Yadkin River, and sometimes they grew homesick, a feeling neither had known before.

In school, Tree Son progressed a little in speaking and understanding spoken English, but quickly gave up on the alphabet and reading from the primer. When the headmaster called on him, he simply turned to Kadomico for help. Nor did he feel that he was missing anything. He attended class only because Kadomico was there. Eventually, the headmaster gave up on him and gave Kadomico his full attention.

Kadomico's natural curiosity rose at every discovery, and he committed them to memory, easily recalling them for re-examination or discussion. He often pondered what to say to his father and grandfather when he returned to the Saponi.

One day, after he had memorized all the strange symbols of the alphabet, the headmaster put three of the symbols together and said, "Boy," then four more and said, "Girl," pointing to a simple drawing of each in the primer. Kadomico saw the connection immediately. He suddenly knew that the symbols were more than just another mysterious, useless way of the English. He saw how setting them up together side by side on the slate had some kind of meaning, like hand signals or motions. He did not yet understand that he was actually reading, but he knew that the symbols were somehow the key to understanding the talking papers. His mind flashed forward, yearning to know more.

It was an awakening. He turned to Tree Son to share the moment, but Tree Son was gazing through the open window, his mind far away. Kadomico moved to the edge of his desk bench and leaned forward in anticipation. He wanted to go back and try to remember everything the headmaster had said about these marks. He tried to ask, but the headmaster angrily rapped his desk for silence and moved on.

After that day and with the additional help from the Adams family, Kadomico's reading in the primer progressed rapidly. He wished that Sam Layton could see and hear him say the words on the school paper. It thrilled him to think of it. It is why Custoga and Choola sent him. He had no way of knowing that his father and grandfather and others of the Saponi would never fully understand his excitement over learning these things. Nor would his newfound ability to read and write stop the white man's movement over their hunting grounds and the threat to the Saponi way of life. He did not yet know that even when he became a reader, it would be many years before his people would understand and accept talking papers as a way of speaking agreements. After that day, the day when he began to read, nothing could diminish Kadomico's elation at his ability to see the word *boy*, without even a picture or diagram to go with it, and know what it meant. It was a good day. Tree Son had recovered from his daydreaming enough to grin at him when the headmaster rapped the desk for attention.

By the time the air turned cold and the days grew short, both boys would be able to manage English well enough to participate in family discussions with the Adams and understand several of the bible stories and church hymns.

One morning as they walked toward the school building, Kadomico said, "Tree Son, the time of winter is near. When it comes, we will leave Williamsburg and return to our people."

"Yes, I am ready," Tree Son replied. "What will you say when we stand before the council, Kadomico?"

"I don't know. There is so much. I do not even know where to begin. Our council must know that the white people are many and more continue to arrive. Sam Layton said that is the most important concern of the Indian.

"All I can say is that I have learned to speak some English and to read and write a little, but I cannot account for the great houses of stone, the endless fields of tobacco, or the steel tools and weapons. How can I explain the work of the blacksmith or this strange church and the priest? I cannot. The Reverend and the Headmaster keep saying that their God is the only true God and that we must learn to accept Jesus and pray to him for forgiveness of our sins. I cannot speak of this. Headmaster says we will learn. They will teach us, he says. Now I only know that the English God is powerful and feared by the English.

"Jock showed me men who were loading and unloading the big canoes called pinnaces. He speaks of commerce, but I do not understand in a way that I can explain it. Before I go before the council, I must speak more openly with my father. He will guide me. What will you say?"

"I will say the way of the English is for the English and the way of the Saponi is for the Saponi. I hate these clothes and the school is worse. I like Matthew, Mark, and Luke, but I am Saponi. I say, leave the English to the English. It is not our way."

Kadomico admired that simplistic view even though caution stirred within him at the notion of "leaving the English to the English." Tree Son had told him that he felt some things needn't be questioned. They were the work of the deities who reside in the sun, wind, fire, rain, thunder, and lightning. Everything that happens, understood or not, could be explained as the work of the Creator. The priests said this, his people said it, and that was good enough for him.

Kadomico realized that Tree Son's faith was unshakeable and not likely to change, but why were these thoughts troubling him? Tree Son's words tugged at his reasoning and roused his curiosity. It surprised him that the difference between his and Tree Son's views could run so deep, but he also noticed that the difference did not seem to matter to either of them except to know that they existed.

That late autumn day, when they were within a few steps of the school, Kadomico stopped and looked at his friend. Tree Son had slowed his walk toward the entrance and was tugging at his stubborn clothes. Still, he was about to sit through another morning in a place he hated, listening to words he didn't understand. Kadomico shook his head as he realized that Tree Son was here only because he had asked him to stay with him. His coal black shoulder-length hair brushed one shoulder then the other as the thought triggered a flood of warm care for such a friend. As he watched, Tree Son suddenly turned, raced toward an ancient mulberry tree and vaulted into the low limbs.

"Better here than there," he teased, certain that Kadomico would be annoyed.

"I know." Kadomico almost whispered the words before he took the first step up to the entrance.

Puzzled, Tree Son slipped back to the ground and silently followed Kadomico into the dark interior of the place that would expand the differences between them, change the course of their lives, and test their friendship.

29

In the light of early morning, Yahou-Lakee sat cross-legged in the Nahyssan longhouse before a small ceremonial fire. Facing him in a semi-circle around the fire were Tonawanda, Red Wolf of the Saponi, Wiwohka of the Occaneechi, and the victorious Nahyssan warriors, including old Tosawi. Hawk, still uncertain of Wiwohka's approval but thrilled to be included here, sat quietly behind Wiwohka.

On Yahou-Lakee's right, the broad-shouldered chief priest of the Nahyssan made an imposing sight under a headdress of elk horns. Skins of perfectly preserved rattlesnakes with fangs glistening in their open-mouthed heads hung from his shoulders and clung to his massive chest as though they grew there. His red and white face paint matched the color of the feathers fastened around his bulging arm muscles with woven bands in several colors and intricate designs. The priest rose slowly before a silent audience and stretched his arms upward and outward. His face was frozen in rapturous reverence to the god of his prayer. In the background, a gourd rattle whispered in rhythm to a barely perceptible drumbeat.

A stillness settled over the council as the priest began a song of Nahyssan victory and war deeds. He sang of the deaths of Nastabon and Sinopa and the capture of Sayen and Tayamiti. As he sang, he sprinkled sacrificial tobacco on the tiny fire. Occasionally, his voice rose in passion, and he splashed the fire with a powder that caused the little fire to hiss and send colored flame and curling smoke upward. For a moment, the room was bathed in a ghostly white light. The rattle and drum beat continued.

The priest raised his arms in a final prayer, resumed his seat alongside Yahou-Lakee, and handed him a long-handled peace pipe with a glistening steel tomahawk blade fashioned opposite the pipe. The steel was a coveted trade item from the English, but the beautifully carved and feather-decorated handle of black locust that had been hand-worn to a golden sheen, was the work of Nahyssan artisans. Yahou-Lakee lit the pipe with a tiny coal from the fire, drew the smoke to his lips, and let it rise slowly past his face with murmurs of approval softly breaking the silence. Without turning his head, he handed the pipe to Red Wolf.

When the last man returned the pipe to the priest, Yahou-Lakee began. He gratefully acknowledged Red Wolf and Wiwohka and their recent acts of courage and skill in battle. He proudly recognized the deeds of Tonawanda and his warriors. Finally, he spoke of Tosawi and Sayen defeating the guard in the Monacan roundhouse. Voices and noises of approbation rose among the council members and Tosawi's breast swelled with pride and with admiration for young Sayen.

"There is much yet to be done, and the suns come quickly," Yahou-Lakee continued. "Tonawanda will speak."

The council members turned their attention expectantly to Tonawanda. He remained sitting until silence settled upon the room. Then, in a low voice charged with the strength of his resolve, he began. "Sayen remains captive to the Monacans. She is recovering with a good family of Monacan people, but the Monacan Chief Massaqua has said that when she is well she belongs to Haw-Chi, War Chief of the Monacan. When Yahou-Lakee speaks with Massaqua, he can offer to buy Sayen's freedom with the weapons we have buried on the trail. There are many steel knives, and tomahawks, war clubs, bows, arrows, spears, and firesticks. There is also powder and ball. It is possible that Haw-Chi will trade."

Yahou-Lakee shifted position, leaned toward Tonawanda and said, "The Monacan are not a peaceful people. They often war against the Iroquois and the Susquehanna, and because of the English strangers, they have moved as far west as they can without climbing into the mountains. Perhaps that is why they guard their hunting grounds closely and deal ruthlessly with trespassers. They hate the English and refuse contact with them, but they do highly value the steel weapons, the firesticks, powder, and ball. Although we have been enemies with the Monacan at one time, we speak the same language and we now face the same threats. I have sent a messenger to the Monacans. I will take Tosawi and two warriors who know where the weapons are, and speak with Massaqua."

Tonawanda continued. "I have seen Tayamiti at the Tuscarora town. He is well. We hold three Tuscarora captives. One of them, called Kajika, is a revered war chief of the Tuscarora. I have offered to exchange Kajika for Tayamiti."

"I understand," Yahou-Lakee replied. "It is right and it will be done, but our people, especially our warriors and the families of Sinopa and Nastabon, seek revenge. It is their right to make these cowardly Tuscarora prisoners pay for wasting the lives of our very young and very old. I will speak to them and keep the prisoners under guard until we see how Tonawanda's offer to the Tuscarora is treated."

Tonawanda responded quickly. "I expect the offer to be accepted. A warrior of Kajika's stature is far more valuable than a young captive. However, unless the bank of the river behind me is lined with our warriors, as soon as Kajika is safely in their canoe, they will attack. I need as many warriors as possible to line that riverbank. The Tuscarora will know then that they risk destruction of their town if they attack."

"I will ask the Saponi council to send their warriors to Tonawanda," Red Wolf said.

"I will speak to the Occaneechi this day and send a messenger to the Tutelo that they might join us," Wiwohka added. "And Hawk will leave now for the Chickahominy town and Williamsburg to speak to Wapiti of the Tutelo."

Hawk caught his breath. He wanted to shout and dance. Wiwokha trusted him and was giving him another task. This is the way of the warrior. He embraced the thought of preparing for war and suppressed his eagerness.

Yahou-Lakee beamed at this simple union forming unexpectedly before him. It more than answered Tonawanda's request. After many dark months of dealing with the powerful English, of devastating disease and the constant threat of attack by Iroquois and other Indian raiders, it was a ray of hope. Pride in his people and a renewed confidence surged within him. The exchange for Tayamiti would take place on the day following the next full moon, time enough to gather the warriors and make the preparations.

Tonawanda continued, "We will remain unseen by the enemy. Two Nahyssan warriors are there now, watching the river. On the day of exchange, Red Wolf and the Saponi will be upstream west of the crossing. Wiwohka, the Occaneechi and the Tutelo will be downstream east. If others come, I will divide them east and west to join you. I will camp north well clear of the crossing point. If the Tuscaroras have crossed the river, we will surround them and attack. If not, we will camp until sunrise, then walk together arms-length apart onto the bank of the Meherrin River."

Yahou-Lakee gave the order for warriors to assemble with Tonawanda the night before the next full moon and immediately dispatched a messenger to alert the Williamsburg authorities that Indians in war paint would move toward the Meherrin River against the Tuscarora. Red Wolf and Wiwohka nodded agreement and repeated their commitment to join Tonawanda with Saponi and Occaneechi warriors. Hawk was eager to go, to be included in these war preparations. The priest stood at Yahou-Lakee's signal of adjournment and made a short plea to the gods for courage, bravery, and protection of these warriors. The Indians rose. Now a brotherhood, they would meet again before the full moon, prepared to face a common enemy. They dispersed in different directions, Yahou-Lakee and Tosawi to the Monacan, Red Wolf to the Saponi, Wiwohka to the Occaneechi and Tutelo, and Hawk back toward Williamsburg to locate Wapiti. .

Hawk found Wapiti with the Chickahominy tribe preparing to leave for the Nahyssan town. After he explained what had happened at the council meeting, they wasted no time. They left immediately for the Tutelo town of Wapiti's people. There they would join the Tutelo warriors for the trip to Tonawanda's camp on the Meherrin. When they reached the Meherrin, Hawk would rejoin Wiwohka and their Occaneechi tribe.

In the Monacan town, the October sun blazed into the cool of early morning giving fair warning that it would be unusually hot for so late in the season. Long before mid-day, under the cloudless sky, the dry earth would feel warm to the bare feet of the children at play in the open spaces near the lodges. Sayen was preparing to leave with Aranck and her family for an overnight trip to a place of many nut trees: hickory, chestnut, and chinquapin. Although they would gather and store the nuts for winter food, Chief Massaqua had ordered the trip for another reason: Sayen was to be kept away from the town while the Nahyssan were there, and they were expected this day.

Still not fully recovered from her wounds and exhaustion, this was Sayen's first day on her feet, and when she stood the walls moved. She blinked her eyes and dropped her head to avoid the dizziness, but the fur mat beneath her blurred. She wanted to sit back down, but she held on to Aranck until her knees became steady enough to support her. Aranck did not restrain her but gave gentle support until Sayen gained an unsteady stance and eased back to a sitting position on the deep furs of the bed. Then Aranck began to speak quietly.

"The young warrior Tadewi, assigned to escort us, will be here soon. We will go to a place to gather hickory, chestnut, and chinquapin. It is not far. If you tire, we will rest. We will bathe in the stream. The water is so cold you will welcome the hot sun. There may be large wild grapes, cold and sweet, resting on the sandy bottom. This night we sleep under the stars."

Aranck and her family had been so protective, caring and attentive that Sayen felt safe with them, and she knew in her heart that the Nahyssans would come for her. She resolved to concentrate on regaining her strength. She cringed when she remembered Haw-Chi. She knew she was not yet strong enough to escape alone through an unknown wilderness, so she was glad to be with Aranck.

As her thoughts gave way to matters of the moment, Sayen took stock of her wounds and asked for water. Touching her hair and the wound on her head, she visualized the bath in the stream. Aranck had made it sound so pleasant. Her mind cleared slowly, but with the clearing came the pain and soreness from the punishments of the past few days. Aranck approached with a carved wooden basin of water and handed her a gourd dipper filled to the brim. Sayen shifted her weight and changed positions as she reached for the soothing drink. Aranck carefully bathed Sayen's face, neck and arms, and watched her take long drinks to ease the dryness in her mouth and throat.

Aranck then woke her daughter, Namid.

"Go and wake your brother. We gather nuts and camp tonight. Tadewi will be here soon."

Namid's eyes flew open at the news of a trip to the nut grove. It was a favored bathing and swimming place in the deep shade of giant sycamores leaning over the water. Muscadine vines, weaving through their topmost branches, dropped the sweet black grapes, fully ripened and bulging with juice, into the cold clear water beneath. Namid remembered that you could see them resting on the bottom, easy to gather. She could not remember if this was the right time for them. It might be, she thought. She remembered that they found them during the last season of the nuts—right there where the stream makes a sharp turn and continually deposits clean white sand along the contour of the curve on that bank. She remembered the place where the path opened into the small clearing among the trees leading to a convenient ford in the shallow water. Just a few steps down stream into the curve, one could swim in the cold waist-deep water, then lie on the warm sand.

Namid shook her brother, but he refused to respond.

"Misae, hurry! We go to the nut grove."

"Misae, Misae! Wake up!"

Seeing her daughter's plight, Aranck tapped a rock twice. Misae heard the command, threw his feet to the bare earth floor, and rubbed his eyes. He and Namid set about their morning chores. Misae, still sleepy-eyed and groggy, reluctantly began gathering water, firewood, and kindling. Namid interrupted her sweeping to give him a gentle swat with her broom of bound dogwood branches. She finished arranging the fur bedding and helped Misae gather the firewood and kindling. Together they ate small bowls of the stew that simmered on the cooking fire.

Aranck poured broth from the cook pot for Sayen, whose appetite had suddenly returned. She filled her stomach with bread made from maize and with broth from the stew. When Tadewi arrived, they set off quickly and as quietly as possible to avoid notice and delay by curious neighbors.

Misae and Namid took turns walking alongside Sayen, offering their shoulder for support, sweeping aside brush in her path and keeping up a friendly chatter. They were concerned and caring. They helped her over or around the occasional deadfall and slipped bits of dried fruit, nuts and parched maize to her.

That night in the flickering light of the campfire she told them about the Tuscarora raid, the death of her friend Sinopa, and the loss of her brother Tayamiti to the Tuscaroras. When she reached the part about Tayamiti, she could not restrain the tears.

Fascinated with her story, Misae and Namid saw that she grieved for her brother who was about the same age as Misae, and they drew closer together, then closer to Sayen to comfort her and to encourage her to continue.

Aranck watched her children become engrossed in Sayen's story and was pleased that they had accepted her and tried to comfort her. Sayen would be welcome in her lodge, but Aranck knew that Haw-Chi would decide. She was grateful that Massaqua had intervened and had made it clear to Haw-Chi that Aranck would care for Sayen until she recovered.

Yahou-Lakee, Tosawi, and two Nahyssan warriors recovered the weapons and ammunition from the fight with Tuscaroras. They took a careful inventory of knives, arrows, bows, spears, muskets, powder, and ball, and spent half a day cleaning them and wrapping them. About thirty paces through the tall grass of the open space near the stream, they dug a shallow trench in the soft sand deposits from past floods. Except for two muskets and a supply of ammunition, they buried the weapons and covered the cache with deadfalls and driftwood. They carefully prepared the approach and surrounding area so that the site was unnoticeable before they set out for the Monacan town.

When they reached the trail fork, they turned north toward the Monacan town and had traveled only a little way when fifteen Monacan warriors appeared in a semi-circle across the trail.

Yahou-Lakee took a deep breath and stepped forward.

"I am Yahou-Lakee, Chief of the Nahyssan."

Without a word, the Monacans surrounded them and motioned them forward. They marched into the town straight toward the longhouse. There they waited while the Monacan officials inside were notified. A warrior quickly returned and motioned Yahou-Lakee forward.

"I go alone," Yahou-Lakee said as he turned to Tosawi. "Do not leave this place." He took one of the muskets wrapped in fur and entered the longhouse where Chief Massaqua sat with the council of seniors. He stopped so that all the council was between him and Massaqua.

"I am Yahou-Lakee, Chief of the Nahyssan. I come in peace to express my appreciation for the Monacan support in our fight against the Tuscaroras. We took this fine English firestick in battle with the Tuscaroras. It is my gift to the great chief of the Monacan people."

"Yahou-Lakee, Chief of the Nahyssan, welcome," Massaqua said as he took up a long-stem pipe of tobacco and motioned Yahou-Lakee to a place before the council fire.

Yahou-Lakee laid the musket and ammunition on the fur mat before Massaqua, took his seat directly opposite Haw-Chi and waited quietly for his turn with the peace pipe.

When the pipe returned to the priest, Massaqua unfolded the bundle, laying aside the soft rabbit skins to expose the oiled steel of the long gun. He held it out with both hands for the others to admire. He examined the firing mechanism and tried the action, then shouldered it to feel the balance and fit. He then handed it to Haw-Chi, who examined it closely and passed it to the next warrior, and so on until the gun had been handled by all.

While the gun was making the rounds, Massaqua turned to Yahou-Lakee and began. "Many winters have passed since the Monacan and the Nahyssan have spoken together. Even now, we Monacans wish to remain apart. We guard our hunting grounds and consider all uninvited who enter them to be our enemies. The English press against us with their traders and settlers, and the neighboring tribes are more careless about boundaries now that the white man has come. Other Algonquin and Siouan people have traded their lands to the English. We will never. The English are our enemy, perhaps the Nahyssan trade with them. Perhaps this firestick was traded, but Monacan will never trade with the English, never give up a single piece of land to them, and will kill them when they come onto our land.

Massaqua fell silent while Yahou-Lakee considered this. Yahou-Lakee waited to see if there was more and there was.

Still looking straight into the eyes of Yahou-Lakee and speaking with a strong voice, Massaqua continued. "We meet with you today because you sent us word that the Tuscaroras were entering our hunting grounds and that you were following them. We were glad to know this. It is right that you spoke, and it is the only reason we allowed your passage and sent Monacan warriors to escort your warriors to the fleeing Tuscaroras."

Yahou-Lakee was not sure where Massaqua was going with this, but it was clear he was not laying the groundwork for a friendly alliance. He knew Haw-Chi by the descriptions Tosawi had given him, and he shifted his eyes from Massaqua to Haw-Chi enough to know the hate that Haw-Chi was feeling. Left up to Haw-Chi, there was little doubt how this visit would be handled. He waited for Massaqua to continue.

"Now you bring a gift and say you come in peace. You also bring Tosawi, the old one that almost killed our sentry, then boldly stepped into the midst of our warriors' victory ceremony and said he would leave with the captive Nahyssan woman. I still am not sure why we let him live."

Haw-Chi grunted and his eyes blazed hate at Massaqua's veiled acknowledgment of Tosawi's courage. Massaqua was growing old and he talked too much. To Haw-Chi, the Nahyssans and anyone else not of the Monacan tribe were enemies, but he remained silent.

Massaqua nodded to Yahou-Lakee who bowed his head in return, rose slowly, and spoke with carefully measured words.

"It is as you say, brave Chief. The Nahyssan and the Monacan have long lived side by side in peace, and I come to acknowledge that and to speak our thanks for the help of the Monacan people. It is also true that Tosawi and all Nahyssans mourn the loss of our daughter to the Tuscarora, but we were glad to learn that the Tuscarora surrendered her to the mighty Monacan War Chief, Haw-Chi, as a war prize. We were pleased when Tosawi told us of your great wisdom, and that she is now recovering with a Monacan family." Yahou-Lakee spoke clearly and carefully, delivering his words without passion, but with deep feeling in a way that Massaqua knew that this Chief of the Nahyssan meant exactly what he said and could be trusted.

Massaqua knew that there would be more about this woman captive and decided to make his position clear. "It is so. What I said to Tosawi remains the truth. This woman you call Sayen will be well cared for by one of our families. Make no mistake. She belongs to the Monacans by fair trade, and here she will stay. When she is well, she will become a member of a Monacan family here or in another Monacan town. We will soon know where she will be and who the family will be. Haw-Chi will tell us," Massaqua said.

There it was, just as Tosawi had said. There was no chance of the Monacans giving up Sayen without a fight and their warrior strength was double the Nahyssan. Sayen's destiny now lay with the Monacans, probably Haw-Chi himself. Fortunately, Massaqua considered the matter closed and had not prepared for negotiations. What happened next would astonish him.

"I understand," Yahou-Lakee said. "Sayen is your captive. However, if you and your War Chief Haw-Chi will agree to exchange this child of the Nahyssan, I will bring you." He stopped, watched the faces of the Monacan chiefs, then laid a green twig with six notches in the soft bark in front of Massaqua and continued. "I will bring you six more of these firesticks with powder and shot." Moving slowly, eyes locked on Massaqua, Yahou-Lakee placed another marked twig alongside the first and continued. "Twelve steel tomahawks," Placing a third marked twig, he said, "eight large steel knives…" Another twig. "…ten bows and ten quivers of arrows."

Yahou-Lakee's eyes remained on Massaqua's face which now showed surprise and confusion. Here was a wealth of arms, more than he could collect in several winters. Satisfied that Massaqua and Haw-Chi understood the meaning of his offer, Yahou-Lakee added the fifth marked twig and said, "And five war clubs in exchange for our daughter, Sayen."

The council members were pointing at the marked stems and murmuring in astonishment at such an offer, so many weapons of steel. Massaqua avoided Haw-Chi's eyes, called for silence, and spoke.

"How is it that the Nahyssan have so many steel weapons of the English?"

"They are weapons taken from the Tuscaroras in our fight in the mountains," Yahou-Lakee said. "If you want them, we will go together with our daughter to the place where the trail divides. There she can return to her people. I will go with you and we will collect what I have promised. If you choose to keep her, I thank you for receiving me, and we will leave immediately."

Yahou-Lakee had stated his offer in simple terms and Massaqua faced an unexpected choice. He knew that "leave immediately" meant war with the Nahyssan, not something that concerned him much, but could he turn down so many treasured steel weapons? Could he seize Yahou-Lakee and Tosawi and force them to disclose the location of the weapons? No. Both would die first.

"You are guests of the Monacan people. The women have prepared a feast. Stay the night, and we will celebrate your victory over the Tuscaroras. When the sun rises, you will have my answer," Massaqua said.

That night Yahou-Lakee and Massaqua spent several private hours in conversation. They spoke frankly about the pressure from the English on their borders, food supplies, and hunting and fishing territories. They spoke of the way many Indian chiefs had sold or traded lands to the English. They talked about the strange sicknesses that seemed to kill their people but not the English. They each had seen the number of their people diminish in just a few winters. Both had been the victim of Iroquois and Susquehanna raids in the past, and both acknowledged the number and power of the English. By midnight, they had formed an unspoken bond.

When Yahou-Lakee stretched out on the soft skins and allowed his body to relax for the first time in many hours, he thought of the events of the past few days and mourned the loss of his people. Only then did he let himself remember the victories and the reassurances of so many neighboring tribes. He felt sure that Massaqua would find a way to win Haw-Chi and the others to accept the weapons and release Sayen, but before he could think through what he might do tomorrow morning, sleep overcame him and he settled into a deep rest.

<u>30</u>

Deputy Sheriff Will James caught up with Governor Nicholson in the dappled shade of the live oaks near the college. Nicholson was just slipping the reins from the hitching rail and was about to mount Cheek for a ride out to Queen Mary's Port.

"Your Excellency, please forgive this interruption, but we have a message from the Nahyssan. They are gathering a large force of armed warriors from several tribes to reclaim a captive Nahyssan boy from the Tuscarora. I have sent a messenger to inform Sheriff Cowles."

Nicholson hesitated, then stepped back and laid a hand on Cheek's withers to let him know he was not going to mount. When Cheek was fresh from a night's rest, a belly full of the choicest feed, and saddled, he wanted to go. He stamped once, sidestepped and shook his head at the delay.

Nicholson smiled at the spirited antics and said, "Deputy James, it looks like you owe Cheek here the apology. Go on, please, when and where?"

"Yahou-Lakee has already sent messengers to several tribes. They are to meet at the next full moon on the Meherrin River. It sounds like armed Indians in war paint will be moving toward our southern frontier. I have messengers ready to alert the militia southward on the Occaneechi Trail and over on the south bank of the James River.

"Where on the Meherrin will they confront the Tuscarora?"

"It was not clear, Your Lordship. Probably near where the Meherrin crosses our Carolina border. That is where the nearest Tuscarora town is located."

"Did the Nahyssans ask for militia support?"

"No, sir."

"If this is true, such Indians moving about out there are sure to cause a reaction by the settlers. You did well to deploy messengers." Nicholson hesitated. "It looks like we have time to inform the militia, and I doubt the Indians will show themselves to the settlers. If they do, the militia is to allow them to pass and avoid involvement unless provoked."

As he spoke, Nicholson thought about the settlers and how serious the situation was. He wondered if this was just another Indian squabble and if it might escalate. Deputy James had mentioned *many* tribes but didn't say how many, their cause, or which tribes they were.

"You had better pay Yahou-Lakee a visit, Deputy. Arrange to join him for this event, but you must withdraw if they engage the Tuscarora. You are not to take sides, just observe. Specifically, we need to know what tribes are involved in this and how many warriors assemble."

"I will see to it, Your Lordship, and I will defer pending matters of the Sheriff's office until I return. Sheriff Cowles is over at Yorktown to find a ship for his crops, but I expect him back soon. Also, the North Carolina colony on the Pamlico River has not yet been notified. The action will not be far from them."

The Governor nodded. "I'll let Sheriff Cowles know. We will get word to the North Carolinians. There are ships leaving the James and York regularly for Charleston and the Caribbean."

Will bowed to the Governor and set out at a trot towards the stables where he almost ran into Jock Adams just leaving. Kadomico and Tree Son were with him.

"My apologies, Jock," said Will.

Jock steadied Will against the near collision and said, "Whoa, Will. What's the rush?"

Will related the news and his task to speak with the Nahyssans.

"You'll need an interpreter to get all those matters attended to. Have you thought of that?"

Will had not, and it certainly was the truth, for he did not speak a word of Siouan. But who?

"You are right, of course, and I had not thought of that. Do you think the school would let me borrow their interpreter?"

Before Jock could reply, Tree Son said, "I go. I speak English. Speak Siouan." It wasn't much English, and what he spoke was broken into syllables most of which were separated by spaces while Tree Son worked on the next syllable. He smiled a pleading smile at Jock.

"It might work, Will. It is obvious that Tree Son understood a good bit of what you said to me. Certainly it is better than no go-between at all, and you are far more likely to get the headmaster's cooperation if it is Tree Son that he is losing rather than his interpreter. Tree Son and Kadomico have been doing a passable job of conversing with my boys. I think you will get a lot of help from Tree Son."

Tree Son was ecstatic. "I go. Get Indian clothes. Come back here for Will James." Both Kadomico and Tree Son were dressed in English clothing, and Tree Son was quick to see the opportunity to shed the woolens. He looked at Kadomico for approval.

"Yes," Kadomico said. "Tree Son can help." He wished he had seen this solution the way Tree Son had seen it. More and more their minds seemed to be on different tracks. He did not know why it saddened him, but it did. Like Hawk, Tree Son would be doing manly things. How he would like to go with Tree Son and Will!

Tree Son saw that Kadomico was troubled. "It is only for three or four suns," he said in Siouan. "I will return for the school."

273

Jock, turned to Will, "I see you are almost ready to travel, Will. Stop by my house. Tree Son will be ready. I'll let the Sheriff and Governor know."

"Thanks, Jock. It will take me another hour to get a trail pack together. We'll ride double."

Jock and the boys walked toward Duke of Gloucester Street. They would be home in a few minutes.

Will walked around the stables. Two mounts remained. They had recently been fed and were waiting to be led out to pasture. He dispatched the waiting messengers, one to take one of the mounts and ride south on the Occaneechi Trail and one to cross the James River and to alert planters on the south bank.

He saddled the remaining mount, which happened to be the mare, Molly, his favorite. They would leave her at the Singleton's plantation at the mouth of the Chickahominy River, ferry across the James, and spend the night at the first plantation they came to.

The Adams family and Kadomico were waiting as Will reined over to the front yard gate. Tree Son had learned about horseback riding from Jock and his sons, so that after greetings were exchanged he stepped anxiously forward. Will freed up a stirrup and said, "Just put your foot in there and I'll give you a lift up behind me."

Tree Son wore buckskin trousers and had a quiver of arrows and his unstrung bow strapped across his bare back. Rebecca had insisted on a pouch of food for them, and Matthew brought it over to the riders and handed it up to Will.

"I thank you, Madam." Will touched the brim his hat. "We'll be off now."

To Jock, this whole business of gathering warriors in large numbers was troublesome. He was glad that Will James was making this trip, and he wished Sam Layton was here.

Will and Tree Son left the mare in the care of the Singletons, and, thanks to their offer of a canoe, they managed to cross the James and gain the nearest plantation before dark.

The next morning they borrowed a saddle horse for the trip up the Appomattox, riding as hard as the narrow trail along the heavily wooded riverbank would permit. They alerted the few settlers they encountered along the way, but did not take time to dismount and visit. Just after sundown, they caught the scent of wood smoke and rode into the first available clearing to check. There, they watched thin white wisps drift upward and vanish, smoke signals to alert the Nahyssan town that strangers had been sighted. They rode on to the first maize field separating them from the town which was situated on a small rise back from the river.

Shortly, people began to gather. Horses and riders were not unknown but still rarely seen in this remote location. A boy broke away from the crowd and approached Tree Son warily. When he realized that Tree Son spoke their language and learned why he was there, he eagerly called another boy and sent him off to alert Tonawanda of the visitors from Williamsburg.

As they drew near the town, Will turn his mount toward the river, stopped and freed up a stirrup for Tree Son to dismount. Instead, Tree Son just leaned into Will enough to bring one leg over the horse's back to join the other and slid on his stomach to the ground, eager to give up that bouncing seat and stretch his leg muscles. His first few steps were unbalanced and his feet wandered aimlessly. He no sooner got them under control than he noticed soreness in his thighs and crotch. Will dismounted and led the horse toward the shallows.

Tree Son greeted the women and children and began chatting freely with them. They remembered him from his previous visit and immediately welcomed him as a guest. Two of the youngest boys pulled on Tree Son's buckskins to get his attention while several of the women came close speaking about the Tuscarora raid and the deaths and captures. They were so excited and talked so fast that Tree Son could barely understand them, but he did learn that Red Wolf, Wiwohka, and Hawk, had been there but had gone away to their homes and that Tonawanda would speak to them.

He called to Will, "They say Yahou-Lakee is not here. Tonawanda is their chief warrior. We will see him."

In the gathering dusk of the still evening, Will slipped the saddle off horse's back and threw it over the limb of a nearby deadfall and began rubbing away the sweat and saddle marks while the horse drank deeply from cool shallows.

"Good enough. I'll stake the horse to pasture and be right with you." Will said, and then he started up the bank toward a sizeable patch of rich long-grass. There he could tether his mount to a young maple tree for the night.

Just as the crowd began to part to make way for a tall Nahyssan warrior, armed only with a sheathed knife, Will walked over to his young interpreter.

"Well, Tree Son, it looks like it is time for you to go to work."

"It is Tonawanda," Tree Son said in his best English. Will raised his open hand in the gesture of peace. He had never met Tonawanda, but from the behavior of the crowd, it was apparent that he was a respected leader, and Will stepped forward to meet him.

"I am Deputy Sheriff Will James. This is my friend Tree Son of the Saponi. I speak for our Governor, Francis Nicholson. I have a message for Chief Yahou-Lakee."

Tree Son stood proudly alongside Will and translated. He spoke a little more loudly than necessary trying to follow Will's tone and emphasis of the names and titles, but it was a credible job.

"Welcome, Will James and Tree Son" Tonawanda said. "Follow me. We will talk, and you will stay for a proper Nahyssan welcome." They walked through the center of the town toward a longhouse stationed at the far wall beyond several cooking fires where women were busy preparing various dishes. Some were drying fish and small animals. Others worked pots or hot stones covered with dough. Children were stacking firewood. Warriors were cleaning and adjusting weapons. Some repairing leggings, moccasins, and breechclouts by the light of the fires. Will noticed the order and industry. Every soul was busy.

They entered the roundhouse alone. Tonawanda led them to the center where the ground was covered with straw and fur mats arranged about a smoldering fire. Tonawanda began relating the story and drawing maps in the sandy floor by motioning and by saying the names of tribes and places. Tree Son was excited to learn about the captives and the fight with the Tuscaroras. To be included in such matters was unusual for one so young. He began to realize the advantages of speaking English, something he had totally missed in the classes at the school. Soon three women came with dried venison, large pots of stew, and several varieties of small nut and fruitcakes.

Tonawanda drew an impressive map in the packed earth near the fire. Will quickly recognized the Atlantic Ocean and the James and several other rivers. He did not understand certain symbols, but by their location, guessed they were landmarks of some sort. By comparing the distances that Tonawanda had shown between Williamsburg and the Nahyssan town, he could see that the trip to the Meherrin was two or three days on foot.

They worked at it until late in the night and resumed the next day. By the time they were finished, Will and Tree Son knew exactly where and when they would meet on the Meherrin, the tribes that were participating, and they had a fair idea of the expected strength. In the process, a kind of understanding and trust grew between them and Tonawanda. In nine days when the moon is full, Will would return and travel with them. Tree Son was disappointed to learn that he would be excluded because the Nahyssans had arranged for an English interpreter to travel with them to speak to any settlers, traders, or militia that they might encounter.

Will and Tree Son departed the next morning to return to Williamsburg.

The fires in the Saponi longhouse burned low over glowing coals of hardwood. Chief Custoga had assembled the council to hear Red Wolf. He assured them that Kadomico was well and engaged in the school, but he concluded that the school was a waste of time—much talk but not of war, hunting, games, or contests.

"They speak only of the English words and the English God," Red Wolf said. "The English are many and many more will come. They clear the land and fence it for themselves. Indians are rarely seen in the town. Most have been killed, died from the white man's sickness, or have been kept in places called reservations," he said. He avoided describing the power and wealth he had observed, said nothing of the cannon, guns, and vast quantities of powder, and did not mention the wonders of the blacksmiths at work.

"How were you treated?" asked Custoga.

"I wanted only to leave that place. Their food is terrible and their houses are like caves—hot and no air."

"Why did you return so soon and without Kadomico?"

This question pleased Red Wolf. It gave him the chance to tell of his part in the Nahyssan battle with the Tuscarora.

"On our way to the English town, we came to the town of the Nahyssan. There we met with Chief Yahou-Lakee. He sends his warm greeting to Custoga and the Saponi. He gave us food, canoes, and warrior escorts to the place where we were to meet Sam Layton. While his warriors were with us, a band of Tuscarora attacked the Nahyssan. Two killed. Two captured. I returned to assist Yahou-Lakee."

Red Wolf continued until he had described the fight with the Tuscaroras in exciting detail. The council members nodded and made an acknowledging noise with gourd rattles, rocks, or sticks at every exploit related to them of this Saponi warrior's bravery and deeds of battle.

Choola, father of Custoga and retired chief of the tribe, was the loudest of all listeners. This was the way of the Saponi. Here was a story to be told and retold. Choola bathed in the memory of such deeds. Custoga, wisely, did not restrain his ancient father's enthusiasm, although listening to Red Wolf he longed all the more to hear his son's version of Williamsburg.

Red Wolf went on to describe the plight of the boy and girl captives, receiving more applause when he related Tosawi's story of the fight Sayen gave the Monacans. He finally came to the deeds of the great warrior Tonawanda and his single-handed confrontation with the whole Tuscarora nation, embellishing and adding so that by the time he finished, every listener had developed an abiding respect and admiration for the Nahyssan warriors and a renewed respect for their own Red Wolf.

Red Wolf continued. "In nine suns when the moon is full," "Tonawanda will return to the Meherrin River, meet the Tuscaroras with his captive Kajika and exchange him for the Nahyssan boy, Tayamiti. Yahou-Lakee asks that all Siouan tribes send warriors to meet him there. Together they will make a great show of strength to the Tuscarora. I will go."

A silence fell over the Council. In just fifty years, war and disease had reduced their count of warriors and hunters to less than forty. This union was important. Brothers in arms against a common enemy gave them a sense of renewed hope and confidence in their ever-present struggle for hunting grounds and the safety of their town and fields of maize and other food.

Custoga agreed to assemble twenty-five warriors to follow him and Red Wolf to the Tonawanda camp near the Meherrin the day before the full moon. Four young women would follow the warriors and tend their campsites.

They had seven suns to prepare. The women would package trail food, repair spare moccasins and leggings, and fill tiny gut pouches with war paint and medicine for the wounded. The priest would prepare sacrificial food, gather their rattles and masks, and mentally rehearse the prayers and stories they would sing. Warriors would assemble war clubs, arrows, greased bows, and secure the weapons they needed for travel and battle.

On the day before departure, a large mound of firewood would be laid in the center of the town. There would be late-night dancing and story-telling at the fire. The next morning, there would be a send-off ceremony and feast honoring the warriors, after which a slow drumbeat would begin and the warriors would pass through the town in single file.

The day before the prisoner exchange, Chiefs Yahou-Lakee and Custoga met at Tonawanda's campsite. It was located about two hundred paces from the Meherrin River and well shielded by the dense forest. They stood knee-deep in a large open meadow of yarrow and golden rod broken here and there by white patches of Queen Anne's Lace. A thick green perimeter of stately red cedars bordered the meadow. The main town of the Tuscaroras occupied high ground across the river.

For Yahou-Lakee and Custoga, it had been a warm day of fast traveling through forests of brilliantly colored falling leaves broken occasionally by soft carpets of pine needles. In the dwindling twilight, each with a band of warriors behind him, they raised their open hands in peace. They stood apart, alone, facing one another. The wrinkles at their eyes and the dusty gray hair mingling with the black beneath their feathered badges of leadership confirmed the years since they had fought together against the Iroquois raiders. Tonawanda laid down a huge stone for the cooking fire and watched.

"I am Yahou-Lakee, Chief of all Nahyssan." The chief raised his voice to be sure that the Saponi warriors heard."

"I am Chief Custoga of the Saponi."

They came together grasping forearms, barely able to conceal their emotions, but making sure to announce their friendship to both bands of warriors. Red Wolf stood close behind Custoga, eager to move his warriors to a campsite and prepare for sun-up.

"Red Wolf spoke of your kindnesses and the help the Nahyssan gave to him. He told us of the attack on your town and the battle with the Tuscarora. We are here to follow Tonawanda."

Yahou-Lakee knew that so many warriors from the Saponi town came at serious risk to the Saponi people. An unprotected town is an easy target for roaming raiders. His thanks were genuine.

"We will be finished here before the sun is high," Yahou-Lakee said. "We have searched carefully. There are no Tuscaroras on this side of the river, and although our strength continues to grow, we will hold Nahyssan vengeance for another time. The Nottoway and Occaneechi are camping to the east. When they arrive, the Shakori, Meherrin, and Monahoc will form a line between our camp and the Occaneechi. Their messengers have told us that they are now preparing campsites."

While they spoke, a runner emerged from the wilderness, approached Tonawanda and reported. "Thirty Tutelo warriors will arrive by nightfall."

Tonawanda gave him instructions. "Say that we are proud to have the Tutelos, and tell them to join the Saponi at the riverside. There they will form a line of campsites—the more campfires, the better. I will visit them this night,"

Red Wolf led the Saponi party back toward the Meherrin and camped a quarter-mile from the point of exchange. The Occhaneechi were camped similarly a quarter mile downstream. Beyond the river bank, campfires began to glow, close enough to the river that the Tuscaroras could see them, but not close enough for them to count the warriors assembling there. Laid with green tree branches, brush, grass, and pine straw, the fires formed clouds of thick smoke that rose upward through the nearly bare limbs of the trees and drifted over the Tuscarora town, warning, threatening, taunting.

When the last light of the setting sun faded away, starlight spread across a clear sky. Soon drums from the camps behind the great black trees began beating a slow call to war. Barely visible from the Tuscarora side of the Meherrin and back-lighted by the fires, black silhouettes of dancing warriors made an eerie scene. By midnight the full moon had risen to light the forest where over three hundred dancers paraded before campfires, grotesque in their costumes, body paint and masks.

Late into the night, Tonawanda walked from camp to camp, meeting the leaders, encouraging the men, and bringing news to them of the extent of this unusual force of Indians, a gathering that would be told and retold among the Indian tribes of Virginia and North Carolina. The message was clear. Make no mistake, Tuscaroras. Only the safe return of Tayamiti will prevent your destruction.

Custoga and Yahou-Lakee also walked the line of camps together and talked past midnight. Before they parted, they had agreed to meet again at the end of the hunting season with eight Siouan chiefs of Virginia and North Carolina. They would talk of their hunting grounds, food supplies and common enemies: the English, Tuscarora, Iroquois and others. They set the time and chose a well-known place on the Roanoke River in Occaneechi territory. The place was within three-day's travel of the eight Siouan tribes and near the North Carolina-Virginia border. It was not far northwest of where they were presently camped.

Deputy Will James could hardly believe the easy discipline, unspoken commands, and orderly procession of so many different tribes. Nor had he or anyone else in Williamsburg seen so many fully armed warriors since the massacre of 1644. He did not feel threatened, but he was uneasy at the size of the army before him when he thought of the damage it could do.

The sun rose in a splendor of warm colors splashing over hills, grassland, and the Meherrin River. War drums began to beat faster as the warriors moved silently past the ashes of the campfires. They spread out arms-length apart on either side of the canoe waiting at the water's edge. When they were in position, Tonawanda appeared with the naked Kajika, his arms bound tightly behind him. Across the river, a band of Tuscarora warriors gathered with a small boy.

31

Will James briefed Sheriff Cowles, and together, they located the Governor at his office. Will James began his report. "Your Lordship, there were well over three hundred warriors there on the bank of that river. I have never witnessed so many armed Indians. I believe more than six tribes were there with their chiefs." Will's excitement caused him to catch his breath between phrases.

"Did the settlers become involved in any way? Were any of them harmed?" Nicholson asked.

"Not a single one that I know of, Your Lordship. The chiefs made it clear that no white man was to be harmed."

"Then I think this may be good news indeed. Go on. Tell me everything you know, especially about the leaders of the tribes."

Will explained as much as he knew of the operation that retrieved a captive Nahyssan boy without firing a shot and named several of the participating tribes and their chiefs. He pointed out their ability to notify so many widely separated tribes in such a short time. It was impressive enough to cause him to question it, but he could not deny that people from as much as three-day's travel came to join Tonawanda on the Meherrin. He emphasized the discipline and military strategies that seemed to be wordlessly executed. Their warriors simply materialized out of the forest, quietly, unobserved, responding to motions of their leaders. How they managed to come so far, from so many directions, and to assemble at exactly the same time and location, he could not explain.

"It was as though they have been preparing for months, but they couldn't have. Yet, they came together and moved like clockwork," Will said.

"Sheriff Cowles, let us take a walk with Will here," Nicholson said, touching his handkerchief to his neck. "These rooms are shielded from what little breeze there is." The sheriff did not miss the Governor's sudden arrangement for privacy, and Nicholson did not disappoint him.

"Will, you say these people are of one language—Siouan?"

"Yes, Your Lordship. It is so."

"And they are mostly located on our borders or the frontier?"

"It is true, Your Lordship."

"And is there any reason you can think of that the chiefs might not want to meet again?"

Will winced at the realization that he had failed to mention the chief's plan to meet again. Of course, it would be important, maybe the most important, and he very much wanted to be seen as one who knew that.

"None, Your Lordship. In fact, they have agreed to meet again on the second full moon. I figure that to be about the 11th day of December. They chose another place not far up the Meherrin River from where they met this time. I believe eight tribes will attend. Custoga of the Saponi and Yahou-Lakee of the Nahyssan seem to be the leaders." Will spoke with the strongest voice he could command to divert attention from his oversight.

"Sheriff, this is better than anything I could have hoped for. In spite of an indifferent House of Burgesses and Council absorbed in their own fortunes, we may yet get something done about our frontier borders and communities. The Indians need protection, hunting grounds, and supplies from the English. We need protection on our frontiers and more land for settlement. There is enough land here for all. As for the supplies, we can easily provide the cloth, guns and steel tools they seek. The only thing missing is an opportunity to sit down and talk it out. Here is such an opportunity. Is it not so, Sheriff?"

"Of course, Your Lordship," Cowles said but he was thinking about his tobacco barns bulging with the recent harvest, disappearing demand, and record low prices. And with piracy raging at an all-time high right in his own backyard, the Governor would do better to focus his energy on the matters at hand. But he wisely held his tongue.

"Deputy Will," Nicholson said, "send word of this to Sam Layton in the Shawnee settlement beyond the western frontier. I want him to know what you have told me. I want him to know that I would welcome him to accompany me to this meeting, or if he prefers, he can come as a representative of the Shawnee. I am sure he would be a welcome addition to this group. Tell him that it is an opportunity for the Indians of Virginia to speak as one to the English. He will understand."

"I will see to it, Your Lordship," Will said.

Turning to Cowles, Nicholson said, "Sheriff, we must contact Yahou-Lakee and Custoga immediately, while they are fresh with this idea of a gathering, and let them know that we wish to speak to them there. We can make a trade agreement with them and provide weapons for mutual protection against outlaw raiders and the Tuscarora. I am thinking of some sort of union among them like the one they just demonstrated, but this one could be specifically for trading and protection on the frontier. They might form a confederation like the Iroquois, maybe make a treaty that provides for boundaries, hunting and fishing rights, a fort, trading posts."

Cowles did not show his concern with this impetuous reaction so typical of Nicholson. When his passion rose on a matter, the man just blocked out all reason and opposition. Now he was about to proceed on serious colony business without counsel of the colony officials, some of whom were Crown appointed and others elected. What worried Cowles most of all was the appearance that he was an accomplice. He decided to risk a caution.

"I take your point, Your Lordship," he said. "Whoever carries your message, the chiefs must find them trustworthy and believable. There is not a man in my acquaintance or employ that can speak to an Indian as an equal or be convincing in his respect and sincerity. Too many carry grievances, whether real, contrived, or mistaken. I know none that I would trust with a mission of this nature. And as you know, you and I will be several more days at the trial of the pirates our navy defeated last summer."

"Find Jock Adams and tell him to see me at once." Nicholson turned in disgust and headed back to the college. He did not want to hear how difficult the sheriff found his idea. A highly decorated and favored soldier in the Kings army, Nicholson expected action when he gave an order. Sheriff Cowles, like most of these fat planters, could use two or three years in His Majesty's army. Where did these nay-saying sheep come from?

Nicholson stood with his hands behind him staring out the window of his office at the college, clearly lost in thought. Jock Adams entered the room."Your Lordship?" he said to the Governor's back.

"Come in, Jock. Sit down. I need your help." Nicholson turned to his visitor and took a seat opposite him at a small table by the window. He went straight to the point, repeating what he had just learned and what he had done about notifying Sam Layton.

"The Virginia government must be represented at that meeting," Nicholson concluded. "I need a man to meet with Yahou-Lakee and Custoga and arrange for me to address that Indian assembly. Can you do that?"

"I can, Your Lordship. I speak but little Siouan and will need an interpreter, one who can be trusted in the presence of these Indian leaders. A wrong word or act can easily be misinterpreted."

"I knew it!" Nicholson loved Jock's enthusiastic response.. "You are a valuable subject of the Crown, Jock Adams. Find your interpreter. He is yours for whatever time you need him, my promise."

Jock didn't hesitate. "Kadomico, son of Chief Custoga, and his friend Tree Son, will accompany me. I will notify the Schoolmaster that they have been granted a two-week leave of absence beginning tomorrow morning."

Nicholson's eyes flew open. He leaned back in his chair, squinted at Jock suspiciously before he recovered enough to realize that he had been checkmated by his own words. Kadomico, the only surviving Indian student, was to be his prize report to the Crown—successful education and conversion of an Indian boy. Now Jock Adams was about to interrupt what looked to be a stand-alone certain success. On the other hand, couldn't this mission become a part of the school's program? The report to the Crown could even be stronger. *Young Indian student, after only eight weeks in training at the College of William and Mary, assists colony officials in negotiations with frontier Indians.* Of course! The King and Queen would be pleased. The colony would have its first trained go-betweens. With the son of the chief of the Saponi assisting Jock Adams, he could count on a certain welcome at the meeting of the Indian chiefs. The headmaster must drop everything and focus the next two weeks on preparing Kadomico for this meeting.

"Done," he said, "And Jock, never mind speaking to the headmaster. I will see him here and explain what is to be done as soon as he is free from classes. Tell Kadomico tonight, and prepare him for extended school days and accelerated learning for the next two weeks."

"Then we leave in two weeks, Your Lordship." Jock bowed and left the room before he let his mind deal with the impact of what had just happened. Immediately, he wished he had said "four weeks" instead of two. It would take some doing to get his affairs in order and prepare for two weeks absence from his business and family. At times like this, he badly needed a partner. He wished Sam Layton had accepted his offer.

As he walked home, Jock recalled that the Governor had not mentioned Tree Son. He smiled at the realization that Tree Son, as a student, had been dismissed in the minds of the Governor, headmaster, and Reverend. So likeable, devoted to Kadomico, and respectful to all, but so oblivious to the business of schooling, they saw him simply as Kadomico's companion, nothing more. Yet, Tree Son had so endeared himself to the Adams family that it was going to be difficult to see him go, and for young Luke who idolized him, it would be very bad indeed. It occurred to Jock that Tree Son might not return with Kadomico, and he winced at the thought.

"Come in, Headmaster." Nicholson waved Arrington to a chair. "Sit down. We have a problem. Reverend Blair will be here shortly."

From the look on Nicholson's face, Arrington worried that this was not going to be pleasant. To be called abruptly to the Governor's office was bad enough. To be called in with the college President, Reverend James Blair, was outright ominous. Nicholson's reputation for firing, arresting, berating, and evicting subjects of the colony was well known. He could be quick, rude, and ruthless, and Arrington searched his immediate past for careless words or deeds that might have caused this summons.

"While we are waiting, tell me how your work is going with the Indians," Nicholson said.

Arrington caught his breath in fear that the Governor was about to reproach him for Tree Son's poor showing. He had reported Tree Son's stubborn resistance to schooling to President Blair, and they had agreed that Tree Son came not as a student but as a companion for Kadomico—strictly in accordance with the Governor's invitation. Nervously, Arrington decided to put the best face possible on the answer.

"Very well indeed, Your Lordship. This remaining student is a credit to his people. He is sincere, curious, and anxious to learn. Still, I am surprised at how much English he understands. Of course, I have devoted many hours to bring about this progress."

"Can he speak English words well enough to be understood?"

"Yes, at this point for the most part he knows only nouns and verbs, but he speaks clearly about daily matters—greetings, go, come, eat, pray, read, write, sleep, work, and so on." Arrington took all the credit, avoiding the Adams family's important influence on Kadomico's progress.

Reverend Blair, president of the college, came to the door. Nicholson neither rose nor looked at him as he waved the president to a seat. That informal treatment and the blatant lack of manners in the presence of the school's headmaster just fueled the president's anger at being summoned by the governor without notice or explanation. Although both he and Nicholson were favorites of the King and had once worked together vigorously to found the College of William and Mary, lately, they opposed each other bitterly in the House and Council meetings. Their close friendship was history now, but they both continued to be active and formidable as ever in the business of Virginia.

Arrington rose respectfully and remained standing until Blair was seated.

"Reverend," Nicholson began, "I hope you will understand and forgive the immediacy of this request for your assistance when you learn of the urgency. As you know, our people continue to die at the hands of the savages on our southern and western frontiers. The wilderness between the rivers and between the coast and the western mountains is all that remains for settlement, but without roads and rivers for supply, building and planting there is too dangerous. A mix of about fifteen Siouan and Algonquian-speaking tribes occupy that land—maybe 3,000 souls in all, if you count the nearby Carolina tribes. They have always been independent and one or two of them shun any sort of contact with the English."

290

"Yes, all that is well known," Blair said. He groaned impatiently. This was more of Nicholson's campaign to send militia and cannon into the wilderness to build new forts and open up new land for settlement. The Council and the House had refused him several times. The costs in men, arms and supplies were simply more than the Colony could bear.

"Most of these tribes are eager to have English supplies and they welcome traders," Nicholson continued. "We have only to organize them into forts and trading posts on our borders to have the protection we need for more wilderness settlements. The possibilities are staggering and the costs most reasonable."

"Come, Governor. Surely you don't think that 3,000 bow-and-arrow savages wandering about in the wilderness at war with each other and the white man can be organized. That is laughable. Be serious."

"They already are, Reverend. They met last week, three hundred armed warriors, six tribes with their chiefs and war chiefs. They met against a common enemy and settled an issue without firing a shot. Deputy Will James witnessed it." Nicholson paused when he saw Blair's expression change from impatience and aggravation to interest and disbelief.

"It is true. They assembled on our southern border and confronted the Tuscarora, more than three hundred, the deputy said, probably six tribes, maybe eight. Furthermore, the chiefs agreed to meet again to discuss their common issues, hunting grounds, fishing, land, and the sicknesses among them. That is what has been missing, Reverend—the ability to work with them as a group."

"You don't see them as a threat?" Blair asked with growing interest.

"No, not at this point anyhow. They need our cloth, steel, and medicines. We need land that is safe to settle and we need protection on our southern border. Can we work these issues out to the advantage of both? We won't know the answer to that until we talk. Adams will leave in two weeks to speak to the two leaders of the assembly: Chief Custoga of the Saponi and Chief

Yahou-Lakee of the Nahyssan. He will arrange for us to address their assembly on the Roanoke River in November."

"I see no harm in that, Governor, and it may have favorable consequences for the colony, but why do you tell me?"

"One of our God-directed and Crown-ordered responsibilities is to convert the savages to Christianity. You have carried this sacred burden almost alone, opening your church and tirelessly promoting the establishment of this college. If we can establish an agreement to work this closely with the Indians, we will open countless opportunities to teach and convert. Your support is critical in the long run. For now, however, Jock Adams needs the help of the student Indian with which Headmaster here has had so much success. We need to accelerate his training over the next two weeks and prepare him to act as a go-between for Jock's visit to the Saponi and Nahyssan. It means that we cut this semester short by two weeks and resume with the spring semester."

"What do you say to that, Headmaster?" Blair asked. For all Nicholson's rudeness and arrogance, the Governor did make a reasonable case for pursuing attendance at this alleged meeting.

"Why yes, Reverend Blair. I can do that. It will just take a bit of rearranging of the school schedules," Arrington said.

"Fine," Nicholson said. "Jock will work with you on what is most critical for Kadomico to know." Then he turned to Blair. "A committee of three councilmen and Jock will meet with me at Dyer's Ordinary for dinner this evening. Can you join us?"

"Yes. I will be there." For the sake of the school, Blair thought it best to stay close to the decisions about to be made in regard to this matter of schooling Indians at the college.

Tree Son lay on his back staring into the unmarked blackness of the room. He, Jock, and Kadomico were to leave at dawn for the Nahyssan town, then on to his Saponi town. He had barely slept. His mind flashed back and forth with visions of the trip back to his people and the life he knew and loved. With eyes wide open, he lay still under a quilted blanket thinking of his favorite fishing places and hunting grounds. This is the time that the nuts of the oaks and hickories beckon the animals. One had only to be still and listen to hear the squirrel cutting the shells high in the massive hardwoods. And with the trees nearly bare of leaves, there was less cover to shield them. Already their fur was thickening in preparation for the winter and would bring a better trade or make a warmer garment. His mind wandered endlessly. Sleep was impossible.

After a while, he gave up and slipped out into the dark, careful not to disturb the Adams family. He had left his travel pack on the front porch. Now, dressed only in his breechclout, he stepped outside the back door holding his buckskins under his arm. He winced at the bitter cold wind, tried to ignore it, but began to shiver. Shivering was a new experience, something he had been conditioned against since infancy. He no longer wore the protective bear grease, his English clothes and indoor living had reduced his tolerance for cold.

He unrolled his buckskin clothing and pulled it on. It helped, but the cold wind whipped at him until he found the protection of the front porch. As he sat alone on the porch this moonless night, he stroked the smooth curves of his bow and anticipated the trip before him. He had said his goodbyes to the Adams boys last night.

Suddenly, the call of the black-billed cuckoo, rapid, repetitive, *coocoocoo*, followed by a single chirp, pierced the night.

Tree Son smiled. He was not the only one who could not sleep. He returned the call and waited until he heard a pebble drop to guide him. He then moved silently toward the gate, straining to see through the cold, foggy darkness, and joined Kadomico, but neither spoke until they were well clear of the house. In the past two weeks, they had barely seen each other. Kadomico had been keeping long hours at the college. He studied after the evening meal break and often arrived at the Adams home after bedtime. To expand his vocabulary beyond the daily usage and church matters, Headmaster Arrington regularly assigned him more than he could possibly accomplish alone.

He learned many of the words of the craftsmen, merchants, and sailors. He learned how to pronounce words of government long before he could understand their meaning: Burgesses, laws, King and Queen, Britain, taxes, crime, barristers and court. Very often, someone from the school or church tutored him. Kadomico willingly immersed himself in these drills to the exclusion of everything else, including his friend Tree Son, who had stopped going to the school.

Now, unable to sleep, they walked silently away from the buildings where barking dogs might betray them, and found a place protected from the wind, part way down in one of the ravines.

"I could not sleep either," Kadomico said. "I heard your restless turning across the room and left there just before you. The buckskins feel good."

"You have not forgotten how to move silently, Kadomico. I did not hear you. I am ready to travel."

"We could not get very far in this mist and darkness, even if Jock was ready." Kadomico replied.

<u>32</u>

Tree Son was glad to be with Kadomico again. "It is good to have some time to talk," he said. "When I went to the Nahyssan town with Deputy Will James, I learned many English words and spoke for him to Tonawanda. You remember Tonawanda. He paddled behind you on the trip to join Sam Layton at the two rivers."

"Yes, he is a great warrior."

"He told me that Chief Yahou-Lakee had gone to the Monacan town and brought Sayen home. He said that to buy her release, they had given the Monacans all the weapons his warriors had taken from the Tuscaroras."

Kadomico was not ready for the reaction that the name Sayen sent surging through his young body. These past days his mind, body, and soul had been immersed in the teachings of the Headmaster and others. Now his heart raced, releasing a flush of blood that made him feel light-headed, and a glaze of moisture formed in his eyes. Fighting to gain control of these strange sensations, he shook his shoulders as though casting off a coverlet and waited for Tree Son to continue.

"Tonawanda is the father of Sayen." Tree Son spoke softly to the misty outline of Kadomico shrouded in darkness.

Her father! Kadomico reeled with the thought. He tried to recall the words he had with Tonawanda on that trip to meet Sam Layton. His mind was not processing the information and he felt confused. He could only remember how strong and powerful Tonawanda looked. He summoned what he could remember of

Tonawanda, and the thoughts rolled like an avalanche. So, both the captives were children of Tonawanda. He remembered being told that Tonawanda led the attack on the Tuscaroras, and afterwards, he led the great gathering of warriors to retrieve the boy, his own son.

What must he think of a Saponi in an English school wearing strange clothes while he, Tonawanda, battled for his people! He had not even gone with Red Wolf and Wiwohka to offer his help. Sayen, daughter of such a warrior as Tonawanda, would choose to be with a skillful hunter, a fierce warrior, not someone who had yet to take a deer or bear. He could never approach Tonawanda for permission to see her.

Following all the fantasies he had dreamed after that first meeting, he had become immersed in learning the way of the English. With the passage of time, his thoughts of Sayen had become less passionate and frequent until, after a while, there were days when he did not think of her at all. Yet, she never faded permanently, and when he did think of her, his pulse quickened. Now he faced reality—for him, she was out of reach. He quickly relived the moment in the canoe when Sayen's raven black hair had brushed his thigh as she bent over the canoe gunwale to place a small gift next to him.

He snapped back to the present when he heard Jock's favorite hound, Red, strike their trail. Immediately the big dog appeared. He scrambled down the steep bank and reared onto Tree Son's shoulders throwing him back into the fresh fallen blanket of leaves.. Jock was laughing as he stood above them on the edge of the steep slope.

"Doesn't surprise me you two want to get an early start, but we English like to eat before we set out on such a trip as we have before us. Come along. Rebecca will have her table set by the time we get back," Jock said.

Jock was dressed in the familiar buckskins of the frontier. Much to Tree Son's relief, Jock had decided earlier that he would not use horses on this trip; too much trouble to care for, and filled with marshes and thick undergrowth in places, the wilderness beyond was good reason to travel light. He had armed himself with pistols instead of his long gun. The boys had bows and arrows. When they ran out of the food Rebecca provided, they would eat whatever the forest and streams offered.

As they returned to his home, Jock's thoughts turned back to his days as a young captive of the Iroquois, adopted into the tribe and in training to be a warrior. During those times, he had learned about trail travel and endurance. He looked forward to being in the company of Indian people over the next few days, confident that Chiefs Yahou-Lakee and Custoga would allow an English representative to attend their meeting in December.

After a good meal, Rebecca, Matthew, and Mark gave them handshakes and pats on the back and best wishes for a safe journey. Refusing to wake so early at Mark's nudging, Luke remained snuggled deeply in his covers. Rebecca defied the usual reserved demeanor of Kadomico and Tree Son and let her maternal instincts and affection for them rule. She hugged them like they were her own. Both boys froze in her embrace, not sure what to do, until Kadomico spoke in English. "Rebecca, you will come to our Saponi town. You will be our family—and Mark, and Matthew, and Luke."

It was not what he meant to say, but what he meant to say was perfectly clear to Rebecca. These were her boys while they were in Williamsburg and they were glad to be. Here was a bond not to be broken.

The rising sun brushed the night away and made the low ground mist easier for travel as the three set out afoot toward the Chickahominy town and the Singleton plantation. There they would cross the James River and move on to the Nahyssan town. They would become as much a part of the country before them as the wild animals living there, equally threatened by missteps, storms, swollen rivers, marshes, and obscure trails. With winter coming, food would soon be scarce in the wilderness. But now in late October, nuts and certain root plants like tuckahoe were plentiful, and with the streams uncommonly low, there would be plenty of fish. They would be on the trail about ten days and visit several tribes, but of these, the Nahyssan and Saponi were the most important.

About a quarter mile before they reached the Singleton house, they came to a large field where several field hands were gleaning maize. Jock sent one of the young field hands running ahead to alert the Singletons of their arrival and let them know that they would need passage to the other side of the James.

Tom Singleton met them well before they arrived. When Jock declined his invitation to visit and asked for a lift over to the other side, Tom changed course. They followed him to the riverbank where he had a twenty-foot dugout canoe. They rested there while Tom found another paddler to help him bring the dugout back.

"Boys, you have the best of me," Jock said as he removed one boot from a painful foot while they rested near the water. "These boots have got to go if I am to survive this trip."

Tree Son laughed. "There is more boot there than is needed to carry you safely, and what is not needed bites you." He spaced his English words to select just the ones required. Jock smiled at the wisdom of one so young. He hoped to find a pair of moccasins in the Nahyssan town.

They camped that night on the Appomattox and feasted from the packs Rebecca had prepared. As they enjoyed the smokeless warmth radiating from a generous circle of hardwood coals, Jock talked about the purpose of this trip.

"What we are trying to do will not be easy," he said. "But there is reason to hope that your people and mine can find a way to work together. Many of the best hunting grounds have already fallen to the white man, sometimes in fair trade but often not. So it will not be easy to earn the trust of your people. Nor will many of the English, especially those who have suffered great personal losses to Indian war parties, be easily convinced that your people can be trusted."

Kadomico asked Jock to explain what he meant by the word trust, since it seemed to be so important to what they were doing on this trip, and they talked for a long time. They practiced translating what they would say to Yahou-Lakee and Custoga. Finally, Jock glanced at Tree Son, long since wrapped in his bearskin enjoying a sound sleep.

"I think Tree Son is setting a fine example. Get some sleep, Kadomico. I'll take the first watch and wake Tree Son for his turn, then get some sleep myself."

"I will, and Tree Son will wake me for my part of the watch."

In the morning, when they had bathed and eaten a little, they set out briskly, inspired by the chill of the late October season. They traveled single file over the narrow trail. As this was Tree Son's second trip over this trail, Jock asked him to lead the way. They traveled most of the day without stopping. By late afternoon, they stepped out of the shrub-and-sapling-bordered trail to a clearing where the ashes of many campfires suggested the popularity of this access to the crystal-like waters of the Appomattox.

"This is where the Nahyssans met us when I came here with Deputy James. Look there!" Tree Son pointed to distant smoke signals that were probably announcing their presence to the town.

Jock barely had time to look before six armed Nahyssans from the town stood before them. The warriors recognized Tree Son from his previous visits. When it was clear who the others were and why they were here, two of the Nahyssans trotted back toward the town. The remaining warriors divided, two in front and two behind to escort them.

When they reached the clearing around the town, Jock motioned the boys to either side of him and they marched three abreast to meet Tonawanda now striding toward them.

"It is Tonawanda," Tree Son said to Jock. "Raise your hand in peace. It means you are our leader."

Tonawanda returned the peace gesture and remained silent.

"Kadomico, say that I am Jock Adams and that I speak for Governor Nicholson of the Virginia Colony. Tell him that the Governor sends his congratulations to Chief Yahou-Lakee and the Nahyssan people for their victory over the Tuscaroras and the return of the Nahyssan children."

Kadomico spoke so easily and clearly that even Tree Son was astonished to hear his friend translating precisely in Siouan.

"Great Warrior, Son of the mighty Chief Yahou-Lakee, father of the famous Sayen who battled against her captives and father of a son captured by the Tuscaroras."

Kadomico continued. "Tonawanda, War Chief of the Nahyssan, this is Jock Adams. He speaks for the leader of the white people who is called Governor. The Governor knows of the brave deeds of Chief Yahou-Lakee and the warriors of the Nahyssan, and he is glad for the return of the Nahyssan captives."

Kadomico translated, instinctively adding the manners and protocols of Indians and those of English. Along with his schooling came a sharp sensitivity to the differences between English and Indian customs. He added and deleted words and gestures as necessary for clarity and to avoid offense or confusion. Jock sensed these changes by watching Kadomico's expression, gestures, and various shifts in the tone of his voice. He was surprised, proud, and immensely pleased at this unexpected skill. It reminded him of Sam Layton. He resolved that on this trip he would begin to learn the Siouan tongue. Rebecca and the boys had already learned many Siouan words from Tree Son and Kadomico, and so could he.

"You are Kadomico. I know you. You rode my canoe to the James River. Many spoke about you when we were on the Meherrin and Deputy Will James and Chief Custoga of the Saponi told of your training with the English."

Tonawanda grasped Kadomico's forearm. This was the highest praise Kadomico had ever known. He had not thought of what he was doing in the school as "training with the English." To be acknowledged in this way by so great a warrior almost overwhelmed him and did overwhelm Tree Son, whose mouth dropped open as Kadomico and Tonawanda stood locked in a gesture of trust and friendship.

"Tell Jock Adams he is welcome. Follow me and we will go to Yahou-Lakee."

They marched abreast of Tonawanda into the little town of bark-covered roundhouses located along the palisade walls. Almost half the town was a cleared space of packed earth where women tended food over small smokeless cooking fires. The townspeople were busy at every-day living. They laughed and chatted, teased and scolded the children at play, and called greetings to Tonawanda and his guests. A group of five older boys trotted toward the entrance, stopped, and then stepped aside to watch their war chief pass. Kadomico heard one of them hiss, "White devil!"

Tonawanda turned his head enough to identify the speaker, and without breaking stride, moved on.

As Jock walked among these people, something long forgotten stirred within him. Naked children of all ages played hard. They ran, jumped, and wrestled with boundless energy. Their laughter, squeals of delight, and calls to each other rang forth as loud as their young lungs would permit. The women were mostly naked to the waist, stirring the pots, kindling the fires, or scraping hides. Some sat sewing, mending, plaiting or occupied with other crafts. They were expert at making most anything useful to them or their families. They watched the antics of the children and smiled or scolded as mothers do, and they chatted continuously while tending their tasks.

The scenes and the scent of the cooking food, mingled with wood smoke, jogged more memories as Jock walked along. He did not notice the nakedness, except he remembered for a moment how much he had enjoyed going without clothes in the warm times when he was an Iroquois Indian boy. It was a feeling of freedom long since forgotten, but at this moment, it seemed real, natural, and not at all strange. It had been such a long time since he had allowed himself to remember. He relished the memory, admired the Nahyssans, and for the moment before reality repossessed him, he felt proud of being an Indian.

Kadomico continued to bask in the unexpected compliment he had received from Tonawanda. He still could not account for it. Tonawanda, and maybe others, seemed to place great value on his training with the English. When his father, Custoga, had met with the tribes on the Meherrin, maybe he had spoken about understanding the way of the English. Maybe that was where Tonawanda formed his opinion.

While these thoughts vied for his attention, he lengthened his stride to match Tonawanda's, and proudly walked alongside him through the town. His mind was still churning with his success as a go-between for Jock when, glancing to his right, he saw Sayen. A curtain of black hair flashing ribbons of sunlight had slipped past her shoulders and rested at her waist, shielding all but the tiny profile of her face, but there was no mistaking her beauty and grace.

She sat on a huge fallen chestnut tree partially shaded among the roundhouses and polished smooth by its use as a convenient bench. He could see only one side of her soft, fringed buckskins, adorned with beads and colored porcupine quills. Her head was bent forward intent on the work in her lap. Her hands were busy with some sort of stitching or lacing. When Tonawanda and his party drew even with her position, she rose, turned her back to them, and walked away.

Stunned, Kadomico lost step with his party and nearly stopped. Tonawanda noticed the interruption. It was only momentary, but it left Kadomico out of step and behind the long strides of Tonawanda and Jock. He hustled forward immediately to regain his position. When he looked back, Sayen had disappeared. At the same time, Tonawanda increased the pace as if to summon Kadomico's wayward attention, and once again, Kadomico adjusted his motion to match the new pace.

Because Kadomico and Tree Son had previously established themselves as friends, Tonawanda postponed the usual peace pipe ceremony reserved for strangers before allowing them to enter the town. He did not go directly to the council longhouse. Instead, he stopped at one of the roundhouses and motioned them to follow. He stooped and entered the small doorway into a room of two single beds set up along the walls end-to-end on each side of a fire pit. They were made of large forked poles for posts with smaller poles lashed to them to support a grid of mixed rawhide straps and strong hand-woven rope made of vegetation fiber. The generous supply of fur on each bed made an inviting place to rest. The only light came from the single doorway and the smoke hole in the ceiling. There in the semi-darkness, the smell of smoke and dust hung heavy. Tonawanda stepped around a small circle of rocks fencing a mound of ash-laden coals and pointed out a well-oiled, smoothly worn turtle shell filled with bits of dried fowl, venison, nuts, and persimmons. Nearby, a wooden basin of fresh water rested on the flat of a split-log table.

A single beam of sunlight from the smoke hole illuminated Tonawanda's face as he spoke. "I have welcomed you as friends, but there are people here who have lost their families to raids by the militia and soldiers of the whites, and some who lost their family to the white man's disease. Those times are many winters past but the memories linger. What you heard came from boys not finished with their warrior training. They have not yet learned when to speak and when to remain silent."

After the translation, Jock replied, "I understand. It is a difficult matter for those who have lost family members."

Tonawanda, spoke directly to Jock. "I go to prepare for the council. When I return, we will go to the longhouse. There Jock will speak to Yahou-Lakee and the council."

Still absorbed in his thoughts of Sayen, Kadomico almost missed what Tonawanda said. Hesitating, he searched his mind for the right words and gave a perfect translation, but Tonawanda turned his back to him, an unmistakable gesture of reproach. Jock motioned acknowledgment to Tonawanda's words as the war chief moved toward the entrance doorway. Ignored but determined to speak to him of Sayen, Kadomico followed the war chief outside.

"Father of Sayen," he called aloud, hoping that his tone of voice was clearly respectful.

Tonawanda stopped and slowly turned, arms folded, face frozen under coal black hair pulled back tight and adorned with feathered symbols of war. His eyes blazed disapproval as he looked down at Kadomico and waited.

Even though he had no fresh kills to underscore his hunting prowess and therefore his worthiness, Kadomico had resolved to ask permission to see Sayen, but Tonawanda's hostility almost disarmed him. Certain that the great warrior had guessed his intention and was about to denounce him forever, he knew better than to show weakness, and Tonawanda was searching his eyes for a sign. Then, from deep within welled a strong sense of confidence. He was Kadomico, Son of Custoga, Chief of all Saponi. He stood erect and uncertain but determined to stand his ground, and to show that he knew his place in the presence of so powerful a person as Tonawanda. He looked back into Tonawanda's eyes without blinking and changed his tactic. The words poured forth.

"Father of Sayen," he repeated softly but distinctly. "This basket belongs to Sayen. I must return it." He held out his open hand with the tiny, exquisitely decorated basket made of white oak splits.

Surprised, the answer Tonawanda had prepared melted uselessly away. He remembered this basket. His daughter had placed it at Kadomico's knees in the canoe the day they left to meet Sam Layton for the trip to Williamsburg. He had wondered at the time why his wife had permitted that impulsive act, but it had happened so fast that they were well underway in midstream before he realized the implication of such a forward gesture by his daughter. It was right that Kadomico return it, but it did not escape him that this was surely a ploy toward gaining favor with Sayen. He had slowly returned Tayamiti to the normal life of a boy training in the weapons and the hunt, but he kept Sayen so close that no young brave of the Nahyssan had dared approach him. He made regular sacrifices and prayed his thanks often to the Creator for his daughter and Tayamiti, and his pride in them knew no bounds.

"The Dance of the Harvest begins when the sun moves below the mountain. After that, we will make sacrifices and take food of the harvest. Sayen's mother will be by my side for the feast. Return the basket to her," Tonawanda's voice was barely above a growl. He turned his back abruptly and walked away.

Kadomico breathed deeply. His confidence had momentarily overcome the uncertainties about his bravery and his right and worthiness to speak to Sayen, and Tonawanda seemed to have accepted his words. However, in truth, his worthiness depended on his proven manhood, hunting skills, endurance, knowledge of the wilderness, and strength. Most of these were known only at his home, and he had not yet even started the huskanaw trial of manhood.

He took comfort in recalling that Tonawanda had grasped his forearm in a gesture of trust and friendship, and spoke of his language skills and the English school.

There! That is where he erred. He had almost failed in his duty to translate for Jock. He should have been right alongside Jock at every turn of the day, listening, translating, and being as inconspicuous as possible, available to Jock at every instant. A great deal depended on Jock's ability to convince the tribes to hear the Governor. Kadomico winced at his negligence and resolved to make amends as he slipped back inside the roundhouse, his confidence renewed that he would hereafter give a good account of himself as a go-between.

"Is all well with Tonawanda?" Jock asked. "His voice seemed to change before he left."

"He may have been displeased because I have been slow to repeat the Siouan he speaks. Also, because he is the father of Sayen, he seemed not to like that I offered to return the basket she gave me when we were first here. I think he is satisfied now and anxious to hear your words from the Governor."

"Well, I hope so. He is a key person. We need to win him to our side. The way he greeted you, I think we can count on him to listen, and from his reputation, I'd say he is able to make things happen," Jock said.

"I will do my best to make it easy for him to understand your message, and I will be next to you at all times," Kadomico said, grateful to have this chance to level with Jock and to put this matter behind him. He was feeling much better, eager to get back in the role of go-between. Nothing could distract him. Now he renewed his resolve to speak for Jock and Yahou-Lakee, to learn the new words, and to understand. The basket became incidental. He would return it tonight and that would be the end of it. He was Jock's go-between, and he could and would do the work well. He and Jock settled down to rehearsing what Jock would say to the council.

33

When Tonawanda returned, they followed him to the council house and stepped inside. Even in this spacious longhouse, the room was full. Yahou-Lakee remained seated, surrounded by council members made up of his war chief, the senior Nahyssan priest, a woman who would speak for the women's council, and several senior warriors and elders. Two other women moved about quietly, ready to respond if needed, and tended the small ceremonial fire around which the members were seated.

Tonawanda led them to a place reserved for Jock near Yahou-Lakee, and positioned Kadomico behind Jock.

"You will stand here so that you may be heard by all," said Tonawanda to Kadomico in a low voice. Hearing this, Tree Son stepped forward to stand behind Kadomico. Tonawanda moved around the circle to a place opposite Jock and took his seat. The priest waited for silence, then rose and prayed a short prayer and sprinkled sacrificial tobacco on the fire. He handed a peace pipe to Tonawanda.

Tonawanda loaded the pipe with rich, freshly cured tobacco. He turned to face Yahou-Lakee, handed him the peace pipe, and said, "Jock Adams comes to the Nahyssan with a message from the leader of the English in Williamsburg. We will hear him and the son of our friend Chief Custoga, the great leader of the Saponi people. His name is Kadomico, Of the People. He speaks the tongue of the English."

Kadomico whispered the words to Jock as Yahou-Lakee began to speak. "It is good that you are here, Jock Adams. Your Deputy Sheriff Will James came with us to face the Tuscarora on the Meherrin, and we are pleased that you come from the Governor in peace." He drew on the pipe stem until white smoke billowed upward and then passed it to Jock.

Again the warm sensations of belonging swept over Jock. He drew from the pipe and passed it on. This was as close to a governing body as he would likely encounter among the Indians. He thought of the House of Burgesses, the Colony Council, the Governor, King, and somehow he knew this gathering met all the people's needs for government directly, simply, and fairly. He didn't dwell on those thoughts except to note how different the two systems of governing were.

In his role as intermediary for much of the colony shipping business, Jock was well informed on most trade issues, and he knew that the color blue was rare and highly prized among the Indians. Trade with them continued to be a very important element of colony commerce. Snapping back to reality, he retrieved a blue silk kerchief from his trail pouch and presented it to Yahou-Lakee.

"Governor Nicholson sends this gift as a token of his esteem for the Nahyssan," Jock said.

Yahou-Lakee let the kerchief unfold and fall into his other hand, as he enjoyed the touch of smooth silk and admired the bristling color with unabashed pleasure. Jock had several of them in his trail pouch, and he retrieved a green one for Tonawanda. The material and colors captured the appreciation of the council. Yahou-Lakee held the silk up for all to see. He moved the cloth enough to show off its folds and changing colors in the firelight, then looked at Jock and smiled his pleasure. Jock was glad to see that the kerchiefs were a good choice for gifts to leaders of the people that he would be meeting on this trip.

A silence fell over the group as the pipe passed from one to another, and when the priest emptied the bowl of ashes and put it aside, Yahou-Lakee nodded to Jock. The council members looked up, and Jock straightened his back, his head held high as he stretched his throat to stop the lump building there. Getting control of himself, he looked at each of the council members as though he was about to speak directly to that person.

"I am Neepaughwheese, Night Walker," began Jock. Kadomico was caught off guard by this news, but he managed the translation perfectly. Idle listeners raised their eyes to be sure where the words came from. Others leaned forward as though they misunderstood. Yahou-Lakee suppressed his disbelief, but wanting an explanation looked at Tonawanda only to see that Tonawanda was also surprised. By custom, speakers could not be interrupted. Jock continued.

"I was raised by the Seneca until I was eight summers. I learned the Seneca had captured me when I was not yet one winter of age. I lived in a Seneca town far from the white man on a river called the Muskingum until white soldiers of the English came and destroyed the town, killed my family, destroyed all the crops , and took many captured white Indians with them back to the land of the whites. I saw these things when I was but eight summers."

Jock paused, and Kadomico said the words or their meaning to the council, but with a difficulty that stemmed largely from his surprise. This was not what they had rehearsed. Knowing how important it was for him to get Jock's words right, he focused hard on them and gave another passable translation.

"Until this very morning, I have not returned to be with Indian people, and as I walked among you today, the teachings of my Seneca mother and uncles came back to me. For a few moments, I again knew the presence of sky, earth, fire, water, and wind as though they were old friends, and with that came a warm kind of peace I have not known since I was a Seneca. For those moments, as I walked among the Nahyssans, it was as though I was in the presence of the Creator."

Kadomico struggled to get the translation right.

"But then I remembered after I was taken back to the English that the Senecas and other nations of Iroquois struck

309

back with terrible revenge, leaving no living person when they raided English settlements. No women, children, or elders lived. They burned crops and buildings, destroyed cattle and other livestock, murdered infants, and scalped their victims and took away the steel tools and guns. The English formed wilderness-wise bands of longknives and returned raid-for-raid, burning, taking captives for slavery, and leaving no life in the towns they destroyed."

Jock paused again for Kadomico and listened closely. Kadomico was striking a rhythm, gesturing and speaking boldly. Jock looked at his audience and found intense interest among them. Some leaned toward him. Some elders had their good ear turned to him. Here was a white man, a leader of white men probably, who had known life as an Indian.

"I was adopted by a settler family here in the Virginia colony when I was a small boy, the same age as Tayamiti, son of your brave war chief. The family treated me kindly and raised me as their son. After several winters, they sent me across the great water to the land of the English King and trained me in the ways of trade because this new land, Virginia, had proved to be so rich in valuable trade items."

So interesting were these revelations to Kadomico that he had to be on guard against further distraction. He had never discussed this background with Jock. Nor could he see how it served the purpose they came for, but he carried on, proud to be speaking for this Neepaughwheese, Night Walker, Jock Adams.

"When I came back, I married a woman of Virginia, and we have three sons. Now, I work with the men of the great ships and the growers of tobacco, maize and timber to bring them together for moving trade items in and out of Virginia. You, the Indians of Virginia, produce many of those trade items. Your furs, canoes, and the bark and roots of plants that have medicinal value, and buckskin clothing are excellent trade items. Iron has recently been discovered in your land and the English blacksmiths can turn it into steel knives and tomahawks. All of these and much more are your trade items. If you wish, you can trade with the

English for firesticks, powder and ball, cloth, iron cook pots, kettles, and steel tools.

Jock continued, "There have been many sicknesses among the tribes, and we have seen whole towns die because of them. The English have strong medicine that sometimes will save lives, and they need more of the valuable roots, bark, and plants of the forest to make medicine that will help.

"You know that the English, Spanish, and French fight for possession of lands that Indians have used since the beginning, and the Indians war against each other and against the white man for the hunting and fishing grounds. You have seen the Tuscarora and Occaneechi fight for control of the southern trade trails. It is the same wherever trade trails exist."

Kadomico was taking the time he needed to get the main thoughts across to the council. Sometimes he added many words of Siouan because there were not words in that language to match what Jock said. He was grateful that, finally, Jock had come to the words they had rehearsed and used only a few strange new words. He would speak to Jock later about the new words, and they would be ready when they spoke to his home Saponi council.

"Governor Nicholson and many other English leaders believe that the wars, sicknesses, and difficult matters of land use, like hunting, fishing, farming and raising livestock, can best be dealt with by working together. He sees ways to improve the trade activities of both the English and the Indian. In addition, Governor Nicholson wishes to work on a way to set up fortifications on our frontier boundaries that would include Indian warriors. Such fortifications would protect both the settlers and the tribes.

"Unfortunately, it is nearly impossible to have separate agreements with each tribe. The land is wide and the tribes are many, but he believes it can be done if all tribes can act as one as you did on the Meherrin against the Tuscarora. He knows that I too believe it is a good thing for the English and Indian to work together. It is why the Governor sent me to ask you for this meeting."

Jock gave the last words a tone of finality. He knew he had hardly touched on the issues facing both the English and Indians. He knew the Church's passion for converting the heathens, the use of rum by cheats and greedy traders, the quick triggers of settlers, and he knew that within Virginia there were no less than fifteen tiny, sovereign tribal nations. He thought of Sam Layton, who had lived through many treaty efforts from New York to Florida in this Eastern Woodland. Sam's words came to him. A meeting may not solve all the issues but it is a start, he thought. Now, it is up to Yahou-Lakee.

Kadomico heard these final words plainly and gave the last sentence his strongest voice, "It is why the Governor sent me to ask you for this meeting."

Yahou-Lakee immediately saw the promise in such a meeting, but he also knew the violent history of English militia and soldiers, broken agreements, raids on their town, robbing winter stores and the cheating traders. In addition, he knew the hatred toward the white man among those who had lost whole families in the English raids. Vengeance was a life-long right and must be satisfied. Still, the bleak prospects of holding their land and vast hunting grounds loomed before him.

Yahou-Lakee spoke directly to Jock. "We are pleased that we might work with others to deal with the sickness, enemy raids, and scarce game and fish. The council will speak to me, and I will have an answer for you before you leave. Now, our fires of prayer and feast are burning. Our people are giving thanks and making sacrifices to the Creator. Go now, and enjoy the Nahyssan welcome and celebration. Join me later for the feast."

Kadomico, Tree Son, and Jock, made their way back to prepare for their departure. Unseen behind a stack of firewood at their roundhouse, three young braves waited. They were about the age and size of Kadomico and had not completed the traditional transition to manhood and warrior status.

312

As Jock and the boys walked over the clean hard-packed earth past roundhouses, people smiled and nodded.

Jock spoke first. "Kadomico, I think you did a good job. The council seemed to understand."

"Yes, I think they understood, but no one knew you had once been a Seneca."

"As I said, when I came into the town, a deep feeling of being a Seneca came back to me. I had not known it even once since I began to live with my English family. I hoped that speaking of it would give me more credit and understanding with the council."

"I think it did. Looking back, I ought to have known it. It is why you and Sam Layton were such good friends, and it is why you and Rebecca took us into your home."

"Are you sure about this?" Tree Son said with a mischievous smile. "No Indian would try to walk so far in moccasins as heavy and hard as wood."

"You have a point, Tree Son. I spoke to Tonawanda about that after the council, and he will see about getting me moccasins for the rest of this trip. Maybe several pair." Jock stooped and entered the roundhouse.

Kadomico was next, but hearing a rustle behind him, he turned just as one of the three young Nahyssans slammed an arrow into the ground signifying "enemy."

"Saponi traitors. Go back. Filthy English devils are our enemy." Bear Claw, the tallest of the three, spat out the words in venomous hatred. His face was a scarred mass of pockmarks.

"We come in peace as guests of Chief Yahou-Lakee," Kadomico said. He moved away from the door, careful to keep Tree Son behind him. "But if you want to make this between you and me." Bear Claw slammed into Kadomico before he finished the sentence, and the two of them crashed to the ground rolling in the dust, their legs and arms locked in death grips. Kadomico twisted to avoid taking the fall on his back under the weight of Bear Claw. Their elbows and hips took the fall, and the shock broke them apart. Bear Claw had a few pounds of muscle on

Kadomico, but Kadomico was faster and gained his feet in time to throw himself back onto Bear Claw, who was struggling to regain his balance. This time Kadomico seized his opponent in a headlock and shifted his weight so that the force of it centered on Bear Claw's neck. At the same time, Kadomico caught a glimpse of Tree Son, stretched and flying, his arms extended to stop a murderous club swung by one of the attackers. A chilling scream erupted from Tree Son as he leaped too late to stop the war club aimed directly at Kadomico's head.

Kadomico felt nothing as he relaxed his hold on Bear Claw and descended into unconsciousness. The wound was open from a point just behind the top of his left ear. From there it sliced upward bleeding slowly with the skull showing in one place. He lay still as death, face down with the left side of his face exposed. The dark blood flowed slowly across the left eye and cheek and into the dust. Jock leaped into the scene, jerked Bear Claw to his feet, and threw him into the bark covering of the roundhouse.

Although too late to stop the deadly club, Tree Son slammed into the one who swung it and seized the would-be killer in an arm lock with his forearm set against the larynx. The sight of the club striking his friend summoned a powerful strength from within to shut off the assailant's breath and obstruct the blood flow as he tightened his grip. Although he could see a bulging eye, gaping mouth, and swelling face it did not satisfy him. He slowly drew his forearm deeper into boy's neck relishing the expectation of death.

Alerted by Tree Son's scream, Tonawanda and several warriors broke through the gathering crowd. The third assailant ran. It took Tonawanda and two warriors to unlock Tree Son from his victim, and several minutes for Tree Son to realize what he had almost done.

Sitting quietly now, he saw Jock take a large cloth from his buckskin shirt and apply it to the wound on Kadomico's head. The sight of blood and the motionless, unresponsive body of his friend sent spasms raging through Tree Son, forcing him to cover his mouth to avoid the screams swelling within his throat. He saw

Tonawanda grasp Bear Claw by his long scalp lock and sling him toward a warrior. Tonawanda called for the medicine woman. He watched a pair of warriors take custody of the two assailants and march them away. A woman came with medicine and poultices. They laid Kadomico on a crude ladder of poles covered with young pine boughs and carried him away.

Tree Son and Jock followed them the short distance to one of the larger roundhouses and remained while the medicine woman attended Kadomico's wound. She had located a place where pressure from her hand slowed the bleeding until it stopped. She cleaned the area around the wound and applied poultices of crushed bark and roots.

Jock and Tree Son, standing well back in the shadows of the room, were surprised when a priest dressed in a wild array of feathers, horns, rattles, and bones of many descriptions, stooped through the little doorway and drew himself up to an awesome sight. He raised his arms and began to shake rattles and slowly twist his body in a sort of dance. When the medicine woman acknowledged him by moving away from Kadomico, the priest began to sing a prayer as he moved back and forth past Kadomico, waving a feathered wand. The healing ceremony went on for several minutes, after which the priest left and the woman turned to Jock.

"The bleeding is stopped. I will call you when he wakes."

It was clear that he could not travel for days, and they agreed that they must wait until they could speak with Kadomico before proceeding to the Saponi town. Kadomico seemed to be breathing quietly. Jock and Tree Son returned to their roundhouse. There they discussed their options, and by the time the harvest ceremony began that night, they had agreed that if Kadomico regained consciousness, they would discuss their plans with him to proceed while he recovered from the head wound.

At the harvest ceremony that night, Yahou-Lakee called Jock and Tree Son to him and, translating through Tree Son, assured Jock that the Nahyssan would welcome Governor Nicholson at their gathering on the Meherrin at the next full moon. As a gift to

315

Governor Nicholson, he gave Jock a richly decorated belt. As wide as a man's hand and a length four times its width, beautiful beadwork and tiny embedded seashells were intricately woven among tinted porcupine quills and brightly dyed soft leather thongs. It was a belt of great value. Tonawanda then turned to the large gathering, made his apologies to Jock, and invited him to the punishment of the assailants. Much to Tree Son's disappointment, Jock refused.

Later at the ceremony, while Jock and Tree Son ate and watched the dancing, Tonawanda approached.

"Tell Jock that, if he wishes, I will go with Kadomico and deliver his message. I will also speak for the Nahyssan at the Saponi council," Tonawanda said.

When Tree Son translated, Jock was so pleased at the offer that he stood and grasped Tonawanda's forearm.

"Yes, yes. Chief Custoga knows you and the Nahyssan people. If you will do that, I will return immediately and report to the Governor the news of Nahyssan support," Jock said.

Tonawanda nodded agreement. "It is a good plan, Jock. I will inform Yahou-Lakee and be ready to go with Kadomico and Tree Son when Kadomico can travel."

That night, after the ceremonial fires had turned to ash and the town slept, Kadomico lay on his side facing outward. They had positioned him there to avoid pressure on the head wound. He woke slowly without moving and kept his eyes closed trying to gather his thoughts from a distant fog, but he could not. Each heartbeat sent a dull ache to his head, a warning to keep still. Except for the pain and the warmth and comfort of the place where he lay, he knew nothing else. The slightest effort to move caused shooting pains to his head.

Eventually, he opened his eyes a little. Sayen was sitting beside him, profiled against the flame light of the small cooking fire. She leaned toward him, and his pulse quickened, causing more pain.

He closed his eyes to savor the dream, but when he opened them again, she was still there, and he heard her say, "Do not speak. You have been wounded. Take this and swallow. It will ease the pain and let you sleep."

She held the stem of a long wooden spoon. The tiny bowl was no wider that the tip of her little finger, but still required effort for Kadomico to close his lips around it and swallow. Sayen withdrew the spoon and repeated the dose just before Kadomico started to slip back into a deep sleep.

He awoke the second time with less pain. Sayen was still there, sitting with her legs crossed on a pallet of soft skins alongside his bed. Her head had dropped so that her chin rested on her chest as she dozed. Slowly and quietly, he turned to see her better, and he lay a long time watching her sleep, relishing her presence.

Outside, the sun struggled with an overcast sky as the morning temperatures of the late fall season drifted uncommonly low. Inside and out, the cook-fires flamed brighter. Kadomico continued to watch Sayen sleep while he studied every feature within his vision. After all those days thinking and dreaming of her, she was here within his reach. He did not want this to end, but as he watched, she lifted her head, and their eyes met for the first time. He knew then that, in every way, Sayen was more than he had dreamed. His innermost fantasies had never disclosed how such a single look from her would flood him with certainty that she was a special gift to any who might know her. This new level of awareness lasted only as long as the brilliant light that flashed the instant their eyes met. She broke the spell when she spoke.

"You are awake."

His mouth felt dry and swollen. Worse yet, when he heard her voice, his thoughts collapsed in a swirl of fragments, and he could not think. Without moving or shifting his eyes, he managed to sound a beginning.

"I I I," he stammered, trying to clear his throat. "I   I am Ka Ka . . . ."

"Yes, you are Kadomico, Son of Custoga, Chief of the Saponi," Sayen said. She retrieved a bit of cloth from a small basin of water and rose to moisten his lips and bathe his face.

Kadomico's eyes followed her every move, fighting back the avalanche of questions forming in his mind.

Sayen handed him a small container of water and continued as though she knew his thoughts.

"You have a serious head wound," she said, while he drank deeply and motioned for more. After three servings of water, Kadomico lay back and relaxed. The exertion had sent his head spinning again, and he closed his eyes to get control. She spoke again.

"The medicine woman left this to help you rest and for the wound to heal."

Kadomico remembered clearly. The potion in the spoon was powerful, but he was not ready to sleep again.

"Please, wait." He rasped the words out with difficulty, but more clearly, now that his throat had found moisture. "The pain is not so bad, and I think I can move about. I need ... ."

"What you need, Kadomico," she said, interrupting him again and gently pressing him back into the covers, "is to be still and quiet. I know about head wounds. Not long ago, I had a wound much like yours. Rest now, and take this medicine. It is not to make you sleep. It is for the wound."

She gave him two doses of the liquid and placed a skin-wrapped container on his covers.

"Use this to relieve yourself while I send for the medicine woman. Afterwards, your friends will come."

She turned and walked away, neither expecting nor allowing further conversation.

Kadomico's face flushed with annoyance and confusion, and a pain shot through his head as he strained to watch her disappear through the little entrance to the roundhouse. He needed to talk. Yet every time he tried to speak she interrupted him and spoke to him as though he were a child. For all her beauty, she could use some training in basic manners. He shifted

318

to a position that enabled him to reach for the skin container and fell back exhausted with the movement. Finally, he managed the relief he needed after his long hours of sleep and hung the skin container on the bedpost.

The medicine woman came in just as he finished. She chattered continuously as she changed the poultices and compression bandages and satisfied herself that the wound had stopped bleeding and draining. Before she finished, Jock and Tree Son entered but not Sayen. The medicine woman continued to talk to no one in particular about the wound, Kadomico's coloring, and the effects of her medicine.

Kadomico looked beyond her and greeted his friend. "Tree Son, you are here.

"It is so, Kadomico, but only because I single handedly defeated the whole force sent against us while you rested on the fellow you nearly killed," Tree Son replied.

Kadomico reached for Tree Son's forearm. "This time I cannot question your words. Maybe I just thought you didn't need my help."

Jock, standing a respectful distance behind Tree Son, smiled with relief to hear Kadomico speak even though he did not understand their Siouan language.

When he realized that he had interrupted the medicine woman, Tree Son stepped back to allow her to finish, but she waved him back to Kadomico's side as she gathered her basket of various medicines and said, "Finish your visit quickly. He needs rest now. I will send Sayen." She took the skin of urine and left.

Kadomico greeted Jock and assured him that the wound was healing. Jock did not comment. Instead, he signaled Tree Son to explain what had happened and waited patiently while Tree Son recounted the attack in Siouan and finished by switching to English to include Jock, saying, "While you slept, the Nahyssans danced and feasted all night."

"And did Tonawanda and Yahou-Lakee agree to Governor Nicholson's proposal?"

"They did approve, and Tonawanda will go to the Saponi people and speak for the Nahyssan," Jock answered.

"Tonawanda told me to return this basket to Red Star, the mother of Sayen, at the ceremony of the harvest, but Sayen was here last night and again this day. Does Tonawanda know?" Kadomico asked.

"This is Tonawanda's roundhouse. He sent you here. No one may see you without his approval. Except for Tree Son and me, Sayen, Red Star, and the medicine woman are the only ones Tonawanda will allow to see you. He has guards posted at the door."

"What of our travel, Jock?" asked Kadomico.

"Earlier this morning, the medicine woman told us it will be six suns before you can travel the wilderness trails to your Saponi town. She says that even then you must be careful and walk because it will be many more suns before the wound is completely healed."

"Then you must leave without me? Tree Son will speak for you?"

"I have spoken with Yahou-Lakee and Tonawanda about that. We believe it is important for you to be there when the Governor's proposal is presented to the Saponi council. In a few days, you will be able to travel. Tonawanda understands my mission and offers to travel with you and Tree Son to the Saponi. I think the three of you are as good, perhaps better, than our original plan.

"It is a good way, Jock. I will be ready to leave sooner than you think."

"Yes, I hope so, and it allows me to return to Williamsburg immediately. The Governor will be able to inform the Council and Burgesses and have more time to prepare for the meeting. You can bring the news to Williamsburg as soon as you have the Saponi decision.

"So I will be on my way today." Jock extended his hand.

Kadomico took the hand as Jock continued.

"Kadomico, your part in this is even greater now. Your people will be proud of what you are doing. However, what happened last night can happen again most anywhere, even in your own town. The hate is strong by a few people on both sides. Now that you know that, be alert. Be sure of the people you trust. You are a vital part of the work in progress to reach understanding and meet the needs of both sides. The meeting on the Meherrin will be the first step. Your friend Sam Layton will be pleased," Jock said.

He gave Kadomico's hand a final firm shake and said, "Goodbye."

Red Star and Sayen passed them at the door. Jock held the skin covering aside and said to Tree Son, "A strikingly beautiful young woman."

"With a powerful warrior for a father," chided Tree Son. "If I were Kadomico, I would worry more about Sayen's father than enemy Indians."

"Kadomico is interested in Sayen?" Jock asked.

"I cannot speak for Kadomico, but since the first time he saw her he has not been the same."

Sayen and Red Star continued into the room moving about busily. Sayen kindled the small cooking fire, folded and stored various sleeping furs and blankets, brought in fresh water, and hung a kettle over the fire. Red Star began slicing food into small bits. They worked silently cooking, cleaning, and putting away until everything not in use was stowed on hangers lashed to the walls. A small pot of simmering mint leaves released pleasant aromas into the room. They worked as though Kadomico did not exist.

He watched without changing positions, well aware that he was in the absolute domain of women. Whatever they did here was not open to question by any man, but after a period of being ignored, he looked for a reason to speak. He shifted the blanket and groaned a little, then coughed just once when the strain sent lightning flashes of pain to the wound. When the pain subsided, he opened his eyes. Red Star was there.

"I am Red Star, Mother of Sayen. You have lost much blood and will remain weak while it rebuilds. Soon you will have food, and then you will sleep for the healing."

Kadomico tried to see where Sayen was. He could hear no movement.

"I thank you for the shelter and for the care I have received. Tonawanda is a great leader." His thoughts were confused, and he was still weak from the loss of blood and the morning visitors, but he wanted to talk with Sayen.

"I think I can sit up and walk now."

Red Star, ignoring his suggestion to walk, worked additional support under his shoulders, and spoke softly. "Sayen is here with food. Afterwards, you will sleep."

Sayen sat by his bed. "This will build your strength," she said. "You will feel much better when you wake." She spooned the fine broth and stew for him. No sooner had he swallowed and prepared to speak, than there at his lips was the next spoonful. Just before he fell asleep he noticed that he was getting drowsy and realized that the medicine had been in his food.

He dreamed he was talking with Sayen on a sunny day by the Yadkin River, when Tonawanda came upon them and took Sayen away. He wanted to explain, but Tonawanda refused to listen. Then Sam Layton came, and he talked to Sam about Sayen. Sam listened, nodding his understanding but did not offer advice.

Then Sam disappeared from his dream and Sayen was there with a tall muscular warrior. Sayen stood looking up at her warrior while Kadomico was trying to explain to her why he had not completed the traditional huskanaw transition to warrior training. They turned away from him, and Tonawanda appeared, ignored Kadomico, and talked manly talk to the warrior. In his dream his heart ached with Sayen's rejection, his gut burned hate toward the warrior, and he cringed at the way Tonawanda and Sayen treated the warrior.

The dream seemed to have lasted a long time. When he woke, the morning light was streaming through the smoke hole in the ceiling. Sayen was sitting at his bedside.

"The medicine is strong," he said.

"It is good you are awake," Sayen said. "Tonawanda will be here soon to speak to you. Here is water and sweet gum twigs for your teeth. I will bring food, and we will see if you can sit up." She placed the urine bag on his lap and left abruptly before he could speak.

He dismissed his frustration and failure to talk with her and turned his attention to the urine bag. Using it, he discovered he was able to sit up, even stand. At first, he staggered a little. His head was clearing, yet the room still swam about him. He gripped one of the wall poles for support until he was ready to return to the bed, glad to sit down and relieved to lie back.

When Sayen returned, she came through the door talking about the food. He had to interrupt her to tell her about standing alone. He thought it would be good news, but, just like in the dream, she did not respond. His frustration resurfaced tenfold. Maybe listening was not possible for this person. Maybe she could only talk. She had not even asked him how he was feeling when he woke—just talk and more talk.

Red Star returned with extra blankets and furs.

"The food is ready, but you must sit up now so it can find its way easily," she said.

As she motioned him up and Sayen began piling support at his back, he said, "Yes, I will sit up, even get up." He was about to say he could walk about now.

"No need to get up. Best you eat then rest. Tonawanda will be here soon," Red Star said. "Drink as much as you like of this water. It will help heal you." She handed him a gourd filled to the brim and motioned him to start.

While he drank, she said, "After this stew, try to rest. Tonawanda will come first, and then the medicine woman will be here later to look at the wound. Rest as much as you can."

The two women cleared away the remaining food and containers and rekindled the fire just as Tonawanda stooped to avoid the low doorway and walked toward Kadomico. Tree Son followed him into the room.

"It is good that your color has returned. Your strength will follow," Tonawanda said.

"I am honored that you are here, and I thank you for these kindnesses," Kadomico replied.

"The youths who attacked you are failures. They resisted our training for warrior status and burn with hate because they cannot join our young warriors. They will ever remain in the fields with the women or become slaves to the elders and the priests. Now they have betrayed their family and defied the Nahyssan tradition of honoring guests. Our people reject them."

"They came at us without warning or reason that I could see. I am told that Tree Son fought well," Kadomico said.

"It is true. Tree Son is brave, strong, and would have killed his enemy if we had not intervened," Tonawanda replied.

Kadomico felt the pain of inadequacy and shame again. The dream was still fresh in his mind, and he was about to admit his own failure to participate in the Saponi huskanaw when Tonawanda continued, "And you might have done the same with the armed enemy even though he out-weighed and out-reached you. It was clear that you had beaten him when his accomplice attacked you. It was then that Tree Son attacked the accomplice. I will speak to Chief Custoga of the Saponi, and you both will be rewarded for these deeds. I am grateful that you defeated these cowardly fools."

Kadomico's eyes widened. He could not find words to reply. Tonawanda saw him as a fighter, also Tree Son, and Sayen surely heard him say the words. They had fought well together, side by side. Tonawanda said the Saponi would recognize these deeds. He said a quick prayer of thanks. He had almost belittled himself before this war chief. He had harbored a powerful self-pity of denial since the first day his father announced that instead of entering into the huskanaw, he would go to Williamsburg. He had been about to draw on the old self-pity and explain his failure as a man. Not so! Far from it, he and Tree Son were warriors. The war chief and others saw it. The realization thrilled him, but he remained composed.

"It is my first battle with an enemy trying to take my life," he said. "I am grateful for the help of those who intervened."

"When you are ready, we will go together to the Saponi town and deliver Jock's message from the Governor," Tonawanda said. He gathered himself to leave. "Until then, you will remain here as my guest."

Kadomico suppressed the exhilaration building within him as he watched Tonawanda twist sideways to get through the little door. With a few words, Tonawanda had erased all doubt about his shortcomings of manliness. With those few words, he also expressed his approval of Kadomico and Tree Son and complimented his conduct in battle, and Sayen had heard all this.

He thought he felt good enough to try to walk, but as soon as Tonawanda left his bedside, Sayen and Red Star appeared with more food, drink, and medicine.

"Not yet," Red Star said. "Take this, and tomorrow you will be strong enough for a walk."

He raised his hand with palm up and open. After all, he now spoke as a warrior and was not to be interrupted. This time someone was going to hear what he had to say.

"Mother of Sayen, I understand, and I am glad of your great healing way and grateful for your care, but I must have another little while before I go back to sleep. Can you stay the medicine long enough for me to rest? I have much to think about to prepare for the trip with War Chief Tonawanda."

"When I return, then, you will take the medicine." Red Star's tone of voice was firm; Kadomico was her patient and these were orders. She said something to Sayen he could not quite hear and left.

Kadomico looked at the food she had left for him. The excitement of the visit with Tonawanda had diminished his appetite, and he set it aside. By straining, he managed to turn enough to see Sayen sitting behind him, her head bent over the beadwork in her lap.

"Sayen, I want to . . . ."

"My mother said you must finish eating," Sayen interrupted. "Then the medicine."

"No!" he exclaimed, "Your mother said take the medicine when she returns." Frustrated with another interruption, he nearly shouted the words.

Sayen suppressed a smile at this bearish response. Maybe the healing had begun.

"It is not good for the wounded Son of the Chief of the Saponi to speak harshly. Eat," she said, quietly as though speaking to an infant.

Kadomico despaired of ever achieving a sensible conversation with either of the two women. It was obvious that Sayen's only interest in him was as a wounded patient. He looked at the tiny basket he had retrieved from his side pouch. He would just leave it by the food, eat, and take the medicine. Tree Son would be there soon and they would talk. It was his last thought before sleep crept over him and reality gave way to dreams.

This time it was of Sayen alone in the wilderness. Animals followed her, and she spoke to them as though they understood. It was the warm season, and she bathed in a shallow stream strewn with convenient outcroppings of flat stones to lie on to dry in the summer sun. He tried to join her, but he became entangled in giant spider webs that disabled his legs. He could only struggle forward by pulling himself from tree to tree. Sayen ignored his plight.

When he woke, the basket was gone. Tree Son was there, his back to Kadomico, talking to Red Star.

"Tree Son! You are here," he exclaimed.

"Yes, while the Son of the Chief of the Saponi sleeps, I, the brave and mighty Tree Son, sharpens his weapons, oils his bow, and repairs his worn moccasins to be ready when he waves us forward to Saponi land."

He was immensely pleased to see Tree Son; the "brave and mighty Tree Son" might have died rather than see him hurt.

He swallowed and replied, "We can talk a little?"

"Yes, we will talk."

"Time enough for talk later," Red Star said, as she inspected and treated the bandaged wound. She and Sayen arranged water and a large shell of food for them and left, passing Tonawanda as he entered the room.

"The medicine woman said you can travel when you feel like it, but there must be no strain on the wound area for many suns," Tonawanda said. "That means no running. Maybe the length of the trip will take twice the time you traveled when you first came here. Sayen will bring medicine and bandages."

Tonawanda could see the astonishment on their faces. Sayen is coming? Why? Could Tree Son not handle the medicine and bandages? Tonawanda read the questions. He knew it did not make much sense. How was he to explain that Sayen was coming because Sayen *wanted* to come. Strong-minded and determined, she had simply told him that he knew he owed Kadomico the best of care, and she certainly could provide that better than he. Besides, why should she not be there to keep her father company on the return trip? Tonawanda had agreed, barely able to hide his pleasure that Sayen would be with them on the trail.

"She is the best one to apply the medicine and bandages," he said, standing prepared to leave. It was a lame explanation, but his voice had the ring of finality. There would be no further discussion.

"My people will be honored to have you and your daughter as guests," Kadomico said. But the news that Sayen would join them lingered in his mind, and he wondered how it came about. Did Tonawanda order her to join them? Could it have been her idea? Observing her command of matters regarding his recovery these past two suns and from what he had heard of her fight with her Monacan sentry, he guessed that it was Sayen's idea, but *why?* Might she just want to be with her father? Maybe she wanted to continue learning and practicing her healing skills. It did not occur to him that *he* might be the reason. However, he did notice the pleasure gradually growing within him as he realized she would travel with them.

The next day Kadomico awoke feeling strong and hungry. Red Star came to his bedside smiling.

"You are better. Will you dress and walk today?" she asked, laying his freshly washed and stretched buckskins across the foot of his bed.

"Yes, yes," he answered, glad to see the unexpected smile and warm greeting. She prepared his food, and later, the two of them walked outside into an early winter sun. He wondered but did not ask about Sayen. The chilly air felt good, but he did not protest when Red Star turned back to the roundhouse. As they neared the entrance, Tree Son appeared. Red Star produced thick furs for sitting and began tending to other chores as Tree Son and Kadomico settled down near the fading coals of the morning cook-fire.

"You look well," Tree Son said. He added kindling to the fire from a nearby supply.

"We can travel soon," Kadomico replied. "When Tonawanda is ready we will go. Our pace will be slow—maybe three days on the trail, or even four, because I will be mostly walking."

"I am glad to go back, Kadomico. I have had enough of the English way. Now, as the time nears, I think of our people, and I am glad we are going home."

The kindling caught fire, sending flames up through the twigs and brightly lighting the room.

"You remember that Jock expects me to return to Williamsburg as soon as we have our people's answer to the Governor's request."

"I know, and if you ask I will come with you, but no more school for me."

Red Star knelt between them. She moved three pottery mugs back from the fire and added a mixture of mint leaves and sassafras roots to each.

"Soon we will have hot tea," she said. "The chill of the season is stubborn this morning." Kadomico began to shiver a little. She placed a light blanket over his shoulders.

328

"I thank you, Red Star," Kadomico said, then turned back to Tree Son. "When I have the council's answer for the Governor, I can come back here with Tonawanda and Sayen, and go on to Williamsburg by canoe. When the school closes for the English winter holiday, I can return home, and we can go together with our leaders to the meeting of many tribes on the Meherrin."

"No doubt we will be important go-betweens." Tree Son, puffed up his chest and raised his nose high to mock the notion.

"It could be," Kadomico replied. "Jock said that the Governor will invite Sam Layton. I hope he will. We have much to learn about the differences between the English and our people, and no one understands them as well as Sam Layton. He calls them dangerous differences, and I know that he will help me to know more about them."

Red Star returned and filled the warm mugs with water and honey. With a long forked stick, she began to retrieve small, round, creek bed stones from the red-hot coals, knocked them free of ash, and placed them in the mugs

They sipped the steaming tea and chatted about the trip to Saponi town.

"I think your people would like to know that you are arriving," Red Star said. "It would give your families and the leaders time to prepare."

"I could do that," Tree Son said, eagerly. "I could go now."

"I am sure that Tonawanda will want us to stay together," Kadomico said. "And it could be a bad thing for you to travel alone in the hunting grounds of others."

"We could stay together until we reach a day's travel farther on to Saponi town, then I could run the remainder of the trip while you rest the night and prepare for your arrival," Tree Son suggested. "That way they would have at least a day's notice."

"Any notice at all would be good," Red Star said. "They will need to prepare food and a place for your guests to sleep."

They agreed to talk to Tonawanda about it.

The next morning Kadomico was up, dressed, and ready for a walk outside before the rest of the roundhouse awoke.

Wrapped in a blanket, he fed the coals on his way out. He untied both the inside and outside skin door-flaps, retied them, and stepped out into the chilly darkness. Sayen watched from her blankets and smiled. Today was the day of preparations. They would probably leave the next day.

On the day of departure, Kadomico walked lively behind Sayen who followed Tree Son to the riverside trail west. Tonawanda walked behind them, keeping all three in sight. There were many rivers and rivulets to cross, almost all of them rich with waterfowl. Sometimes the trail faded to small animal tracks. At other times there was no trail for a while, then the land opened to rolling hills and grassland, and always the creeks drained the land, splashing clear, sweet water around huge boulders of limestone. By nightfall, they were well past the point where the trail turned south away from the river.

They made camp. Sayen started a fire, and while it burned down to roasting coals, she skinned a squirrel that Tonawanda has taken earlier. She also prepared the birds the men killed by firing arrows into a cloud of migrating pigeons so thick that one arrow would sometimes take two of them. Sayen skillfully turned it all into tasty food.

Each day they rested two or three times. They traveled unchallenged and without incident. They were on the trail four days before Tree Son departed at mid-day, trotting briskly for Saponi town. At night when they camped, Sayen was so busy tending Kadomico's wound from her medicine pouch and preparing food there was little exchange of words between them.

After Tree Son left the group, Kadomico took the lead position, and the three continued to travel at a walk until sundown. They would reach the Saponi town at mid-day. That night at the last campfire of the trip, they rested in the warmth of their fire as the last of the sunlight disappeared and darkness descended. They were in Saponi hunting grounds now, well known to Kadomico, and they relaxed by the cook fire waiting for pieces of turkey from Tonawanda's morning kill to roast on green hickory sticks.

"The wound is dry now and the swelling is almost gone," Sayen said, as she applied more of Red Star's ointment to the wound and bathed the surrounding area.

"It will be a good thing for you to know my father, Chief Custoga, and my mother, Tanaka. It will give them the chance to thank you for the care you have shown," Kadomico said, looking from one to the other.

Tonawanda said, "But it was in our town that you were attacked, and I must explain that to Chief Custoga. He is entitled to revenge."

"Perhaps, but in truth, is not revenge mine rather than his, and have I not stated my satisfaction to you?" Kadomico replied.

Tonawanda saw the fact of this, and marked it down as another quality of this unusual young warrior's character. He thinks fast and true.

"I see your point, but I must speak to your father about this and answer any questions he has. We shall see." Tonawanda was anxious to make amends if needed. Much depended on Chief Custoga and the Saponi council.

Sayen listened and learned. It was clear to her that Tonawanda approved of Kadomico and his assignment to live among the English. She had sensed it the day they came striding past her in the town corridor and later at the council. She saw it amplified after the three bad young Nahyssans attacked him. Since Kadomico had been a guest in their roundhouse, Sayen and Red Star had talked about it, and watched Kadomico win Tonawanda's growing respect. Now on the trail it was even more evident to Sayen. She also knew that Kadomico was still recovering and faced many challenges the next day before his family and the council. When he joined his family, there was not much more she could do for him, but she would watch him closely. As she eased into her blankets spread over a cushion of pine boughs, she remembered that day she had waded out and placed the tiny basket of bread next to his knee in the canoe. She had been right in her feelings then.

The next day they broke camp at first light, shifted their buckskins against the chill, and struck the trail without eating. They walked at a brisk pace with a cold light wind at their backs. The morning light came on fast under a clear sky as they moved south out of the forest into a treeless expanse of brown switch grass and straw finely peppered with other wild grasses and golden rod. Kadomico's heart warmed at the sight of the familiar hunting ground. This was perfect cover and feeding for quail, pheasant, grouse, and wild turkey. He hoped to flush some of them to show Sayen and Tonawanda their number and beauty.

Halfway through the mile-long expanse they would turn west through more foothills of the mountains. It would be less than half a day on to the Saponi town.

The trail west led them up a forested hillside to an overlook that exposed brown fields, and several small creeks. Beyond them, a shallow river marked the rise of a forested mountainside. Below them, on their side of the river, a small valley lay flat and remained high to the very edge of the river. And there, after a hundred years of moving south and west, stood the many roundhouses of Saponi town, safe from flood and surprise attack.

Kadomico stood quietly observing the scene, and for the first time he understood the threat to his people. There was nowhere else to move. To north, south, and east all the hunting grounds were claimed and the west was blocked by mountains. He thought back over the beautiful valleys of land he had just crossed, so easily converted to English farms, and the forest with rich stands of great pine and chestnut oak trees, so tall that a squirrel in their tops would be a difficult target. Such trees would fall quickly to English steel saws and axes, and they were sure to come.

Consumed by the realization, he was startled at the touch of Tonawanda's hand on his shoulder.

"We go now?" Tonawanda asked quietly.

"Yes, we go," Kadomico replied, hesitating for a moment before he turned and walked forward.

Standing behind them, Sayen had watched Kadomico survey his homeland. Now back on the trail, she followed her father and Kadomico down to the valley, secure in the knowledge that they had formed a lasting friendship.

When they broke out of the forest onto the field that had been gleaned of beans, squash, and maize, Tree Son and White Water came racing over the fallen stalks. Behind them were a colorful escort of warriors led by Red Wolf to officially welcome Tonawanda and Sayen.

Kadomico pried White Water's arms from around his neck and held them at length.

"I must see how beautiful my sister has grown," he said.

White Water wiped her tearing eyes, "You are hurt," she said.

"No, No, I am almost healed now," Kadomico said as he knelt to be at eye level with her.

"But Tree Son said you cannot run."

"Very soon I will race you," he said. When he looked up, Red Wolf and his delegation were welcoming Tonawanda and Sayen.

Tree Son stood aside waiting for Kadomico to reassure White Water before he spoke.

"You look well, Kadomico. Your family is waiting. Chief Custoga has sent the best hunters for fresh meat for a feast tonight. Red Wolf will settle Sayen and Tonawanda in the guest roundhouse. Afterwards they will take them to the longhouse to meet the council. The sun will be low by then, so you will have some time with your family before you speak."

White Water wiped away the last of her tears with one arm and, now well behind the others, she, Kadomico, and Tree Son started toward the town.

"It is good that you came before us, Tree Son. I will be with my family first, but we need to talk with my father quickly to prepare for the council. Can you be there?"

"I can. I will be there." He was pleased that Kadomico included him. All eyes of the town would be on Kadomico and Tonawanda. "I met with the council yesterday. I answered questions, but sometimes I just said that you would speak for both of us today."

"And I will," Kadomico replied, as they walked toward the town, with White Water holding Kadomico's hand and biting back the questions flashing through her mind while he spoke with Tree Son. She sensed that Kadomico had changed. He did not tease or laugh. She tried to tell him about the rabbit she had snared, and she started to tell him how she had learned to stitch and lace, but although he looked at her and listened, he seemed not to hear.

As they approached Kadomico's home, Tree Son stopped and said, "I will come back when my shadow is a little longer."

Tanaka suppressed the natural emotions of a proud mother as she stood outside her doorway with a light, brightly colored cloth of the English fastened under her chin and flowing down over her shoulders to her waist.

"Mother, I come," Kadomico said, cherishing the moment.

They embraced before Tanaka made the traditional response, "Kadomico, you are here."

Custoga stepped through the doorway and grasped Kadomico's forearm in welcome.

White Water who had not stopped talking during their walk, fell silent during the greetings and disappeared as they continued their welcomes inside. No one noticed that she had found a place in the shadows of the large room where she let the tears return. She didn't know why. She just knew that Kadomico was different, and she did not understand.

When Tree Son returned, Tanaka kindled the fire and made a hot tea for them. When she handed Custoga a mug of the steaming drink, she brought her lips close to his ear and whispered. "Kadomico is troubled. Be easy."

Custoga said, "You and Tree Son have done well. Red Wolf brought good news of your time in Williamsburg. We know that it was strange and difficult, but the Creator and the teachings of the Saponi guided you both. Your people are proud. Tonight we will celebrate."

Kadomico began, "It is true, Father, that we have seen the English and much of their way. I think the council will ask me to speak about it. Although Tree Son was not directed to stay with me, without his help I could not have withstood the difficulties I faced in their town, and I want him to be with me when I face the council."

"Tree Son will be with you at the council, and they are proud of you both. Your meeting with them will not be difficult, but if you wish to talk to me about what you will say, we have plenty of time," Custoga said.

Kadomico began telling Custoga that he and Tree Son had learned to speak enough English that they had been chosen to translate for Jock on this trip. He explained that he now understood talking papers, and that he had learned to make some of the marks used on them, and the more he talked the more easily the words came to him. Custoga listened, proud and pleased, but also, with intense interest as his son spoke. The words flowed evenly from one subject to the next.

Kadomico spoke for a long time about the school, the food and Carrie, Hawk, Shanda, Wiwohka, and Wapiti. He described Governor Nicholson, Sam Layton, Jock, and his family, and the schoolmaster and their priest, emphasizing the way of their preaching, praying, and singing. He talked of fields of crops and animals raised for food, so many that the English need not hunt. He spoke of the ships and their cargos and how there were many on both the York and James Rivers at all times. "They bring English things and people and carry away the crops, especially tobacco and trees from the forest," he told Custoga.

When Custoga asked about their treatment, Kadomico assured him that all those things promised by the Governor had been provided to them: food, housing, school, clothing, and hospitable reception of friends and family. He also described the incident caused by bad Luther Rawlings the day they. He told of their welcome by the beautiful Mary Stilson, and the generous and friendly hospitality of Jock's family. He included many others who helped and heaped friendship and understanding on them.

"You have seen many things and learned much," Custoga said.

Kadomico's head dropped as though he were searching for more words. Custoga waited.

"Father, what I have said is true. It is what I have seen and learned, but I have seen much more that I do not understand. I cannot describe the ease with which the English destroy the hunting grounds and spoil the streams. And I cannot explain the great houses of stone, the steel they use to make things, or the animals they slaughter for food but also keep to work and ride. I have seen these things but I cannot account for such great numbers of them—far more than they can use. I need to learn more before I speak to the council of these matters."

"You have spoken well, Kadomico," Custoga said. "I will tell the council that you will return to Williamsburg to complete the work they expected."

Kadomico took a deep breath. "Father, I must tell you that I also now believe the English are certain to claim the very land we live on, and I doubt they are more than a few winters from coming here."

"How can you be so sure?" Custoga asked, well aware of what a statement like that would cause among his people.

"I have just traveled from Williamsburg here. I saw the great fields and houses on both sides of the rivers. They are thick for almost a full day's downstream canoe trip to Williamsburg. Although they become less numerous upstream on the Appomattox, every location where tree stands are sparse or the land is completely open, there are marks where settlers have been. When we turned south away from the river, we traveled two days through many open fields with creeks. Those are the places settlers could fence at once and begin growing crops and animals. The English are many, and many more come each day.

When I stood on the overlook this morning, I realized that once they see our land, they will come."

"Kadomico, it is possible that what you realized this morning will happen, but we do not know that. It is something that the council members must decide, but it is important to tell them everything that you have seen. The evidence and reason in your words will lead them to the right conclusions."

Kadomico brightened. Of course, it was his duty to give the council the information and let them decide. He knew that the council was composed of wise men with many winters of experience in protecting their hunting grounds and defending their people.

34

That night at the welcome ceremony and feast, Custoga arranged places for his guests and for several tribe officials, the priest, four senior warriors, his father Choola, and a senior woman of the Women's Council. The drums, rattles, and songs filled the night air with merriment. Elder men and women gathered in clusters in the outer rim of firelight, clear of the dancers circling the fire. Women and children tended the fire, and the fresh meat and fish roasting over the pits cast tantalizing aromas. Senior warriors told stories of tribal history, and the priest, adorned with brilliantly colored feathers and intricate beadwork, prayed and offered sacrifices. The Saponi people were relaxed and enjoying themselves after the hard work of the harvest and the first of the long hunts to store winter meat. They celebrated the return of Kadomico and Tree Son, and it was their pleasure to honor visitors of their language, and especially such a visitor as Tonawanda, now the legendary leader against the enemy Tuscaroras for the spectacular release of his son.

Sayen, sitting near her father, saw Kadomico rise from his place on the opposite side of the dancers and go toward the steaming food. She did likewise, never letting her eyes shift away from him until she reached his side.

"Before the sun rises," Kadomico said, "I will go to a place unknown to most."

"Sleep well." Sayen smiled up at him, carved a large slice of meat from the roasting venison, and placed it on his plate of woven wood splits. She carved another for Tonawanda and turned away to rejoin him.

Kadomico, keenly aware that Tonawanda was watching them, forced himself to look away from Sayen.

The next morning, Tanaka watched from her bed as her son rose silently from his blanket, picked up his bow and quiver of arrows, and stepped out into the predawn chill. He raised his arms, yawned, and stretched his body several ways, enjoying the strength that had returned. He did not notice the movement alongside a nearby roundhouse.

He made no sound as he walked the smooth open corridor toward the town entrance. There he glanced toward the Yadkin River running unseen in the still darkness, then turned away to start climbing. He followed an obscure animal trail upward through straw, golden rod, and briar patches until they gave way to clear ground richly strewn with laurel and dogwood growing in thickets among huge outcroppings of limestone. Finally, he stopped and rested. The first light of day melted the blackness around him into the gray shapes of white oak and shagbark hickory. The stand of laurel on his left grew thick from the ground upward well beyond his reach forming a perfect shield for the solid rock overlook.

In the spring, the flowering dogwood and evergreen laurel at this untended wonderland was something only the Creator could make, and the toughest warrior would be reverent here. After the laurel thicket, a floor of solid limestone led past more shrubs and a towering white oak on his left. Beyond the old oak on his left, a vast rock cliff rose higher yet and formed the north side of a breathtaking vista east and south across the valley and river below.

Kadomico laid aside his bow, quiver of arrows, and walked past the old oak. When he sensed a warm reassurance and confidence that the Creator was with him, he stopped and listened. The scene began to work its spell on him. After a while, he raised his arms upward and spoke softly.

"Great Spirit, Maker of rivers and valleys and mountains, while I was away I did not remember your works and I forgot the wonders that you have given. I want never again to forget. If it is the will of my people, I will go back and learn the way of the English, but always I will remember this place and be grateful for your gift. Now I seek your guidance. Help me to understand the guidance you offer, and give me the strength and knowledge to follow it."

As he turned back to gather tinder for a sacrificial fire, the first light of dawn bathed the scene in reflected sunlight to announce the rising sun. Birds were moving, but the air was still. He took a step before he saw Sayen standing there quietly, smiling. Even in the dim light of dawn, her tawny buckskin dress and flowing black hair stood out against the dark green background of laurel.

An avalanche of thoughts descended on Kadomico, her safety, her purpose, Tonawanda, and his own family, but none of these practical matters lingered in his mind. Her smile said everything, and suddenly it was as though they had been together like this all his life, and he knew it would remain so no matter the circumstances before them. All questions and concerns evaporated.

"I am here," she said.

He took her hand, and they turned toward the east to watch the beginning of a new day.

EPILOGUE

Our fictitious characters, Kadomico and Sayen, married after two more years during which Kadomico continued studying at William and Mary College. In 1714, Virginia Governor Spotswood was finally able to open Fort Christana near the Virginia-North Carolina border to the many tribes. It happened exactly as Governor Nicholson and the tribal Chiefs had envisioned at their first assembly of Siouan-speaking tribes on the Meherrin River in December, 1700.

Kadomico's ten-year-old son was among the first to attend the new Indian school at Fort Christana. By then, Kadomico was an experienced warrior, a busy interpreter, a trusted go-between, a skilled negotiator for his people, and an ardent student. In 1723, the 37-year-old Kadomico was present when the Brafferton Indian School opened at the College of William and Mary.

Settlers called them Indians, but they called each other by their tribal names and they still do: Mattaponi, Monacan, Occaneechi, Tutelo, Chickahominy, Nansemond, Pamunkey, Rappahannock, Meherrin, Tuscarora, Saponi, a strong manifestation of a people, once independent and sovereign.

BIBLIOGRAPHICAL NOTE

During the research and writing of this novel, I found the following works to be rich with examples and descriptions of life in the Virginia and North Carolina colonies. I am particularly grateful to these writers and historians.

Robert Beverly, *The History and Present State of Virginia, 1705;* Edited by Louis B. Wright, 1947

John Lawson, *History of North Carolina, 1709;* Edited by Frances Latham Harriss, 1937

James Axtell, *The Invasion Within, 1985*

Martha W. McCartney, *A History of Green Spring Plantation, 1998*

Helen Roundtree, *The Powhatan Indians of Virginia, 1989*

John Swanton, *The Indians of Southeastern United States, 1946*

Jamestown Narratives, The First Decade, 1607-1617; Edited with commentary by Edward Wright Haile, 1998

The Virginia Indian Heritage Trail, 2007; Edited by Karenne Wood

John W. Reps, *Tidewater Towns: City Planning in Colonial Virginia and Maryland, 1972*

ACKNOWLEDGMENTS

I thank Johnnie James Laird for proof reading with extraordinary patience and unrelenting encouragement.

Jeffrey McCall Laird provided the maps and geographic advice without which this book would have been much longer and more complicated.

Williamsburg Writers: John Conlee, professor, writer, lecturer; Alastair Connell, physician, writer, lecturer; Kathrine Fournier, author; Charles Geraud, writer, retired U.S. Marine aviator; Aleck Loker, physicist, lecturer, author; Sally Stiles, writer, instructor, editor. Over the three years this book was a work-in-progress, these friends, all of whom are writers, edited, critiqued, suggested, and were continuously available when I needed help. I cannot repay such a huge debt, but I am all the more grateful for their help and friendship.

Del Moore, reference librarian, and staff of John D. Rockefeller Jr. Library, Williamsburg, VA have at their service a national treasure of source information on the colonial period. They guided me through countless efforts to confirm data and information, but missteps, errors, and any other questionable wording you may find in this writing is entirely my own mistake.

I thank Beverly Hancock, Curator, Wake Forest University Museum, North Carolina, for *A History of North Carolina (1705)*, by John Lawson. It became an indispensible companion throughout the writing of this book.

Andrew Mackie, Yadkin County Historian, North Carolina guided me to period Indian settlements and the Trading Ford, well known to those who followed the Indian trading trails in 1700.

I am grateful to the Staff and Interpreters of Henricus Historical Park, Virginia, Monacan Village at Natural Bridge, VA, Jamestown Settlement Museum and Indian Village, and Mariners Museum, Newport News, VA.

I thank Roger Conlee, Journalist, Writer, and Historian for marketing guidance and editorial assistance.

College of William and Mary Swem Library, Special Collections and Research Center provided valuable accounts of the establishment of the college and Governor Nicholson's efforts to accomplish the education and conversion of neighboring Indians.